# DIVINE
# SOUL SONGS

# DIVINE
# SOUL SONGS

*Sacred Practical Treasures to Heal,*
*Rejuvenate, and Transform You,*
*Humanity, Mother Earth,*
*and All Universes*

# Dr. Zhi Gang Sha

**ATRIA** BOOKS

New York   London   Toronto   Sydney

Heaven's Library
Toronto

**ATRIA** BOOKS
A Division of Simon & Schuster, Inc.
1230 Avenue of the Americas
New York, NY 10020

Heaven's Library
Toronto, ON

The information contained in this book is intended to be educational and not for
diagnosis, prescription, or treatment of any health disorder whatsoever. This information
should not replace consultation with a competent health-care professional. The content
of the book is intended to be used as an adjunct to a rational and responsible health-care
program prescribed by a health-care practitioner. The author and publisher are in
no way liable for any misuse of the material.

First Atria Books hardcover edition June 2009

**ATRIA** BOOKS and colophon are trademarks of Simon & Schuster, Inc.
Heaven's Library and Soul Power Series are trademarks of Heaven's Library Publication Corp.

For information about special discounts for bulk purchases,
please contact Simon & Schuster Special Sales at 1-866-506-1949
or business@simonandschuster.com.

The Simon & Schuster Speakers Bureau can bring authors to your live event.
For more information or to book an event, contact the Simon & Schuster Speakers Bureau
at 1-866-248-3049 or visit our website at www.simonspeakers.com.

Designed by Davina Mock-Maniscalco
Photos, charts, and music courtesy of the author

Manufactured in the United States of America

10  9  8  7  6  5  4  3  2  1

Library of Congress Cataloging-in-Publication Data

Sha, Zhi Gang.
Divine soul songs : sacred practical treasures to heal, rejuvenate, and transform you,
humanity, Mother Earth, and all universes / Zhi Gang Sha.
p.   cm.
Includes bibliographical references.
1. Spiritual life.  2. Spiritual healing.  3. Chants—Texts.  I. Title.
BL624.S4754   2009
204'.32—dc22                           2008052068

ISBN 978-1-4391-2965-4

# Contents

Soul Power Series                                              xv

How to Receive the Divine Soul Downloads Offered
    in the Books of the Soul Power Series                      xxix

• What to Expect After You Receive Divine Soul
    Downloads                                                  xxxii

Foreword to the Soul Power Series by
    Dr. Michael Bernard Beckwith                               xxxv

Foreword to *Divine Soul Songs* by Dr. Maya Angelou           xxxvii

How to Read This Book                                         xxxix

Introduction                                                  xliii

• Energy Reactions in the Body                                lvii

• The Importance of Practice                                  lxii

• You Are in My Workshop                                      lxiii

• Soul Healing, Soul Enlightenment, and
    Divine Soul Songs                                         lxvii

*1: Soul Secrets, Wisdom, Knowledge, and Practices
    of Soul Song*                                                    *1*

What Is Soul Song?                                                     1

The Power and Significance of Soul Song                               7

Bring Out Your Own Soul Song                                          9

Apply Your Soul Song to Heal, Rejuvenate,
    and Transform You, Humanity, Mother Earth,
    and All Universes                                                13

*2: The First Three Divine Soul Songs for Humanity,
    Mother Earth, and All Universes*                                *21*

The Power and Significance of the Divine
    Soul Song *Love, Peace and Harmony*                              21

  • How I Received This First Divine Soul Song                        28

  • Apply the Divine Soul Song *Love, Peace
      and Harmony* to Heal, Rejuvenate, and
      Transform You, Humanity, Mother Earth,
      and All Universes                                              31

  • Go into the Divine Condition                                     37

  • Apply the Divine Soul Song *Love, Peace and
      Harmony* to Remove Selfishness and Greed                       38

The Power and Significance of the Divine Soul
    Song *God Gives His Heart to Me*                                 44

  • How I Received This Second Divine Soul Song                      51

  • Apply the Divine Soul Song *God Gives His Heart
      to Me* to Heal, Rejuvenate, and Transform You,
      Humanity, Mother Earth, and All Universes                      54

  • Apply the Divine Soul Song *God Gives His
      Heart to Me* to Remove Mind-sets, Ego,
      and Attachment                                                 65

- Apply the Divine Soul Download of the Divine
  Soul Song *God Gives His Heart to Me* to Heal
  and Transform Life                                    78
- Soul Transformation for Past, Present, and
  Future                                                87

The Power and Significance of the Divine Soul
Song of Compassion                                      91

- Teachings and Blessings of Compassion
  I Have Received                                       91
- How I Received This Third Divine Soul Song            98
- Apply the Divine Soul Song of Compassion
  to Heal, Rejuvenate, and Transform You,
  Humanity, Mother Earth, and All Universes             99
- Divine Soul Download of the Divine Soul Song
  of Compassion                                        103

3: *Divine Soul Songs of Divine Universal Laws*        *107*

The First Divine Universal Law:
The Universal Law of Yin Yang                          107

- Basic Philosophy and Concepts of Yin Yang            108

Divine Soul Song of Yin Yang                           110

- How I Received the Divine Soul Song of
  Yin Yang                                             110
- Practice the Divine Soul Song of Yin Yang            119
- The Power and Significance of the Seven
  Soul Houses                                          129
- Secret Wisdom of Yin Yang                            133
- A Top Divine Practice of the Divine Soul Song
  of Yin Yang Revealed As I Wrote This Book            136

- The Power and Significance of the Divine
  Sacred *Tian Di Ren* Soul Practice to Reach
  the Tao                                                    142
- Apply the Divine Soul Song of Yin Yang to Heal
  and Transform You, Humanity, Mother Earth,
  and All Universes                                          154
- Divine Soul Downloads of the Divine Soul Song
  of Yin Yang                                                157
- Apply Divine Soul Downloads of the Divine
  Soul Song of Yin Yang to Heal You, Others,
  Humanity, Mother Earth, and All Universes                  167
- Another Sacred Practice to Heal, Rejuvenate,
  and Transform Your Soul, Mind, and Body
  Just Revealed                                              184

The Second Divine Universal Law:
The Universal Law of Five Elements                           199
- Basic Concepts of Five Elements                            199

Divine Soul Song of Five Elements                            202
- How I Received the Divine Soul Song of
  Five Elements                                              202
- Practice the Divine Soul Song of Five
  Elements                                                   205
- Apply the Divine Soul Song of Five Elements
  to Heal, Rejuvenate, and Transform You,
  Humanity, Mother Earth, and All Universes                  212
- Divine Soul Downloads of the Divine Soul
  Song of Five Elements                                      216
- Apply Divine Soul Downloads of the Divine
  Soul Song of Five Elements to Heal,

Rejuvenate, and Transform You, Humanity,
    Mother Earth, and All Universes                    217
The World Soul Healing, Peace and Enlightenment
    Movement                                          228
The Third Divine Universal Law: The Universal
    Law of Message Energy Matter                      229
    • Message Energy Matter Theory                    229
    • The Power of Soul                                231
Divine Soul Song of Message Energy Matter             237
    • How I Received the Divine Soul Song of
        Message Energy Matter                          238
    • Apply the Divine Soul Song of Message Energy
        Matter to Heal, Rejuvenate, and Transform
        You, Humanity, Mother Earth, and All
        Universes                                      240
    • Divine Soul Download of the Divine Soul
        Song of Message Energy Matter                 242
The Fourth Divine Universal Law:
    The Universal Law of Universal Service            244
Divine Soul Song of Universal Service                 245
    • How I Received the Divine Soul Song of
        Universal Service                              245
    • Apply the Divine Soul Song of Universal
        Service to Heal, Rejuvenate, and Transform
        You, Humanity, Mother Earth, and All
        Universes                                      246
    • Divine Soul Download of the Divine Soul Song
        of Universal Service                           247
Summary                                                251

**4: *Experiences of Divine Soul Song***                  **253**
     Healing                                      254
     Rejuvenation                                 263
     Transformation of Relationships              267
     Transformation of Finances                   272
     Enlightenment                                273


Conclusion                                        287
Acknowledgments                                   291
A Special Gift                                    295
Dr. Sha's Teachings and Services                  297

# List of Figures

Figure 1    Body Power Technique to Calm a Strong
            Energy Reaction in the Body

Figure 2    Divine Soul Song *Love, Peace and Harmony*

Figure 3    Divine Soul Song for World Soul Healing,
            Peace and Enlightenment

Figure 4    Divine Soul Song *God Gives His Heart
            to Me*

Figure 5    Divine Soul Song of Compassion

Figure 6    Seven Houses of the Soul and Wai Jiao

Figure 7    Divine Soul Song of Yin Yang

Figure 8    Energy Circle of the Divine Soul Song
            of Yin Yang

Figure 9    Matter Circle of the Divine Soul Song
            of Yin Yang

Figure 10  Divine Soul Song of Yin Yang—Body Power for First Soul House

Figure 11  Divine Soul Song of Yin Yang—Body Power for Second Soul House

Figure 12  Divine Soul Song of Yin Yang—Body Power for Third Soul House

Figure 13  Divine Soul Song of Yin Yang—Body Power for Fourth Soul House

Figure 14  Divine Soul Song of Yin Yang—Body Power for Fifth Soul House

Figure 15  Divine Soul Song of Yin Yang—Body Power for Sixth Soul House

Figure 16  Divine Soul Song of Yin Yang—Body Power for Seventh Soul House

Figure 17  Divine Soul Song of Yin Yang—Body Power for Wai Jiao

Figure 18  Divine Soul Song of Yin Yang—Body Power for Energy and Matter Circles

Figure 19  Yin Yang Symbol

Figure 20  Divine Sacred *Tian Di Ren* Soul Practice to Reach the Tao

Figure 21  Divine Sacred *Tian Di Ren* Soul Practice to Reach the Tao: Circle 1 Mind Power

Figure 22  Divine Sacred *Tian Di Ren* Soul Practice to Reach the Tao: Circle 2 Mind Power

Figure 23   Divine Sacred *Tian Di Ren* Soul Practice to Reach the Tao: Circle 3 Mind Power

Figure 24   Divine Sacred *Tian Di Ren* Soul Practice to Reach the Tao: Circle 4 Mind Power

Figure 25   Universal Connection Hand Position

Figure 26   Universal Connection for the First Soul House

Figure 27   Universal Connection for the Second Soul House

Figure 28   Universal Connection for the Third Soul House

Figure 29   Universal Connection for the Fourth Soul House

Figure 30   Universal Connection for the Fifth Soul House

Figure 31   Universal Connection for the Sixth Soul House

Figure 32   Universal Connection for the Seventh Soul House

Figure 33   Universal Connection for the Wai Jiao

Figure 34   Divine Soul Song of Five Elements

Figure 35   Divine Soul Song of Wood Element— Body Power for *Jiao*

Figure 36   Divine Soul Song of Fire Element— Body Power for *Zhi*

Figure 37   Divine Soul Song of Earth Element— Body Power for *Gong*

Figure 38   Divine Soul Song of Metal Element— Body Power for *Shang*

Figure 39   Divine Soul Song of Water Element— Body Power for *Yu*

Figure 40    Divine Soul Song *Ai* for All Five Elements—
Body Power for *Ai*

Figure 41    Divine Soul Song of Message Energy Matter

Figure 42    Divine Soul Song of Universal Service

# Soul Power Series

THE PURPOSE OF life is to serve. I have committed my life to this purpose. Service is my life mission.

My total life mission is to transform the consciousness of humanity and all souls in the universe and enlighten them, in order to create love, peace, and harmony for humanity, Mother Earth, and all universes. This mission includes three empowerments.

My first empowerment is to teach *universal service* to empower people to be unconditional universal servants. The message of universal service is:

> *I serve humanity and all universes unconditionally.*
> *You serve humanity and all universes unconditionally.*
> *Together we serve humanity and all souls in all universes unconditionally.*

My second empowerment is to teach *healing* to empower people to heal themselves and heal others. The message of healing is:

*I have the power to heal myself.*
*You have the power to heal yourself.*
*Together we have the power to heal the world.*

My third empowerment is to teach *the power of soul,* which includes soul secrets, wisdom, knowledge, and practices, and to transmit Divine Soul Power to empower people to transform every aspect of their lives and enlighten their souls, hearts, minds, and bodies.

The message of Soul Power is:

> *I have the Soul Power to transform my consciousness*
> *and every aspect of my life and enlighten my soul,*
> *heart, mind, and body.*
> *You have the Soul Power to transform your conscious-*
> *ness and every aspect of your life and enlighten your*
> *soul, heart, mind, and body.*
> *Together we have the Soul Power to transform con-*
> *sciousness and every aspect of all life and enlighten*
> *humanity and all souls.*

**To teach the power of soul is my most important empowerment.** It is the key for my total life mission. The power of soul is the key for transforming physical life and spiritual life. It is the key for transforming and enlightening humanity and every soul in all universes.

The beginning of the twenty-first century is the transition period into a new era for humanity, Mother Earth, and all universes. This era is named the Soul Light Era. The Soul Light Era began on August 8, 2003. It will last fifteen thousand years. Natural disasters—including tsunamis, hurricanes, cyclones, earthquakes, floods, tornados, hail, blizzards, fires, drought, extreme temperatures, famine, and disease—political, religious, and ethnic wars, terrorism, proliferation of nuclear weapons, economic challenges, pollution, vanishing plant and animal species, and other such upheavals are part of this transition. In addition, millions of people are suffering from depression, anxiety, fear, anger, and worry. They suffer from pain, chronic conditions, and life-threatening illnesses. Humanity needs help. The consciousness of humanity needs to be transformed. The suffering of humanity needs to be removed.

The books of the Soul Power Series are brought to you by Heaven's Library and Atria Books. They reveal soul secrets and teach soul wisdom, soul knowledge, and soul practices for your daily life. The power of soul can heal, prevent illness, rejuvenate, prolong life, and transform consciousness and every aspect of life, including relationships and finances. The power of soul is vital to serving humanity and Mother Earth during this transition period. The power of soul will awaken and transform the consciousness of humanity and all souls.

In the twentieth century and for centuries before, *mind over matter* played a vital role in healing, rejuvenation, and life transformation. In the Soul Light Era, *soul over matter*—Soul Power—will play *the* vital role to heal, rejuvenate, and transform all life.

There are countless souls on Mother Earth—souls of human beings, souls of animals, souls of other living things, and souls of inanimate things. *Everyone and everything has a soul.*

Every soul has its own frequency and power. Jesus had miraculous healing power. We have heard many heart-touching stories of lives saved by Guan Yin's[1] compassion. Mother Mary's love has created many heart-moving stories. All of these great souls were given Divine Soul Power to serve humanity. In all of the world's great religions and spiritual traditions, including Buddhism, Taoism, Christianity, Judaism, Hinduism, Islam, and more, there are similar accounts of great spiritual healing and blessing power.

I honor every religion and every spiritual tradition. However, I am not teaching religion. I am teaching Soul Power, which includes soul secrets, soul wisdom, soul knowledge, and soul practices. Your soul has the power to heal, rejuvenate, and transform life. An animal's soul has the power to heal, rejuvenate, and transform life. The souls of the sun, the moon, an ocean, a tree, and a mountain have the power to heal, rejuvenate, and transform life. The souls of healing angels, ascended masters, holy saints, Taoist saints, Hindu saints, buddhas, and other high-level spiritual beings have great Soul Power to heal, rejuvenate, and transform life.

Every soul has its own standing. Spiritual standing, or soul standing, has countless layers. Soul Power also has layers. Not every soul can perform miracles like those performed by Jesus, Guan Yin, and Mother Mary. Soul Power depends on the soul's spiritual standing in Heaven. The higher a soul stands in Heaven, the more Soul Power that soul is given by the Divine. Jesus, Guan Yin, and Mother Mary all have a very high spiritual standing.

Who determines a soul's spiritual standing? Who gives the appropriate Soul Power to a soul? Who decides the direction for humanity, Mother Earth, and the universes? The top leader of the spiritual world is the decision maker. This top leader is the

---

1. Guan Yin is known as the Bodhisattva of Compassion and, in the West, as the Goddess of Mercy.

Divine. The Divine is the creator and manifester of all universes.

In the Soul Light Era, all souls will join as one and align their consciousness with divine consciousness. At this historic time, the Divine has decided to transmit the Divine's soul treasures to humanity and all souls to help humanity and all souls go through Mother Earth's transition.

Let me share two personal stories with you to explain how I reached this understanding.

First, in April 2003, I held a Power Healing workshop for about one hundred people at Land of Medicine Buddha, a retreat center in Soquel, California. As I was teaching, the Divine appeared. I told the students, "The Divine is here. Could you give me a moment?" I knelt and bowed down to the floor to honor the Divine. (At age six, I was taught to bow down to my tai chi masters. At age ten, I bowed down to my qi gong masters. At age twelve, I bowed down to my kung fu masters. Being Chinese, I learned this courtesy throughout my childhood.) I explained to the students, "Please understand that this is the way I honor the Divine, my spiritual fathers, and my spiritual mothers. Now I will have a conversation with the Divine."

I began by saying silently, "Dear Divine, I am very honored you are here."

The Divine, who was in front of me above my head, replied, "Zhi Gang, I come today to pass a spiritual law to you."

I said, "I am honored to receive this spiritual law."

The Divine continued, "This spiritual law is named the Universal Law of Universal Service. It is one of the highest spiritual laws in the universe. It applies to the spiritual world and the physical world."

The Divine pointed to the Divine. "I am a universal servant."

The Divine pointed to me. "You are a universal servant." The Divine swept a hand in front of the Divine. "Everyone and everything is a universal servant. A universal servant offers universal service unconditionally. Universal service includes universal love, forgiveness, peace, healing, blessing, harmony, and enlightenment. *If one offers a little service, one receives little blessing from the universe and from me. If one offers more service, one receives more blessing. If one offers unconditional service, one receives unlimited blessing.*"

The Divine paused for a moment before continuing. "There is another kind of service, which is unpleasant service. Unpleasant service includes killing, harming, taking advantage of others, cheating, stealing, complaining, and more. If one offers a little unpleasant service, one learns little lessons from the universe and from me. If one offers more unpleasant service, one learns more lessons. If one offers huge unpleasant service, one learns huge lessons."

I asked, "What kinds of lessons could one learn?"

The Divine replied, "The lessons include sickness, accidents, injuries, financial challenges, broken relationships, emotional imbalances, mental confusion, and any kind of disorder in one's life." The Divine emphasized, "This is how the universe operates. This is one of my most important spiritual laws for all souls in the universe to follow."

After the Divine delivered this universal law, I immediately made a silent vow to the Divine:

> *Dear Divine,*
> *I am extremely honored to receive your Law of Universal Service. I make a vow to you, to all humanity, and to all souls in all universes that I will be an unconditional*

*universal servant. I will give my total GOLD* [gratitude, obedience, loyalty, devotion] *to you and to serving you. I am honored to be your servant and a servant of all humanity and all souls.*

Hearing this, the Divine smiled and left.

My second story happened three months later, in July 2003, while I was holding a Soul Study workshop near Toronto. The Divine came again. I again explained to my students that the Divine had appeared, and asked them to wait a moment while I bowed down 108 times and listened to the Divine's message. On this occasion, the Divine told me, "Zhi Gang, I come today to choose you as my direct servant, vehicle, and channel."

I was deeply moved and said to the Divine, "I am honored. What does it mean to be your direct servant, vehicle, and channel?"

The Divine replied, "When you offer healing and blessing to others, call me. I will come instantly to offer my healing and blessing to them."

I was deeply touched and replied, "Thank you so much for choosing me as your direct servant."

The Divine continued, "I can offer my healing and blessing by transmitting my permanent healing and blessing treasures."

I asked, "How do you do this?"

The Divine answered, "Select a person and I will give you a demonstration."

I asked for a volunteer with serious health challenges. A man named Walter raised his hand. He stood up and explained that he had liver cancer, with a two-by-three-centimeter malignant tumor that had just been diagnosed from a biopsy.

Then I asked the Divine, "Please bless Walter. Please show me how you transmit your permanent treasures." Immediately, I saw the Divine send a beam of light from the Divine's heart to Walter's liver. The beam shot into his liver, where it turned into a golden light ball that instantly started spinning. Walter's entire liver shone with beautiful golden light.

The Divine asked me, "Do you understand what software is?"

I was surprised by this question but replied, "I do not understand much about computers. I just know that software is a computer program. I have heard about accounting software, office software, and graphic design software."

"Yes," the Divine said. "Software is a program. Because you asked me to, I transmitted or downloaded my Soul Software for Liver to Walter. It is one of my permanent healing and blessing treasures. You asked me. I did the job. This is what it means for you to be my chosen direct servant and channel."

I was astonished. Excited, inspired, and humbled, I said to the Divine, "I am so honored to be your direct servant. How blessed I am to be chosen." Almost speechless, I asked the Divine, "Why did you choose me?"

"I chose you," said the Divine, "because you have served humanity for more than one thousand lifetimes. You have been very committed to serving my mission through all of your lifetimes. I am choosing you in this life to be my direct servant. You will transmit countless permanent healing and blessing treasures from me to humanity and all souls. This is the honor I give to you now."

I was moved to tears. I immediately bowed down 108 times again and made a silent vow:

> *Dear Divine,*
>
> *I cannot bow down to you enough for the honor you have given to me. No words can express my greatest gratitude. How blessed I am to be your direct servant to download your permanent healing and blessing treasures to humanity and all souls! Humanity and all souls will receive your huge blessings through my service as your direct servant. I give my total life to you and to humanity. I will accomplish your tasks. I will be a pure servant to humanity and all souls.*

I bowed again. Then I asked the Divine, "How should Walter use his Soul Software?"

"Walter must spend time to practice with my Soul Software," said the Divine. "Tell him that simply to receive my Soul Software does not mean he will recover. He must practice with this treasure every day to restore his health, step by step."

I asked, "How should he practice?"

The Divine gave me this guidance: "Tell Walter to chant repeatedly: *Divine Liver Soul Software heals me. Divine Liver Soul Software heals me. Divine Liver Soul Software heals me. Divine Liver Soul Software heals me.*"

I asked, "For how long should Walter chant?"

The Divine answered, "At least two hours a day. The longer

he practices, the better. If Walter does this, he could recover in three to six months."

I shared this information with Walter, who was excited and deeply moved. Walter said, "I will practice two hours or more each day."

Finally I asked the Divine, "How does the Soul Software work?"

The Divine replied, "My Soul Software is a golden healing ball that rotates and clears energy and spiritual blockages in Walter's liver."

I again bowed to the Divine 108 times. Then I stood up and offered three Soul Softwares to every participant in the workshop as divine gifts. Upon seeing this, the Divine smiled and left.

Walter immediately began to practice as directed for at least two hours every day. Two and a half months later, a CT scan and an MRI showed that his liver cancer had completely disappeared. At the end of 2006 I met Walter again at a signing in Toronto for my book *Soul Mind Body Medicine*. In May 2008 Walter attended one of my events at the Unity Church of Truth in Toronto. On both occasions Walter told me that there was still no sign of cancer in his liver. For nearly five years his Divine Soul Download healed his liver cancer. He was very grateful to the Divine.

This major event of being chosen as a direct divine servant happened in July 2003. As I mentioned, a new era for Mother Earth and the universe, the Soul Light Era, began on August 8, 2003. The timing may look like a coincidence but I believe there could be an underlying spiritual reason. Since July 2003 I have offered divine transmissions to humanity almost every day. I have offered more than ten divine transmissions to all souls in all universes.

I share this story with you to introduce the power of divine transmissions or Divine Soul Downloads. Now let me share the commitment that I made in *Soul Wisdom*, the first book of my Soul Power Series, and that I have renewed in every one of my books since:

**From now on, I will offer Divine Soul Downloads in every book I write.**

Divine Soul Downloads are permanent divine healing and blessing treasures for transforming your life. There is an ancient saying: *If you want to know whether a pear is sweet, taste it.* If you want to know the power of Divine Soul Downloads, experience it.

Divine Soul Downloads carry divine frequency with divine love, forgiveness, compassion, and light. Divine frequency transforms the frequency of all life. Divine love melts all blockages, including energy and spiritual blockages, and transforms all lives. Divine forgiveness brings inner peace and inner joy. Divine compassion boosts energy, stamina, vitality, and immunity. Divine light heals, prevents sickness, rejuvenates, and prolongs life.

A Divine Soul Download is a new soul created from the heart of the Divine. The Divine Soul Download transmitted to Walter was a Soul Software. Since then, I have transmitted several other types of Divine Soul Downloads, including Divine Soul Herbs, Divine Soul Acupuncture, and Divine Soul Transplants.

A Divine Soul Transplant is a new divine soul of an organ, a part of the body, a bodily system, cells, DNA, RNA, the smallest matter in cells, or the spaces between cells. When it is transmitted, it replaces the recipient's original soul of the organ, part of the body, system, cells, DNA, RNA, smallest matter in cells, or spaces between cells. A new divine soul can also replace the soul of a home or a business. A new divine soul can be transmitted to a pet, a mountain, a city, or a country to replace their original souls. A new divine soul can even replace the soul of Mother Earth.

*Everyone and everything has a soul.* The Divine can download any soul you can conceive of. These Divine Soul Downloads are permanent divine healing, blessing, and life-transforming treasures. They can transform the lives of anyone and anything. Because the Divine created these divine soul treasures, they carry Divine Soul Power, which is the greatest Soul Power among all souls. All souls in the highest layers of Heaven will support and assist Divine Soul Downloads. Divine Soul Downloads are the crown jewel of Soul Power.

Divine Soul Downloads are divine presence. The more Divine Soul Downloads you receive, the faster your soul, heart, mind, and body will be transformed. The more Divine Soul Downloads your home or business receives and the more Divine Soul Downloads a city or country receives, the faster their souls, hearts, minds, and bodies will be transformed.

In the Soul Light Era, the evolution of humanity will be created by Divine Soul Power. Soul Power will transform humanity. Soul Power will transform animals. Soul Power will transform nature and the environment. Soul Power will assume the leading role in every field of human endeavor. Humanity will deeply understand that *the soul is the boss.*

Soul Power, including soul secrets, soul wisdom, soul knowledge, and soul practices, will transform every aspect of human life. Soul Power will transform every aspect of organizations and societies. Soul Power will transform cities, countries, Mother Earth, all planets, stars, galaxies, and all universes. Divine Soul Power, including Divine Soul Downloads, will lead this transformation.

I am honored to have been chosen as a divine servant to offer Divine Soul Downloads to humanity, to relationships, to homes, to businesses, to pets, to cities, to countries, and more. In the last few years I have already transmitted countless divine souls to humanity and to all universes. I repeat to you now: *I will offer Divine Soul Downloads within each and every book of the Soul Power Series.* Clear instructions on how to receive these Divine Soul Downloads will be provided in the next section. "How to Receive the Divine Soul Downloads Offered in the Books of the Soul Power Series," as well as on the appropriate pages of each book.

I am a servant of humanity. I am a servant of the universe. I am a servant of the Divine. I am extremely honored to be a servant of all souls. I commit my total life and being as an unconditional universal servant.

I will continue to offer Divine Soul Downloads for my entire life. I will offer more and more Divine Soul Downloads to every soul. I will offer Divine Soul Downloads for every aspect of life for every soul.

I am honored to be a servant of Divine Soul Downloads.

Human beings, organizations, cities, and countries will receive more and more Divine Soul Downloads, which can transform every aspect of their lives and enlighten their souls, hearts, minds, and bodies. The Soul Light Era will shine Soul Power. The books in the Soul Power Series will spread Divine Soul Downloads, together with Soul Power—soul secrets, soul wisdom, soul knowledge, and soul practices—to serve humanity, Mother Earth, and all universes. The Soul Power Series is a pure servant for humanity and all souls. The Soul Power Series is honored to be a total GOLD[2] servant for the Divine, humanity, and all souls.

---

2. Total GOLD means total gratitude, total obedience, total loyalty, and total devotion to the Divine.

The final goal of the Soul Light Era is to join every soul as one in love, peace, and harmony. This means that the consciousness of every soul will be totally aligned with divine consciousness. There will be difficulties and challenges on the path to this final goal. Together we will overcome them. We call all souls of humanity and all souls in all universes to offer unconditional universal service, including universal love, forgiveness, peace, healing, blessing, harmony, and enlightenment. The more we offer unconditional universal service, the faster we will achieve this goal.

The Divine gives the Divine's heart to us. The Divine gives the Divine's love to us. The Divine gives Divine Soul Downloads to us. Our hearts meld with the Divine's heart. Our souls meld with the Divine's soul. Our consciousnesses align with the Divine's consciousness. We will join hearts and souls together to create love, peace, and harmony for humanity, Mother Earth, and all universes.

> *I love my heart and soul*
> *I love all humanity*
> *Join hearts and souls together*
> *Love, peace and harmony*
> *Love, peace and harmony*

Love all humanity. Love all souls. Thank all humanity. Thank all souls.

Thank you. Thank you. Thank you.

Zhi Gang Sha

# How to Receive the Divine Soul Downloads Offered in the Books of the Soul Power Series

*T*HE BOOKS OF the Soul Power Series are unique. For the first time in history, the Divine is downloading the Divine's soul treasures to readers as they read these books. Every book in the Soul Power Series will include Divine Soul Downloads that have been preprogrammed. When you read the appropriate paragraphs and pause for a minute, divine gifts will be transmitted to your soul.

In April 2005 the Divine told me to "leave Divine Soul Downloads to history." I thought, "A human being's life is limited. Even if I live a long, long life, I will go back to Heaven one day. How can I leave Divine Soul Downloads to history?"

In the beginning of 2008, as I was editing the paperback edition of *Soul Wisdom*, the Divine suddenly told me: "Zhi Gang, offer my downloads within this book." The Divine said, "I will preprogram my downloads in the book. Any reader can receive them as he or she reads the special pages." At the moment the Divine gave me this direction, I understood how I could leave Divine Soul Downloads to history.

Preprogrammed Divine Soul Downloads are permanently stored within this book and every book in the Soul Power Series. If people read this book thousands of years from now, they will still receive the Divine Soul Downloads. As long as this book exists and is read, readers will receive the Divine Soul Downloads.

Allow me to explain further. The Divine has placed a permanent blessing within certain paragraphs in these books. These blessings allow you to receive Divine Soul Downloads as permanent gifts to your soul. Because these divine treasures reside with your soul, you can access them twenty-four hours a day—as often as you like, wherever you are—for healing, blessing, and life transformation.

It is very easy to receive the Divine Soul Downloads in these books. After you read the special paragraphs where they are preprogrammed, close your eyes. Receive the special download. It is also easy to apply these divine treasures. After you receive a Divine Soul Download, I will immediately show you how to apply it for healing, blessing, and life transformation.

You have free will. If you are not ready to receive a Divine Soul Download, simply say *I am not ready to receive this gift.* You can then continue to read the special download paragraphs, but you will not receive the gifts they contain. The Divine does not offer Divine Soul Downloads to those who are not ready or not willing to receive the Divine's treasures. However, the moment you are ready, you can simply go back to the relevant paragraphs and tell the Divine *I am ready.* You will then receive the stored special download when you reread the paragraphs.

The Divine has agreed to offer specific Divine Soul Downloads in these books to all readers who are willing to receive them. The Divine has unlimited treasures. However, you can receive only the ones designated in these pages. Please do not ask for different or additional gifts. It will not work.

After receiving and practicing with the Divine Soul Downloads in these books, you could experience remarkable healing results in your physical, emotional, mental, and spiritual bodies. You could receive incredible blessings for your love relationships and other relationships. You could receive financial blessings and all kinds of other blessings.

Divine Soul Downloads are unlimited. There can be a Divine Soul Download for anything that exists in the physical world. The reason for this is very simple. *Everything has a soul.* A house has a soul. The Divine can download a soul to your house that can transform its energy. The Divine can download a soul to your business that can transform your business. If you are wearing a ring, that ring has a soul. If the Divine downloads a new divine soul to your ring, you can ask the divine soul in your ring to offer divine healing and blessing.

I am honored to have been chosen as a servant of humanity and the Divine to offer Divine Soul Downloads. For the rest of my life, I will continue to offer Divine Soul Downloads. I will offer more and more of them. I will offer Divine Soul Downloads for every aspect of every life.

I am honored to be a servant of Divine Soul Downloads.

## What to Expect After You Receive Divine Soul Downloads

Divine Soul Downloads are new souls created from the heart of the Divine. When these souls are transmitted, you may feel a strong vibration. For example, you could feel warm or excited. Your body could shake a little. If you are not sensitive, you may not feel anything. Advanced spiritual beings with an open Third Eye can actually see a huge golden, rainbow, or purple light soul enter your body.

These divine souls are your yin companions[3] for life. They will stay with your soul forever. Even after your physical life ends, these divine treasures will continue to accompany your soul into your next life and all of your future lives. In these books, I will teach you how to invoke these divine souls anytime, anywhere to give you divine healing or blessing in this life. You also can invoke these souls to leave your body to offer divine healing or blessing to others. These divine souls have extraordinary abilities to heal, bless, and transform. If you develop advanced spiritual abilities in your next life, you will discover that you have these divine souls with you. Then you will be able to invoke these divine souls in the same way in your future lifetimes to heal, bless, and transform every aspect of your life.

It is a great honor to have a divine soul downloaded to your own soul. The divine soul is a pure soul without bad karma. The divine soul carries divine healing and blessing abilities. The download does not have any side effects. You are given love and light with divine frequency. You are given divine abilities to serve yourself and others. Therefore, humanity is extremely honored

---

3. A yang companion is a physical being, such as a family member, friend, or pet. A yin companion is a soul companion without a physical form, such as your spiritual fathers and mothers in Heaven.

that the Divine is offering the Divine's downloads. I am extremely honored to be a servant of the Divine, of you, of all humanity, and of all souls to offer Divine Soul Downloads. I cannot thank the Divine enough. I cannot thank you, all humanity, and all souls enough for the opportunity to serve.

Thank you. Thank you. Thank you.

# Foreword to the Soul Power Series

$\mathcal{I}$ HAVE ADMIRED DR. Zhi Gang Sha's work for some years now. In fact, I clearly remember the first time I heard him describe his soul healing system, Soul Mind Body Medicine. I knew immediately that I wanted to support this gifted healer and his mission, so I introduced him to my spiritual community at Agape. Ever since, it has been my joy to witness how those who apply his teachings and techniques experience increased energy, joy, harmony, and peace in their lives.

Dr. Sha's techniques awaken the healing power already present in all of us, empowering us to put our overall well-being in our own hands. His explanation of energy and message, and how they link consciousness, mind, body, and spirit, forms a dynamic information network in language that is easy to understand and, more important, to apply.

Dr. Sha's time-tested results have proven to thousands of students and readers that healing energies and messages exist within specific sounds, movements, and affirmative perceptions. Weaving in his own personal experiences, Dr. Sha's theories and practices of working directly with the life-force energy and spirit are practical, holistic, and profound. His recognition that Soul Power is most important for every aspect of life is vital to meeting the challenges of twenty-first-century living.

The worldwide representative of his renowned teacher, Dr. Zhi Chen Guo, one of the greatest qi gong masters and healers in the world, Dr. Sha is himself a master of ancient disciplines such as tai chi, qi gong, kung fu, the *I Ching,* and feng shui. He has blended the soul of his culture's natural healing methods with his training as a Western physician, and generously offers his wisdom to us through the books in his Soul Power Series. His contribution to those in the healing professions is undeniable, and the way in which he empowers his readers to understand themselves, their feelings, and the connection between their bodies, minds, and spirits is his gift to the world.

Through his Soul Power Series, Dr. Sha guides the reader into a consciousness of healing not only of body, mind, and spirit, but also of the heart. I consider his healing path to be a universal spiritual practice, a journey into genuine transformation. His professional integrity and compassionate heart are at the root of his being a servant of humankind, and my heartfelt wish for his readers is that they accept his invitation to awaken the power of the soul and realize the natural beauty of their existence.

*Dr. Michael Bernard Beckwith*
*Founder, Agape International Spiritual Center*

# Foreword to Divine Soul Songs

"Gᴏᴅ ᴛᴏʟᴅ ᴍᴇ to heal His people, and I have taken that order seriously." That was Dr. Zhi Gang Sha's introduction to me. His statement was so simple and offered with such sincerity, that I believed him to be honest and faith-driven.

He travels the world over helping the rich and poor to find health. He accepts all, rejecting none.

We, the human race, need more Zhi Gang Sha.

—Dr. Maya Angelou

# How to Read This Book

$\mathcal{I}$N EVERY BOOK of my Soul Power Series, I reveal soul secrets and teach soul wisdom, soul knowledge, and soul practices. Secret and sacred wisdom and knowledge are important. *Practice is even more important.* Since ancient times, serious Buddhist, Taoist, qi gong, and kung fu practitioners have spent hours and hours a day in practice. Their dedication empowers them to develop and transform their frequency, their consciousness, and their purification further and further. In the modern world, successful professionals in every field similarly spend hours a day for months and years in practice. Their commitment empowers them to develop and transform their power and abilities further and further.

Every book in my Soul Power Series offers new approaches to healing, rejuvenation, and life transformation. Along with the teachings of sacred wisdom and knowledge, I also offer Divine Soul Downloads as a servant, vehicle, and channel of the Divine. I am honored to serve you through these books. However, *the most important service offered in these books is the practices.* This is especially true of this book, *Divine Soul Songs*. In this book I lead you in dozens of practices. If you spend four or five minutes to do each practice, I fully understand that it will take you some time to finish all of them. Do a few practices today. Tomorrow do another few practices. Do a few more the day after tomorrow. The practices are vital. If you do not do them, how can you experience their power and benefits? If you do not experience their power and benefits, how can you fully understand and absorb the teaching?

My message to you is that as you read this book, make sure you do not miss the practices. I deliberately guide you in this book to do spiritual practices using the power of soul for healing, preventing sickness, prolonging life, and transforming every aspect of life, including relationships and finances. Reading this book is like being at a workshop with me. When you go to a workshop and the teacher leads you in a meditation or practice, you do not run off to do something else, do you?

Do not rush through this book. Do every practice I ask you to do. You will receive ten, fifty, a hundred times the benefit that you would receive if you simply read through the book quickly. Especially, to receive Divine Soul Downloads does not mean you automatically receive their benefits. You must invoke them and practice with them to experience and receive divine healing and blessing. Remember also that going through this book just once is not enough. My advanced students go through my books many times. Every time they read and do the practices, they reach more and more "aha" moments. They receive more and more remarkable healing, purification, and life transformation results.

These are important messages for you to remember as you read this book. I wish each of you will receive great healing, rejuvenation, purification, and life transformation by doing the practices in this book. Receive the benefits of *soul over matter,* which is the power of soul.

Practice. Practice. Practice.

Experience. Experience. Experience.

Benefit. Benefit. Benefit.

Hao! Hao! Hao!

Thank you. Thank you. Thank you.

# *Introduction*

MILLIONS OF PEOPLE around the world are searching for soul secrets, wisdom, knowledge, and practices to fulfill their spiritual journeys. They really want to know the purpose of life. They want their spiritual journeys to be deeply blessed. They also want to transform every aspect of their physical lives. They want health. They want happiness. They want to rejuvenate. They want to prolong life. They want good relationships. They want financial abundance.

Why do so many people care about their spiritual journeys? They realize that physical life is short, while soul life is eternal. A human being's soul has experienced hundreds and perhaps even more than a thousand lifetimes as a human being. Why does a soul have to repeat life as a human being again and again? The reason is that a soul needs to be purified, and purified more and more. To be human is to be given a great opportunity for purification of soul, heart, mind, and body.

Why does a soul need to be purified? A soul needs to be purified in order to raise its spiritual standing higher and higher in Heaven.

Why does a soul need to uplift its standing to higher and higher layers of Heaven? The Divine resides in Tian Wai Tian (pronounced *tyen why tyen*), which is at the top of Heaven. "Tian" literally means *Heaven*. "Wai" means *beyond*. So Tian Wai Tian means *Heaven beyond Heaven*. Tian Wai Tian is the divine realm. Souls that reach Tian Wai Tian stop reincarnation. They continue to serve humanity, Mother Earth, and all universes. However, they will not become a human being any more. They will offer great service in soul form. If you call them, they will come from Tian Wai Tian to serve you. After serving you, they will return to Heaven's temple in Tian Wai Tian to continue to do Xiu Lian.

Xiu Lian (pronounced *shew lyen*) is an ancient spiritual term. "Xiu" means *purification*. "Lian" means *practice*. Xiu Lian represents the totality of the spiritual journey. It includes the cultivation and purification of your soul, heart, mind, and body. Xiu Lian is the process and practice of purification to uplift your spiritual standing.

Neither you nor your soul can decide your spiritual standing. The Akashic Records decide your spiritual standing. The Akashic Records are a special place in Heaven where all of your lives are recorded, including all of your activities, behaviors, and thoughts. They also decide your spiritual standing in Heaven based on your life records.

As I write this, there are about 6.7 billion human beings on Mother Earth. Our souls reside in Jiu Tian (pronounced *joe tyen*). "Jiu" means *nine*. Again, "tian" means *Heaven*. So Jiu Tian is the nine layers of Heaven. As I have shared in the first three books of

my Soul Power Series,[4] souls in Jiu Tian must reincarnate. After
your physical life ends, your soul will stay in Jiu Tian for a while.
How long it stays depends on how much good service you gave
humanity, Mother Earth, and universes. The better you serve in
this physical life, the longer you will stay in Heaven, but you will
return as a human being again.

Your soul has and will continue to reincarnate again and
again to purify. It will continue to gain more wisdom. It will have
the opportunity to offer more service to humanity, Mother Earth,
and universes. Do a good job and your soul will be uplifted
higher and higher in Heaven. Moving to Tian Wai Tian, the divine realm, is your soul's direction, desire, and final destiny.

Millions of people are searching for soul wisdom, knowledge,
and practices to fulfill their spiritual journeys because millions of
souls have realized that their journey is to move toward the divine realm.

Why do souls have this realization? Because they understand
the benefits of reaching the divine realm:

- Souls who reach the divine realm (Tian Wai Tian)
  stop reincarnation.
  Souls who reach the divine realm will not become
  a human being anymore, but such souls become very
  powerful high-level servants. It is not difficult to understand this. To reach the divine realm a soul must
  have great purity and be an unconditional universal
  servant.

---

4. Zhi Gang Sha, 2008–2009, *Soul Wisdom, Soul Communication,* and *The Power of Soul,* New
York/Toronto: Atria Books/Heaven's Library.

Millions of people pray to the Divine for blessings. When you pray to the Divine, the Divine will respond. The Divine will come to bless you and then return to the Divine's temple in Heaven. The Divine blesses us in soul form. The Divine is an unconditional universal servant. In a similar way, all souls in Tian Wai Tian bless us in soul form. All souls in Tian Wai Tian are unconditional universal servants. The Divine is the highest soul.

- Souls who reach the divine realm are closer to the Divine.

    To be closer to the Divine is to be more aligned with the Divine in soul, heart, mind, and body. To be closer to the Divine is to be given great abilities to serve through transmissions of Divine Soul Power. Souls who reach Tian Wai Tian receive special teachings, blessings, and further purification directly from the Divine. Imagine the honor of receiving direct divine teaching, blessing, and empowerment. No words can explain this greatest honor and blessing further. What more can a soul wish for or receive? This is why moving to the divine realm is the direction, desire, and destiny of every soul.

It is easy to understand the benefits of reaching the divine realm. It is not easy to receive them. As I shared in the beginning section of this book on the Soul Power Series, the Soul Light Era, a new era for Mother Earth and all universes, began on August 8, 2003. It will last fifteen thousand years. In the Soul Light Era many more people will realize the importance of the spiritual journey. Almost all souls of humanity are eager to move higher and higher in the spiritual realms toward the divine realm.

It is very difficult to move to the divine realm. To be uplifted to Tian Wai Tian is the greatest honor and blessing attainable in one's spiritual journey. The Divine will select only the purest souls who have offered the greatest service to humanity, Mother Earth, and universes to be uplifted to Tian Wai Tian.

In the previous fifteen-thousand-year era that ended on August 8, 2003, the only two souls to be uplifted to Tian Wai Tian were the top spiritual leaders in Jiu Tian. These two beings are named Niu Wa Niang Niang (pronounced *new wah nyung nyung*) and Yuan Shi Tian Zun (pronounced *yuahn shee tyen zuen*).

Let me share with you part of the incredible stories of these two great beings. Legends about Niu Wa Niang Niang can be found in ancient Chinese records. Niu Wa Niang Niang had the head of a human being and the body of a snake. She was a very quiet person. Although she did not speak much, she had a very big heart with deep love and compassion.

In that distant and very ancient time, it was known that Heaven was supported by four huge columns, but they broke and collapsed. Half of Heaven then fell down to Mother Earth, leaving a big hole in Heaven and forming a big opening in Mother Earth. This event also caused huge forest fires and floods. Wild animals became very disturbed and began to attack and hurt people.

During this time of great disasters, Niu Wa Niang Niang selected five different-colored stones from a special river and cooked them down to create a glue-like substance. She used this glue to plug the hole in Heaven. She then cut four legs from a huge sea turtle and placed them in the four directions so that they could hold up Heaven. She killed a monstrous black dragon that was menacing people, and she also repelled the wild animals. She collected reeds and burned them, using the ashes to block the floods. Due to her efforts, the disasters stopped.

The above story was taken from a historical Chinese book. As I was writing *Divine Soul Songs,* I asked Marilyn Smith, one of my top teachers, to do soul communication with the soul of Niu Wa Niang Niang. The second book of my Soul Power Series, *Soul Communication: Opening Your Spiritual Channels for Success and Fulfillment,* teaches how to open your spiritual channels to communicate directly with the universe. If you open your spiritual channels, you will able to converse directly with every soul in the universe and with the Divine. This is true soul communication ability.

Marilyn called the soul of Niu Wa Niang Niang. The following words come directly from Niu Wa Niang Niang's soul speaking through Marilyn's soul communication:

> *Greetings. I am honored to share some of my story. Great natural disasters actually happened. The turmoil in the heavens was also very real and it caused great problems on Earth. People felt as though the sky had fallen in. I used my powers to stop the turmoil that was experienced on Earth as natural disasters. The wild animals also became very dangerous because they could not find food. They were attacking anyone and anything to get food. When I calmed the turmoil in Heaven, the rivers and all things in nature returned to their proper behavior. The natural disasters on*

*Earth ended, and there was food for the animals once again.*

*You now know that what I did was to use the power of soul. In those ancient days, people did not know about soul power, so they created the stories you have read to explain as best they could the things that I accomplished. I did all of these things and much more.*

I also asked Francisco Quintero, another of my top teachers, to connect with the soul of Niu Wa Niang Niang. The following words come directly from Niu Wa Niang Niang's soul speaking through Francisco's soul communication:

*I was sent to Mother Earth to assist humanity during a difficult time many thousands of years ago. It was a time when Heaven opened and humanity was ready to begin to uplift their souls. It was I who created a strong foundation on Mother Earth because I noticed that there was light on Mother Earth and the souls of humanity did not know how to work with this light.*

*I helped humanity by connecting their souls to Heaven. I did this by creating a temple on Earth that allowed the Divine to shine through. At the same time, I killed a black dragon, allowing many demons, monsters, and wild animals to be removed from Mother Earth. I gave people the skills to clear their own demons and monsters. To help bring people closer to Heaven, I had to create a temple. For the pillars of the temple, I used the legs of the sea turtle because they brought ancient wisdom and long life. People came to these temples to receive the ancient wisdom and to get closer to God. This was the beginning of a beautiful era that brought people closer to God.*

Now let me share the legend of Yuan Shi Tian Zun. Pan Gu Zhen Ren was the first embodiment of Yuan Shi Tian Zun. This was as a bird. Pan Gu Zhen Ren spent many years in an egg. He extended his arms and legs to try to crack the egg and break free. In doing this he was actually expanding Heaven and Earth.

Before the universe was created, everything was blurred, formless, and chaotic. There were no stars, no sun, no moon, and no Mother Earth. Pan Gu Zhen Ren was the essence of the universe. He absorbed heavenly chi and also drank of the Earth's spring. The essence of Pan Gu Zhen Ren flowed through the universe. After he created Heaven and Earth, he left his body behind and transported his soul to Heaven. Various parts of Pan Gu's body became the sun, the moon, the stars, the rivers, the mountains, the thunder, the lightning, and the wind. Pan Gu's body became all that was created upon Mother Earth. Meanwhile, his soul flowed freely throughout the universe. After millions and millions of years, Pan Gu Zhen Ren met a holy woman named Tai Yuan Yu Niu. He transformed into light and went into Tai Yuan's body. After twelve years of being in Tai Yuan Yu Niu's body, he was born as Yuan Shi Tian Zun.

Yuan Shi Tian Zun was the first Taoist saint and the original king of Heaven. Many call him the grandfather of Heaven. "Yuan Shi" means *originator*. "Tian" means *Heaven* and "Zun" means *revered*. Yuan Shi Tian Zun gave birth to Tian Huang Zhi Wang Mu. Tian Huang Zhi Wang Mu, who was Heaven's mother, gave birth in turn to Earth's king. Earth's king gave birth in turn to a human king.

Yuan Shi Tian Zun was the first to reach immortality. He had very high powers and has helped people in all eras. As every new era came about, Yuan Shi Tian Zun would embody and offer his help. Yuan Shi Tian Zun has served for countless years.

Yuan Shi Tian Zun had many high-level disciples, including Tai Shang Lao Jun, Tai Shang Zhang Ren, Tian Huang Zhen Ren, and Wu Fang Wu Di. In Taoist temples, you can see portrayals of Yuan Shi Tian Zun. He always sits in the center with Ling Bao Tian Zun to the right and Tao Te Zhen Jun to the left. They are considered the three highest saints in the Taoist pantheon.

Now let us hear direct divine teaching about Yuan Shi Tian Zun through Marilyn's soul communication:

*Yuan Shi Tian Zun came directly from the source and creator of all that exists. The Creator placed divine energy, light, and life within a woman who gave birth to the one who is called Yuan Shi Tian Zun. No physical father was involved. The role of the father was performed by the light, life, and energy of the Creator.*

*Yuan Shi Tian Zun has been present from the beginning of creation. He has had a special role in the unfolding of creation and the development of wisdom among humanity. He has served all of creation through its many different stages. He has given guidance, direction, and blessings. He is doing this for humanity at this time.*

*Yuan Shi Tian Zun is one of the very few who has passed to the heavenly realms without experiencing death. He is known as an immortal. His presence with humanity at this time will assist us in many ways. One of those ways is to teach us the wisdom of immortality.*

*Yuan Shi Tian Zun has had a special role in directing creation on Mother Earth and the universe. He continues*

*that role very seriously. At this time humanity can partici-*
*pate in his teachings. He is very present with humanity,*
*Mother Earth, and all universes.*

I asked Francisco to connect directly with the soul of Yuan
Shi Tian Zun. The following words come directly from Yuan
Shi Tian Zun's soul speaking through Francisco's soul communi-
cation:

> *I was born from creation. I was the first soul to be born. I*
> *was born from the heart of the Divine. This was my very*
> *first incarnation as a soul. I incarnated as a human soul*
> *billions of years ago. I did this to assist humanity. I brought*
> *with me the sacred treasures, practical wisdom, and soul*
> *secrets needed to uplift humanity.*
>
> *I taught humanity wisdom and shared with them*
> *treasures to purify their hearts. I was a spiritual leader and*
> *a divine servant. In this lifetime, I made a vow to assist*
> *humanity to enlighten their souls. I have served countless*
> *beings, including all souls of humanity. I now sit in the*
> *divine realm overseeing and guiding the saints on Mother*
> *Earth.*

I also asked Peter Hudoba, another one of my top teachers,
to directly connect with the soul of Yuan Shi Tian Zun. Here are
more words from Yuan Shi Tian Zun's soul speaking through
Peter's soul communication:

> *I am one of the creators of the universe. I am part of*
> *the emanation from the divine realm. I was one of the*

original ones. I helped create the universe through my special form and special position as an advisor to Heaven's king.

Ever since, one of my roles has been to be in charge of the original yuan qi, which is original qi or original spiritual qi. I have passed through the barrier separating the highest levels of the universe and humanity many times, always as a supportive leader. I have always guided people indirectly through the Source. My desire has been to bring all souls to the highest purity, and I have given numerous teachings to many souls in many parts of the universes.

As I mentioned, I have been teaching indirectly. My greatest ambition has always been to create a huge highest divine realm and to help bring many souls there. However, this task has been very difficult to advance because many souls reject the idea of the highest levels of purity. I have been one of the highest advisors to the king of Heaven, helping to supply energies to the universe. I have been in charge of the army of heavenly scholars and warriors to defend the realm of the highest purity. Even in the Soul World my guidance has remained indirect.

I have not written many books, but some of them are in the heavenly library where they remain hidden with their secrets. These books describe reaching the highest levels of enlightenment through the process of self-cultivation and aligning oneself with the flow of Tao. My ambition has always been to establish a realm of highest purity in the Soul World; I have never focused on the material *world. I am currently assisting the Highest Divine in the purification process of thousands of souls in the highest levels of the universe. The transition that is occurring on Earth is also occurring in Heaven. Pu Ti Lao Zu is in charge of Mother Earth's transition. I am in charge of Heaven's transition.*

The Divine must send a personal order to uplift a soul to Tian Wai Tian. Such a Divine Order is given to the Akashic Records. At the same time, the Divine will transmit major divine soul treasures to the soul to be uplifted. These treasures empower that soul to offer greater service. Then that soul can be uplifted to the divine realm.

If you call on Niu Wa Niang Niang or Yuan Shi Tian Zun to bless your life, you will understand better what I am sharing here. Invoke them. Spend three minutes with them to experience their power. Then you will understand that the souls in Tian Wai Tian are powerful servants beyond comprehension. They are purest divine servants. Call them and they will respond, just as when you call the Divine, the Divine will respond.

Join me in experiencing their Soul Power now. In the first practice in this book, you will ask Niu Wa Niang Niang to boost your energy, stamina, vitality, and immunity. Here is how to do it. Say *hello* to Niu Wa Niang Niang:

*Dear Niu Wa Niang Niang,*
*I love you, honor you, and appreciate you.*
*Could you give me a blessing for three minutes to boost my*
    *energy, stamina, vitality, and immunity?*

*I am very grateful.*
*Thank you.*

Then completely relax. Close your eyes. Go into a calm, meditative state. Silently chant for three minutes:

*Niu Wa Niang Niang, boost my energy, stamina,*
　　*vitality, and immunity.*
*Niu Wa Niang Niang, boost my energy, stamina,*
　　*vitality, and immunity.*
*Niu Wa Niang Niang, boost my energy, stamina,*
　　*vitality, and immunity.*
*Niu Wa Niang Niang, boost my energy, stamina,*
　　*vitality, and immunity . . .*

After three minutes say:

*Hao! Hao! Hao!*
*Thank you. Thank you. Thank you.*
*Gong song. Gong song. Gong song.*

"Hao" (pronounced *how*) means *good, perfect* in Chinese.

The first "thank you" is to the Divine. The second "thank you" is to Niu Wa Niang Niang. The third "thank you" is to your own soul.

We will close every practice in this book in this way.

"Gong song" (pronounced *gohng sohng*) means *return with respect.* You are returning Niu Wa Niang Niang to her Heaven's temple in Tian Wai Tian with great respect, gratitude, and honor for her having come to offer you her blessing.

If you did this three-minute practice with me and your Third Eye[5] is open, you saw the huge soul of Niu Wa Niang Niang blessing you. If you could not see her soul, you may have seen light of various colors—golden, rainbow, purple, or even crystal light. If you could not see light, you may have felt some tingling or vibration. If you are not sensitive, you may not have felt anything. This does not mean you did not receive Niu Wa Niang Niang's blessing. Everyone is different, so everyone could have unique feelings and reactions. Everybody could receive different levels of blessing for energy, stamina, vitality, and immunity. Some highly developed spiritual beings and advanced energy healers and practitioners could feel their bodies shaking. Some people could feel a gentle and refined vibration in their bodies.

I would like to emphasize what I explained earlier in the section "How to Read This Book." I will give you many practices in this book for boosting your energy, stamina, vitality, and immunity. I will also give many practices for healing your physical, emotional, mental, and spiritual bodies. Please remember my guidance and follow the directions to do the practices. Really do them with me. Do not simply read through the text. If you simply read without practicing, you will miss the essence of this book.

This book gives you and humanity healing, rejuvenation, and life transformation on the spot as you read it. When I ask you to do a practice—as I just did by asking you to ask Niu Wa Niang Niang to bless your energy, stamina, vitality, and

---

5. The Third Eye, one of the body's major spiritual centers, is a cherry-sized energy center located in the center of your head. After you open and develop the Third Eye, you will be able to see images of the spiritual world.

immunity—do the practice exactly as I ask you to. You will receive benefits beyond words and comprehension.

This book literally brings Heaven to Mother Earth. This book brings the top saints in all layers of Heaven to you. This book brings divine blessings directly to you. Receive soul blessings on the spot in this book. Healing could happen on the spot. Rejuvenation is happening on the spot. Life transformation will happen on the spot. Why? Because you are applying your Soul Power, saints' Soul Power, and Divine Soul Power.

## Energy Reactions in the Body

In receiving the blessings and doing the practices in this book, divine frequency and divine light will come to you. Energy and spiritual blockages can be removed or reduced. Individuals can have a variety of responses, including seeing images and feeling energy in the body. I would like to offer some teaching and guidance about energy reactions in the body.

- Generally speaking, people who are sensitive, fatigued, or weak have more dramatic energy reactions to soul blessings.

  When you practice and receive soul blessings from saints, Divine Soul Songs, Divine Soul Downloads, and more, your body could shake and vibrate dramatically. If this causes you some discomfort, let me show you a simple way to calm your body. Immediately put your right middle fingertip on the center of the top of your head and your left middle fingertip on your navel. (See figure 1 in the insert.) Call divine love and light:

*Dear Divine Love and Light,*
*Calm me. Calm me. Calm me. Calm me . . .*

Within one minute your body's reaction should calm down. Then concentrate on your Lower Dan Tian. (The Lower Dan Tian is a foundational energy center that is centered 1.5 *cun* below the navel and 2.5 *cun*—pronounced *tsuen*—inside the abdomen. The *cun* is a unit of measurement used in traditional Chinese medicine. One *cun* is defined as the width of the top joint of the thumb at its widest part. Although this varies from person to person, it is roughly equivalent to one inch. The Lower Dan Tian is roughly the size of your fist. The Lower Dan Tian is foundational for one's energy, stamina, vitality, and immunity, and so it is a key for long life.)

Visualize all light from the universe concentrating in your Lower Dan Tian. The purpose of doing this is to accumulate universal energy to build your foundational center of energy, stamina, vitality, and immunity. In the same way, if you do any energy healing or spiritual healing, at the end spend one minute concentrating on the Lower Dan Tian. This is called *shou gong* (pronounced *show gohng*), which means *close the practice*.

- People who are healthy and physically strong may not feel a clear vibration when they receive soul blessings in this book.

  This is perfect. Generally speaking, physically strong people are not sensitive to energy and spiritual blessings. But if you do not feel too much, it does not mean you are not receiving the benefits of the blessings. You are still receiving great benefits for healing, rejuvenating, and transforming your frequency to higher and more refined levels. Continue to practice as I teach in this book. You will feel more and more. You may not feel a clear vibration for quite a long time. It could take years. But if you continue to practice, one day you will feel such a dramatic vibration that you could be scared.

Whatever your energy reaction, there is no need to be scared. Let me share my personal experience with you. I have practiced tai chi since age six. I started to practice qi gong at age ten. In my journey of energy and spiritual practice, I have experienced sweating and strong vibration many times. In 1994 I went back to China to see my most beloved spiritual father, Master and Dr. Zhi Chen Guo. Twenty thousand people were practicing together at his clinic in Hebei province. Suddenly my body started to shake like a machine. I shook for six days. I never believed I could shake like that. That was a big blessing. It was a major energy and spiritual development for my body.

If you have a strong reaction, I showed you the technique to calm your body just now. If you shake so much that you cannot handle it, apply this technique right away. It will help you stop shaking. If using the technique for one minute is not enough to calm your body, continue to practice for a few more minutes. Gentle shaking for a few days is okay. That is your body's development. If you reach the condition of strong shaking, I congratulate you. Sometimes the body will go through strong shaking a few times for further and further development.

After experiencing dramatic shaking one time or perhaps a few times, you could then experience a very refined vibration when you do energy or spiritual practices. If you reach the condition of a refined vibration, a very slight tingling sensation, or itchiness, I congratulate you again. Itchiness is a very important signal that the frequency of the energy in your body is transforming to a significantly higher level.

In summary, in most cases the development of one's energy response to soul blessings is a process from no feeling to a little feeling, then to a strong feeling, to shaking, and finally to a refined feeling. Going through this process will deeply transform the frequency of your body's energy centers, soul houses (I will explain the seven soul houses in chapter 3), systems, organs, cells, cell units, DNA, RNA, and smallest matter. When you reach a truly advanced level in your body's energy development, then every moment you do an energy or spiritual practice you will feel a "tiny," refined tingling vibration in your whole body, from head to toe and skin to bone. This gentle vibration produces a gentle heat that is very comfortable. Words cannot explain that comfort enough.

This is the process for advanced energy and spiritual practice. Many people who do not do energy or spiritual practices may never shake once in their entire lives. But because millions of people are searching for spiritual secrets, wisdom, and practices to fulfill their spiritual journeys, and because millions of people are doing various kinds of energy and spiritual practices such as qi gong, yoga, meditation, chanting, and more from all kinds of spiritual groups and teachings, I am sharing these secrets for these practitioners and for you. When you advance in the process and reach the condition of great sensitivity and strong shaking, do not be afraid. Without the secret wisdom and knowledge I have shared, you may not be prepared for this condition. You could be very scared, which is not good for you. We have experience with hundreds of thousands of people practicing in China and worldwide. We have experience with all kinds of energy and spiritual reactions. Therefore, I share this teaching to give guidance for advanced energy and spiritual practitioners. Whatever kind of reaction happens during your practice, it is right for your journey. If you feel uncomfortable, use the calming technique right away: put your right middle fingertip on the center of the top of your head and your left middle fingertip on your navel, ask divine love and light to calm you, and finally focus on your Lower Dan Tian.

If you want to receive my advanced energy and spiritual training, I welcome you to join my various training programs, including Soul Healing and Enlightenment retreats, Opening Your Spiritual Channels workshops, various teleclasses, and more. It has been nearly fifty years since I began my energy and spiritual journey with tai chi practice at age six. I have constantly received guidance from my spiritual fathers and mothers in the Soul World and from many great physical masters and teachers. Even though I am now a teacher myself and have taught many thousands of people worldwide, I am still receiving constant guidance from my teachers and from the Divine. In the energy and spiritual journey you do need a teacher to guide you. It will save you lots of time and effort. It will help you avoid making mistakes. You will progress much faster. There are many great teachers worldwide. Find the proper teacher to guide you in your energy and spiritual journey. I wish you great success in your energy practice and in your spiritual journey.

Hao!

## The Importance of Practice

As I have already said, this book has more practical exercises than any other book I have written. There are thousands of books in history that give so many secrets and so much wisdom. They are great, but I feel it is important to transform the direction of my books more toward practice. Simply do the practices to heal and transform your life. The one-sentence secret is:

### To practice is to transform.

I cannot emphasize enough that this book is leading you to practice. Do not read through the practices quickly. You will not receive their benefits. You will not receive maximum benefits from the teaching. Spend the time. Follow my instructions. Do each practice—a few minutes here and a few minutes there. It is just as though you are in my workshop. I intend to make this book just like a live workshop with me. You may be reading my book in your home, your office, a hotel room, or on the beach. It doesn't matter where you are if you do the practices the way I am asking you to. You will receive exactly the same teaching and blessings as you would in my workshops.

Every book in my Soul Power Series offers new teachings of *soul over matter*. Soul can heal. Soul can transform every aspect of your life. Soul healing and soul transformation are not limited by time or space. Wherever you are, I am offering you teaching. Wherever you are, I am offering you service. Wherever you are, saints are blessing you. Wherever you are, the Divine is blessing you. To offer you these blessings and service, the new direction I am taking, starting with this book, is to transform my books to be just like live workshops. When you are in a workshop, the teacher may guide you to meditate. If the teacher wants to spend three minutes leading you in a meditation, you will spend three minutes meditating with the teacher. When you read this book, if I ask you to do three minutes of singing or chanting, please do it. You will be singing or chanting the words of many Divine Soul Songs. It is just like I am singing with you in a workshop. When you do the practices, the Divine is with you because in this book I will offer many Divine Soul Downloads, which are permanent divine soul treasures. Every moment you practice, you are receiving blessings from divine frequency and divine vibration with divine love, forgiveness, compassion, and light.

## You Are in My Workshop

Now I would like you to experience the new direction I am taking in this book. Imagine you are in a workshop with me. Let us practice together. You can also call my soul anytime to support your practice. My soul is your servant. On page 335 of my book *Soul Mind Body Medicine*,[6] I have offered my soul in service to humanity and all souls twenty-four hours per day each and every day. Call my soul. My soul is a servant for you, for all humanity, and for all souls.

---

6. Zhi Gang Sha, 2006, *Soul Mind Body Medicine: A Complete Soul Healing System for Optimum Health and Vitality*, Novato, California: New World Library.

Let us do the second practice in this book. You can ask Niu
Wa Niang Niang to give you love. Niu Wa Niang Niang is a divine daughter. She carries divine love.

> *Dear Niu Wa Niang Niang,*
> *I love you, honor you, and appreciate you.*
> *Could you give me your love for three minutes to heal*
>     *or bless _____ (make a request for healing or*
>     *blessing)?*
> *I am very grateful.*
> *Thank you.*

Then completely relax. Close your eyes. Go into a calm,
meditative state. Silently chant for three minutes:

> *Niu Wa Niang Niang's love, heal and bless me.*
> *Niu Wa Niang Niang's love, heal and bless me.*
> *Niu Wa Niang Niang's love, heal and bless me.*
> *Niu Wa Niang Niang's love, heal and bless me . . .*

After three minutes, close:

> *Hao! Hao! Hao!*
> *Thank you. Thank you. Thank you.*
> *Gong song. Gong song. Gong song.*

Now join me in asking Yuan Shi Tian Zun to bless our lives.
Let us ask him to give us a healing:

> *Dear Yuan Shi Tian Zun,*
> *I love you, honor you, and appreciate you.*

*Could you heal my _____ (make your request for*
  *healing)?*
*I am very grateful.*
*Thank you.*

Then chant repeatedly for three minutes, silently or aloud:

*Yuan Shi Tian Zun, heal my _____.*
*Yuan Shi Tian Zun, heal my _____.*
*Yuan Shi Tian Zun, heal my _____.*
*Yuan Shi Tian Zun, heal my _____ . . .*

After three minutes, close this practice:

*Hao! Hao! Hao!*
*Thank you. Thank you. Thank you.*
*Gong song. Gong song. Gong song.*

Next let us ask Yuan Shi Tian Zun to bless our relationships:

*Dear Yuan Shi Tian Zun,*
*I love you, honor you, and appreciate you.*
*Could you bless my relationship with _____ (name a*
  *person)?*
*I am very grateful.*
*Thank you.*

Relax completely. Close your eyes. Go into a calm, meditative state. Silently chant for three minutes:

*Yuan Shi Tian Zun, bless my relationship with*
     _____ (name the person).
*Yuan Shi Tian Zun, bless my relationship with*

     _____.

*Yuan Shi Tian Zun, bless my relationship with*

     _____.

*Yuan Shi Tian Zun, bless my relationship with*

     _____ . . .

After three minutes, close this practice:

*Hao! Hao! Hao!*
*Thank you. Thank you. Thank you.*
*Gong song. Gong song. Gong song.*

These practices use the secret Say Hello formula that I revealed in my book *Soul Mind Body Medicine*, which was published two years before the Soul Power Series was introduced. In that book, I introduced the Say Hello Healing and Say Hello Blessing technique:

1. Say hello.
2. Give love.
3. Make an affirmation or a request or give an order.
4. Express gratitude and courtesy.

The Say Hello formula is one of the simplest Soul Power techniques, yet it is one of the most powerful techniques for healing, rejuvenation, and life transformation, including transformation of relationships and finances. We will use this formula in every practice in this book.

## Soul Healing, Soul Enlightenment, and Divine Soul Songs

Every religion and spiritual group has its great teachers. Some of the best known include Jesus, Mary, buddhas such as Shi Jia Mo Ni Fuo[7] and Guan Yin, and many more. They continue to serve humanity and all souls. The Divine promotes them because of their service. Without service, one's spiritual standing cannot be uplifted. Only with service to humanity and all souls can your spiritual standing be uplifted. To uplift your spiritual standing is to reach soul enlightenment and advanced soul enlightenment. In the teaching of the Soul Power Series, the Divine asked me in 2008 to focus my service on soul healing and enlightenment. Soul healing is to remove the suffering of humanity. Soul enlightenment is to uplift one's soul standing. Physical life is to serve soul life. To uplift one's soul standing to the divine realm is the ultimate goal for one's spiritual journey.

My most beloved spiritual father, Dr. and Master Zhi Chen Guo, taught me many soul secrets in China. He, my other physical spiritual fathers and mothers, and Heaven's spiritual fathers and mothers prepared me to purify my soul, heart, mind, and body to be a better servant. All my lifetimes of commitment to serve humanity, Mother Earth, universes, and the Divine enabled me to be selected by the Divine as a servant of humanity and all souls. In July 2003 I was chosen as a divine servant. I was chosen as the servant to transmit divine soul treasures to humanity and all souls to facilitate my total mission:

---

7. Shi Jia Mo Ni Fuo, the Chinese name of the founder of Buddhism, is also known as Shakyamuni and Siddhartha Gautama. His name in Chinese is pronounced *shee jya maw nee fwaw*.

**To transform the consciousness of humanity and all souls**
**and enlighten them, in order to create**
**love, peace and harmony for**
**humanity, Mother Earth, and all universes.**

In 2008 the Divine directly told me to focus on the Soul Power Series for my entire life. The major service of the Soul Power Series and of my total mission is to offer soul healing and enlightenment. I was honored to receive this divine task. I continue to offer this teaching and service. I continue to train and certify Master Teachers and Healers of Soul Healing and Enlightenment and Divine Master Teachers and Healers who can also travel worldwide to offer soul healing and enlightenment service.

Soul healing is to remove the suffering of humanity. People are suffering in so many ways. In April 2007 I gave a speech at the international medical conference on "Meeting the Global Challenge of Cancer" at the United Nations. According to the World Health Organization, more people die from cancer worldwide than from malaria and AIDS combined. Cancer is not an epidemic, but it is everywhere. I met a renowned professor and researcher at UCLA who shared with me that two of the major sufferings of humanity are depression and anxiety. Millions of people suffer from them. There are so many chronic and life-threatening conditions. People everywhere are suffering.

The Divine asked me to offer the teaching of soul healing and enlightenment through the Soul Power Series. The Divine is giving the Divine's soul healing treasures to humanity as self-healing and healing tools. The message of healing is:

*I have the power to heal myself.*
*You have the power to heal yourself.*
*Together we have the power to heal the world.*

In this book the Divine is giving humanity Divine Soul Songs to further empower people to do soul self-healing. I am extremely grateful for all divine soul treasures. I am extremely honored to be a servant of humanity.

Soul enlightenment is to uplift your soul standing in Heaven. It could take hundreds of lifetimes to reach enlightenment. Now the Divine has chosen to send the Divine's order to enlighten those who are ready in an instant. There has never been a single saint who could enlighten a soul in this way. The Divine is enlightening souls now through a Divine Order. I am a chosen servant and vehicle for the Divine to offer the Divine's enlightenment. I can never express my gratitude enough for this honor. I am extremely privileged. I am most humbled.

In summary, to offer soul healing is to remove the suffering of humanity. To offer soul enlightenment is to uplift the soul toward the divine realm, Tian Wai Tian. This is a divine task given to me and my team. We will work together with millions of spiritual beings worldwide and all spiritual fathers and mothers on Mother Earth and in Heaven to serve and accomplish this divine direction.

This book reveals divine soul treasures that are tools to purify your soul, heart, mind, and body. This book will also help you gain divine abilities to serve. The more service you give, the faster your soul can be uplifted. The Divine Soul Songs shared in this book are practical treasures and divine tools for soul healing and enlightenment. The more you practice with these treasures, the faster you can heal. You can use these treasures to heal yourself and others. You can use these treasures to rejuvenate your soul, heart, mind, and body and the souls, hearts, minds, and bodies of others. You can use these treasures to bless and transform every aspect of your life, including relationships, finances, and more.

These treasures are so simple and practical. The results you receive from applying them could be profound and beyond description.

Enjoy them. Practice with them. Benefit from them. Use these divine treasures to serve yourself, your loved ones, and others.

Now let us sing together the first Divine Soul Song that the Divine gave to me, *Love, Peace and Harmony*. I will discuss this song in depth in chapter 2. The music for this Divine Soul Song is provided in figure 2 in the insert. You may also listen to an excerpt of *Love, Peace and Harmony* on the first track of the audio CD enclosed within this book. You may obtain a full-length CD of me singing this Divine Soul Song with a beautifully arranged instrumental accompaniment by visiting my Soul Song website, www.MasterShaSoulSong.com.

*I love my heart and soul*
*I love all humanity*
*Join hearts and souls together*
*Love, peace and harmony*
*Love, peace and harmony*

Thank you. Thank you. Thank you.

The first *thank you* is for the Divine. The second *thank you* is for all holy saints, Taoist saints, buddhas, healing angels, ascended masters, lamas, gurus, and all spiritual teachers on Mother Earth and in all layers of Heaven. The third *thank you* is for your own soul, heart, mind, and body and for all your loved ones.

It is my great honor to serve you.

It is my great honor to serve humanity, Mother Earth, and all universes.

I am extremely honored to be your servant.

Hao!

# DIVINE
# SOUL SONGS

# Soul Secrets, Wisdom, Knowledge, and Practices of Soul Song

On September 10, 2005, the Divine gave me the first Divine Soul Song, which begins *Lu La Lu La Li* in the Divine's Soul Language. The translated title of this Divine Soul Song is *Love, Peace and Harmony*. Since that day the Divine has given me many more Divine Soul Songs. Soul Song has already served thousands of people well. Within a few years I believe Soul Song will serve millions of people worldwide with remarkable, heart-touching results for healing, rejuvenation, and life transformation. Soul Song carries Soul Power beyond comprehension. Soul Song offers breakthrough soul service for humanity, Mother Earth, and all universes.

## What Is Soul Song?

Soul Song is the song of one's soul. When you sing a Soul Song, your soul is singing. When I sing a Soul Song, my soul is singing.

If a group of people sing their Soul Songs, every soul in that group is singing. The Divine sings Divine Soul Songs.

Soul Song is the song of one's Soul Language. Soul Language is the language and soul communication tool of the Soul World. If you speak Soul Language, the souls of other people understand it, the souls of saints understand it, and the Divine understands it. *Soul Wisdom,* the first book of my Soul Power Series, reveals secret and sacred wisdom, knowledge, and practices of Soul Language, Soul Song, Soul Tapping, Soul Movement, and Soul Dance. These practical soul treasures have received great responses from people worldwide. They continue to serve humanity. The power of these soul treasures has been expressed in thousands of heart-touching and moving stories. Later in this chapter I will lead you in a practice to bring out your Soul Language and your Soul Song.

The soul is the boss of a human being. Soul Song is effective because it carries Soul Power. I have trained and certified hundreds of Soul Song Singers worldwide. They and thousands of other people are singing Soul Songs to heal and transform their own lives and the lives of others. Soul Song is one's soul mantra. Divine Soul Songs are the Divine's soul mantras. Mantra is an ancient spiritual practice. For thousands of years, renowned Hindu, Buddhist, Taoist, and other spiritual leaders in many different traditions have shared their mantras to serve millions of people.

I shared a few of the most important mantras in history in my book *Power Healing.*[1] One of them is *A Mi Tuo Fuo* (pronounced *ah mee twaw fwaw*). A Mi Tuo Fuo (Amitabha in San-

---

1. Zhi Gang Sha, 2002, *Power Healing: The Four Keys to Energizing Your Body, Mind & Spirit,* San Francisco: HarperSanFrancisco.

skrit) is the buddha who leads the Pure Land in Heaven. In his physical life on Mother Earth, he was an emperor. After he met his spiritual mentor, he gave up his emperor's position to follow his spiritual teacher, with the goal of reaching his soul enlightenment. He made forty-eight vows to Heaven and the universe. He created the Pure Land, a spiritual world in Heaven that is named Ji Le Shi Jie (pronounced *jee luh shee jyeh*) in Chinese. "Ji" means *the most.* "Le" means *happiness.* "Shi Jie" means *world.* Ji Le Shi Jie is the *world of most happiness.* In this place there are no ego, no fighting, and no attachment. A Mi Tuo Fuo has gathered countless buddhas, bodhisattvas, and other high-level souls in his realm to do Xiu Lian (spiritual practice) to advance their soul journeys.

Shi Jia Mo Ni Fuo, the founder of Buddhism, introduced A Mi Tuo Fuo's teachings to his students. Millions of students of Buddhism have received great benefits from these teachings to fulfill their spiritual journeys. Buddhist teaching is to teach students to become buddhas, which is to reach soul enlightenment. Shi Jia Mo Ni Fuo taught eighty-four thousand ways to fulfill your spiritual journey. One of the secret ways is to chant *A Mi Tuo Fuo.* This unique teaching is direct and extremely powerful: to become a buddha, chant *A Mi Tuo Fuo.* A Mi Tuo Fuo is the top buddha in the Buddhist realm. To chant *A Mi Tuo Fuo* repeatedly is to purify your heart completely. When you are upset, chant *A Mi Tuo Fuo* to balance your emotions. When you are sick, chant *A Mi Tuo Fuo* to receive spiritual healing from A Mi Tuo Fuo. When you are overly excited, chant *A Mi Tuo Fuo* to calm yourself down.

How does this work? When you chant *A Mi Tuo Fuo,* the soul of A Mi Tuo Fuo is healing you, blessing you, and transforming you. To chant *A Mi Tuo Fuo* repeatedly is to make a direct soul-to-soul and heart-to-heart connection with A Mi Tuo Fuo. When you chant *A Mi Tuo Fuo,* A Mi Tuo Fuo's soul knows what you need. Sometimes you may not have a particular request for A Mi Tuo Fuo's blessing. You are just chanting *A Mi Tuo Fuo.* The moment you do this, you are calling A Mi Tuo Fuo. His soul will respond and appear. His soul will instantly know what you need. He will give you love, forgiveness, compassion, and light. He will offer his soul service to heal and transform your life.

How simple it is! How profound a teaching it is. How powerful a technique it is. I have studied Buddhism. I have chanted *A Mi Tuo Fuo* a lot throughout my life. I have received blessings from A Mi Tuo Fuo that are beyond comprehension. I cannot honor Shi Jia Mo Ni Fuo enough for sharing the secret teaching, practice, and life-transforming power of chanting *A Mi Tuo Fuo.* Millions of people in history have received remarkable healing, blessing, life transformation, and soul enlightenment by chanting *A Mi Tuo Fuo.* I cannot honor this teaching enough.

I am sharing this Buddhist teaching, but that does not mean I am teaching Buddhism. I am teaching soul secrets, wisdom, knowledge, and practices. There are many powerful ancient mantras of ancient saints. There are powerful mantras of Taoist saints. There are sacred mantras of Hindu saints. There are sacred mantras of other spiritual groups and belief systems. I use the example of A Mi Tuo Fuo to share with you and humanity that chanting is one of the most powerful soul treasures for healing, blessing, and transforming all lives.

Soul Song or soul mantra carries soul frequency with love, forgiveness, compassion, and light, which can remove blockages in your soul, your energy, and your matter for healing, rejuvenating, and transforming your health and every aspect of your life.

Every person has his or her own soul. Every being has a soul.

Every inanimate thing has a soul. *Everything* has a soul. Every soul carries Soul Power. Every soul's power is different. There are layers in Heaven. The Divine resides at the top. Buddhas, holy saints, Taoist saints, and other high-level beings reside at levels under the Divine. Human beings' souls reside under the saints' souls in Heaven.

Why are Jesus, Mary, A Mi Tuo Fuo, Shi Jia Mo Ni Fuo, and Guan Yin (pronounced *gwahn yeen;* she is known as Avalokiteshvara in Sanskrit and Chenrezig in Tibetan) special? Because the Divine transmitted divine power to them. The Divine has transmitted the Divine's power to every saint. Different saints have received different powers from the Divine. The Divine has transmitted the Divine's healing power to Jesus. The Divine has transmitted the Divine's love power to Mary. The Divine has transmitted the Divine's purification power to A Mi Tuo Fuo. The Divine has transmitted the Divine's education power to Shi Jia Mo Ni Fuo. The Divine has transmitted the Divine's compassion power to Guan Yin. (Guan Yin's new name in the Soul Light Era is Ling Hui Sheng Shi—pronounced *ling hway shung shr*—which means *Soul Intelligence Saint Servant.*) There are many saints who have received different powers from the Divine. They are all chosen servants of the Divine. They are chosen servants for humanity and all souls. Because of their total commitment to serve the Divine, humanity, and all souls, they are given special powers from the Divine. They have served humanity with their special powers with many heart-touching and moving results. Therefore, millions of people love them, honor them, respect them, and follow their teachings. The more service they give, the more power the Divine transmits to them. The more power they have, the better service they can give to humanity and all souls. I share this teaching to reveal a top secret to you and humanity:

## Real Soul Power is given by the Divine.

One must offer total GOLD (gratitude, obedience, loyalty, and devotion) service to humanity and all souls. Then the Divine will transmit power to such a one.

In July 2003 the Divine chose me as the Divine's servant to transmit Divine Soul Power to humanity and all souls. I have transmitted divine soul healing power to create more than seven hundred Divine Healers for humanity. I have transmitted divine soul writing power to create more than one hundred Divine Writers. I have transmitted divine soul singing power to create a few hundred Divine Soul Song Singers. I have transmitted countless divine souls to humanity and all souls for divine soul healing, rejuvenation, and life transformation. I am a servant of the Divine. The Divine gave me the greatest honor. I ask; the Divine transmits. I cannot honor the Divine enough for being a chosen servant of humanity and all souls.

Divine souls carry divine frequency with divine love, forgiveness, compassion, and light. Divine frequency transforms the frequency of our souls, hearts, minds, and bodies. Divine Soul Songs are the Soul Songs that the Divine sings. The Divine's Soul Songs carry the Divine's frequency with the Divine's love, forgiveness, compassion, and light.

Let me summarize the essence of what I am sharing here:

- To chant *A Mi Tuo Fuo* is to receive total healing, purification, and enlightenment in order to become a buddha.
- The Divine has transmitted or downloaded power to Jesus, Mary, A Mi Tuo Fuo, Shi Jia Mo Ni Fuo, Guan

Yin, and other high-level beings. After receiving the Divine's downloads, they carry divine power.

- In July 2003 I was given the honor to transmit divine power to chosen ones. The recipients carry divine power as Divine Soul Healing Teachers and Healers, Divine Writers, Divine Editors, Divine Soul Song Singers, and more.

The purpose of this book is to teach Divine Soul Songs and transmit Divine Soul Song power to you and every reader in order to empower every reader to carry divine power.

Divine Soul Songs can heal, rejuvenate, and transform you, humanity, Mother Earth, and all universes.

## The Power and Significance of Soul Song

Soul Song works because Soul Song carries soul frequency with love, forgiveness, compassion, and light. A human being consists of soul, mind, and body. Soul is the boss.

**Heal the soul first; then healing of the mind and body will follow.**

**Transform the soul first; then transformation of every aspect of life will follow.**

Soul frequency transforms the frequency of one's heart, mind, and body. Love melts all blockages and transforms all life. Forgiveness brings inner peace and joy. Compassion boosts energy, stamina, vitality, and immunity. Light heals, prevents sickness, rejuvenates, prolongs life, and transforms every aspect of life, including relationships and finances.

Human beings and everything in the universe consist of soul, mind, and body. Soul, mind, and body are made of message, energy, and matter. A soul is the essence of a being. A soul has its own message and energy. It also has its own matter. The matter of the soul is the tiniest or most refined matter. A mind is the consciousness of a being. A consciousness has its own message and energy. It also has its own matter, which is also tinier and more refined than the matter of the body. A body has its own message and energy. It also is made of matter.

As I taught in my book *Soul Mind Body Medicine*, sicknesses can be divided into three types:

- message blockages
- energy blockages
- matter blockages

Message blockages are spiritual blockages, which are bad karma. Soul Mind Body Medicine states:

**When a person has a spiritual blockage,
that person has a sickness of the soul.**

When the soul is sick, sickness could also appear at the mind and body levels now, or it could manifest later. As long as a person has a spiritual blockage, sooner or later it *will* affect the mind and body. To remove spiritual blockages is to heal the soul. *Heal the soul first; then healing of the mind and body will follow.*

Energy blockages are chi blockages. In traditional Chinese medicine and other ancient philosophies, chi is vital energy and life force. Actually, chi is tiny or refined matter. It flows in the body through the cells and the spaces between the cells and the organs. *The Yellow Emperor's Internal Classic,* the authoritative book of traditional Chinese medicine, states: *If chi flows, one is healthy. If chi is blocked, one is sick.* This theory has guided traditional Chinese medicine for five thousand years. Remove energy blockages for healing. Time has proven that this theory is absolutely correct. It has served millions of people throughout history.

Matter blockages occur inside the cells. Each cell is made up of various units such as a nucleus, mitochondria, Golgi apparati, and other organelles. The nucleus includes DNA and RNA. There are various liquids and proteins within a cell. A cell is made of matter. Matter blockages cause sickness. Remove matter blockages for healing.

A Soul Song can heal by removing message, energy, and matter blockages through its vibration and frequency. It can influence, balance, and harmonize soul, mind, and body. These benefits can be applied to all life. For example, a business, a relationship—anything and everything consists of message, energy, and matter. Because Soul Song can remove the blockages of message, energy, and matter, it can offer healing and transformation to every aspect of life. It can prevent sickness, rejuvenate, prolong life, purify soul, heart, mind, and body, enlighten soul, heart, mind, and body, and more.

## Bring Out Your Own Soul Song

I shared much wisdom about Soul Song in *Soul Wisdom,* the first book in my Soul Power Series. Here I would simply like to give you a direct practice to bring out your Soul Song.

The first step is to bring out your Soul Language. Apply the secret divine code San San Jiu Liu Ba Yao Wu, which is Chinese for 3396815 and is pronounced *sahn sahn joe lew bah yow woo*. Each number in this secret code vibrates a different part of the body. San vibrates the chest. Jiu vibrates the lower abdomen. Liu vibrates the area of the ribs (the right and left sides of the body). Ba vibrates the navel area. Yao vibrates the head. Wu vibrates the stomach area. These physical vibratory effects offer great benefits for healing. But far beyond that, San San Jiu Liu Ba Yao Wu is a divine code for opening your Soul Language and all of your soul communication channels and for unlocking all of the potential power of your soul.

Let's prepare to practice now! Please read the entire practice first to get an idea of what you will be doing.

Ready? Let's practice now!

Relax. Sit or stand comfortably.

Chant *San San Jiu Liu Ba Yao Wu* repeatedly:

> *San San Jiu Liu Ba Yao Wu*
> *San San Jiu Liu Ba Yao Wu*
> *San San Jiu Liu Ba Yao Wu*
> *San San Jiu Liu Ba Yao Wu . . .*

Chant faster!

> *San San Jiu Liu Ba Yao Wu*
> *San San Jiu Liu Ba Yao Wu*
> *San San Jiu Liu Ba Yao Wu*
> *San San Jiu Liu Ba Yao Wu . . .*

Chant *San San Jiu Liu Ba Yao Wu* faster and faster!!

> *San San Jiu Liu Ba Yao Wu*
> *San San Jiu Liu Ba Yao Wu*

> *San San Jiu Liu Ba Yao Wu*
> *San San Jiu Liu Ba Yao Wu . . .*

Chant *San San Jiu Liu Ba Yao Wu* repeatedly as fast as you can!!!!

> *San San Jiu Liu Ba Yao Wu*
> *San San Jiu Liu Ba Yao Wu*
> *San San Jiu Liu Ba Yao Wu*
> *San San Jiu Liu Ba Yao Wu . . .*

As you chant faster and faster, let go of any conscious intent to pronounce the individual words clearly. As you chant as fast as you can, suddenly you may hear a very special voice that you never heard before. That special voice could sound very strange. Do not be surprised. Congratulations! That voice is your soul voice. Your soul is speaking its Soul Language. To confirm that you are really speaking Soul Language, repeat *San San Jiu Liu Ba Yao Wu* clearly again. Then chant as fast as you can once again. If that special voice comes out again, that confirms you are speaking Soul Language.

I taught this wisdom and practice in my book *Soul Wisdom,*[2] with additional teachings in my book *Soul Communication.*[3] Thousands of people worldwide have used this technique to bring out their Soul Language. Bringing out your Soul Language is the first step in developing the potential power of your soul.

You can learn many profound secrets about Soul Language in

---

2. Zhi Gang Sha, 2008, *Soul Wisdom: Practical Soul Treasures to Transform Your Life,* New York/ Toronto: Atria Books and Heaven's Library Publications.
3. Zhi Gang Sha, 2008, *Soul Communication: Opening Your Spiritual Channels for Success and Fulfillment,* New York/Toronto: Atria Books and Heaven's Library Publications.

*Soul Wisdom*. Most people can bring out their Soul Language very quickly. If your Soul Language has not come out, do the preceding practice more. You can also go back to *Soul Wisdom*. I offered Divine Soul Downloads in that book to empower every reader to bring out their Soul Language and to translate Soul Language. Bringing out and translating Soul Language are vital for developing the potential power of your soul.

Once you have brought out your Soul Language, it is very easy to bring out your Soul Song. The second step is simply to ask your soul to express your Soul Language in song. Say *hello* to your Soul Language:

> *Dear soul, mind, and body of my Soul Language,*[4]
> *I love you, honor you, and appreciate you.*
> *Please turn my Soul Language into Soul Song.*
> *I am very grateful.*
> *Thank you.*

Then right away *sing* your Soul Language. Your Soul Language will instantly turn to Soul Song. This *is* your Soul Song. Your Soul Song can change. The more you sing it, the more it may change.

Soul Song carries soul frequency with love, forgiveness, compassion, and light to heal, prevent sickness, rejuvenate, prolong life, and transform every aspect of life, including relationships and finances. In one sentence:

---

4. Soul Language has a soul. Soul Language has a mind. Soul Language has a body. In fact, everyone and everything has a soul, mind, and body. A soul is a light being. A mind is the consciousness of a being. A physical body is made of matter. The body of a mind is made of tiny or refined matter. The body of a soul is made of very tiny matter.

**Soul Song can offer healing, rejuvenation, and transformation to you, humanity, Mother Earth, and all universes.**

## Apply Your Soul Song to Heal, Rejuvenate, and Transform You, Humanity, Mother Earth, and All Universes

This is the way to apply your Soul Song to heal yourself:

*Dear my beloved Soul Song,*
*I love you and appreciate you.*
*You have the power to heal* _____ (make a
  request for healing yourself).
*Do a good job.*
*Thank you.*

Then sing your Soul Song for three minutes. You can sing aloud, silently, or both ways. As I emphasized earlier, spend three minutes to do it now. In this book I ask you to practice many different times for at least three minutes. It is very important to do the practices to experience the power of your own Soul Song and, later in this book, the power of Divine Soul Songs.

After singing for three minutes, close the practice:

*Hao! Hao! Hao!*
*Thank you. Thank you. Thank you.*

Generally speaking, for self-healing and healing others, sing three to five minutes per time, three to five times per day. For chronic and life-threatening conditions, practice two hours or more in total per day, as Walter did with his Divine Soul Download for his liver cancer. There is no time limit. The more and the longer you sing, the better.

Next let me show you how to apply your Soul Song for rejuvenation:

> *Dear my beloved Soul Song,*
> *I love you and appreciate you.*
> *You have the power to rejuvenate my soul, mind, and*
>     *body.*
> *Do a good job.*
> *Thank you.*

Then sing your Soul Song for three minutes, silently or aloud. After singing for three minutes, close the practice:

> *Hao! Hao! Hao!*
> *Thank you. Thank you. Thank you.*

For rejuvenation, sing three to five minutes per time, three to five times per day. There is no time limit. The more and the longer you sing, the better.

The next practice is to apply your Soul Song to transform your relationships:

> *Dear my beloved Soul Song,*
> *I love you and appreciate you.*
> *You have the power to transform my relationships.*
> *Please bless my relationships to be more loving, forgiv-*
>     *ing, compassionate, and caring.*
> *Do a good job.*
> *Thank you.*

Then sing your Soul Song for at least three minutes. Close the practice in the usual way. Again, there is no time limit. The more you sing, the more transformation your relationships could receive.

Next, this is the way to apply your Soul Song to transform your finances. You can request a general blessing as you just did for relationships or you can make a specific request. For example:

> *Dear my beloved Soul Song,*
> *I love you and appreciate you.*
> *You have the power to help me find the best job.*
> *Do a good job.*
> *Thank you.*

Then start to sing your Soul Song for three minutes, the longer, the better.

You can always sing aloud or silently. Both ways work.

This is the way to apply your Soul Song to offer healing to a loved one:

> *Dear my beloved Soul Song,*
> *I love you and appreciate you.*
> *You have the power to heal my brother, my friend . . .*
>     (make specific requests).
> *Do a good job.*
> *Thank you.*

Sing your Soul Song for at least three minutes. You can visualize your brother or friend as being completely healthy and filled with golden light. After three minutes, close the practice in the usual way.

This is the way to apply your Soul Song to offer healing to humanity:

> *Dear my beloved Soul Song,*
> *I love you and appreciate you.*
> *You have the power to offer healing to humanity.*
> *Do a good job.*
> *Thank you.*

Then sing your Soul Song for three minutes or more. After singing for at least three minutes, close:

> *Hao! Hao! Hao!*
> *Thank you. Thank you. Thank you.*

Singing your Soul Song in this way to offer healing to a loved one, a friend, humanity, Mother Earth, and all universes is unconditional service. You offer service without asking for anything in return. The recipient of your service may not even know about it. What is happening as you do these practices? Your Soul Song carries soul frequency with love, forgiveness, compassion, and light. The frequency and vibration of your Soul Song are radiating to your loved one, your friend, all humanity, Mother Earth, and all universes. The Akashic Records (the place in Heaven where all of one's activities, behaviors, and thoughts from all of one's lifetimes are recorded) records your service. Your book in the Akashic Records and your soul are given virtue, which is spiritual currency in the form of beautiful divine soul flowers. Virtue will nourish your soul. Virtue will bless and transform every aspect of your life.

I shared the Universal Law of Universal Service, which is the fourth major universal law, in the beginning section of this book on the Soul Power Series. I will discuss this universal law further in chapter 3. The essence of this universal law is that the more one serves, the more blessings and life transformation one will receive.

Millions of people are searching for life transformation. Thousands of great teachers, books, workshops, seminars, and retreats are teaching life transformation. I honor each teacher and each teaching. What I would like to share with you is that life transformation can be summarized in a one-sentence secret:

**To serve is to transform every aspect of your life.**

Now join me in singing our Soul Songs to offer healing to Mother Earth:

> *Dear my beloved Soul Song,*
> *I love you and appreciate you.*
> *You have the power to offer healing to Mother Earth.*
> *Do a good job.*
> *Thank you.*

Then sing your Soul Song for three minutes or more. Close the practice in the usual way.

Finally, let us apply Soul Song to offer healing to all universes:

> *Dear my beloved Soul Song,*
> *I love you and appreciate you.*
> *You have the power to offer healing to all universes.*
> *Do a good job.*
> *Thank you.*

Then sing your Soul Song. Generally speaking, sing your Soul Song for three to five minutes, three to five times per day. Close:

> *Hao! Hao! Hao!*
> *Thank you. Thank you. Thank you.*

If your Third Eye is open, you could see light radiating from your soul to entire universes as you sing your Soul Song. You could be very excited to actually see that you can serve universes simply by singing your Soul Song. Remember, all universes are made of message, energy, and matter. Your Soul Song carries its own frequency and vibration with love, forgiveness, compassion, and light. It can vibrate, balance, and harmonize the message, energy, and matter of all universes. It may be hard for many people to believe that one person's Soul Song can serve countless universes, but it is a fact.

In July 2008 I received further divine teaching about the power of Soul Song to heal, rejuvenate, and transform all lives. I was holding a Soul Healing and Enlightenment retreat in Germany for my devoted German students and other European students. One morning just before the retreat began, the Divine gave me the following new divine poem with the melody to make it a Divine Soul Song. This Divine Soul Song is entitled "Divine Soul Song for World Soul Healing, Peace and Enlightenment." (See figure 3 in the insert.)

> *Chanting chanting chanting*
> *Divine chanting is healing*
> *Chanting chanting chanting*
> *Divine chanting is rejuvenating*

*Singing singing singing*
*Divine singing is transforming*
*Singing singing singing*
*Divine singing is enlightening*

*Humanity is waiting for divine chanting*
*All souls are waiting for divine singing*
*Divine chanting removes all blockages*
*Divine singing brings inner joy*

*Divine is chanting and singing*
*Humanity and all souls are nourishing*
*Humanity and all souls are chanting and singing*
*World love, peace and harmony are coming*

*World love, peace and harmony are coming*

*World love, peace and harmony are coming*

This new Divine Soul Song clearly expresses the power and significance of singing and even simply chanting the words to Soul Songs and Divine Soul Songs.

Millions of people throughout history have chanted mantras for healing and purification and to advance their spiritual journeys. Your Soul Song is your own soul mantra. Divine Soul Songs are the Divine's soul mantras.

*To sing and chant is to serve.*
*To sing and chant is to heal.*
*To sing and chant is to prevent sickness.*
*To sing and chant is to rejuvenate.*

*To sing and chant is to prolong life.*
*To sing and chant is to transform relationships.*
*To sing and chant is to transform finances.*
*To sing and chant is to transform every aspect of life.*
*To sing and chant is to purify your soul, heart, mind,*
    *and body.*
*To sing and chant is to reach soul enlightenment.*

Especially, when you sing and chant Divine Soul Songs, you are offering divine healing, blessing, and transformation to you, humanity, Mother Earth, and all universes.

Now I am ready to introduce and teach Divine Soul Songs.

# The First Three Divine Soul Songs for Humanity, Mother Earth, and All Universes

*I*N CHAPTER 1 I explained what Soul Song is. I described its power and significance. I led you in various practices of singing your own Soul Songs so that you could experience their power. Divine Soul Songs are Soul Songs sung by the Divine. The Divine has taught me many Divine Soul Songs. In this chapter I will reveal and share with humanity three of the most important Divine Soul Songs that I have received so far. You will experience the power of Divine Soul Songs.

## The Power and Significance of the Divine Soul Song *Love, Peace and Harmony*

On September 10, 2005, I received the first Divine Soul Song in the Divine's Soul Language:

*Lu La Lu La Li*
*Lu La Lu La La Li*
*Lu La Lu La Li Lu La*
*Lu La Li Lu La*
*Lu La Li Lu La*

The English translation of these lyrics is:

*I love my heart and soul*
*I love all humanity*
*Join hearts and souls together*
*Love, peace and harmony*
*Love, peace and harmony*

In this and in every Divine Soul Song, the Divine sings the Divine's Soul Language. Every Divine Soul Song carries a wave of divine frequency and vibration to bless humanity, souls, and all universes. When you sing *Love, Peace and Harmony,* its divine power can remove life blockages to transform your life.

This and any Divine Soul Song can be sung with a melody or chanted without melody—simply repeat the words without singing a melody. The power is the same.

Let me explain why. Soul Song is the song of Soul Language. Divine Soul Song is the Divine's song of the Divine's Soul Language. The Divine has given a melody for the words of every Divine Soul Song. The melodies of all Divine Soul Songs are beautiful and heart-touching. I do not know how to read music, but the Divine gives me the melodies. Sometimes I hear them. Sometimes I sing them out directly.

Singing the Divine Soul Songs in this book is the natural way to practice. But there is another way to practice, which is to simply chant the words of the Soul Song. Singing Divine Soul Songs is beautiful. Chanting the words of Divine Soul Songs is also beautiful. Divine Soul Songs carry divine consciousness, frequency, and vibration with divine love, forgiveness, compassion, and light. Whether you sing or chant a Divine Soul Song, its divine qualities and power are present. Therefore, singing Divine Soul Songs and chanting the words of Divine Soul Songs are the two ways to practice Divine Soul Songs in this book and in your daily practice of Divine Soul Songs for life. Both ways are perfect. Both ways work.

To return to the Divine Soul Song *Love, Peace and Harmony,* its first line, *Lu La Lu La Li,* means *I love my heart and soul.* Love melts all blockages and transforms all life. Love your soul. Soul is the boss. Love your soul to heal your soul. Love your soul to transform your soul. *Heal the soul first; then healing of the mind and body will follow. Transform the soul first; then transformation of every aspect of life will follow.* The first line of this Divine Soul Song is a priceless divine soul treasure for healing and life transformation.

The founder of Buddhism, Shi Jia Mo Ni Fuo, offered forty-nine years of teaching in his time on Mother Earth. One of his profound sacred teachings was:

**All sicknesses are due to the heart.**
**To heal the heart is to heal all sicknesses.**

The authoritative text of traditional Chinese medicine, *The Yellow Emperor's Internal Classic,* revealed that:

**The heart houses the soul and mind.**

The Divine guided me to do and teach soul healing. *Heal and transform the soul first; then healing and transformation of every aspect of life will follow.* The first line of the Divine Soul Song *Love, Peace and Harmony, Lu La Lu La La Li, I love my heart and soul,* gives humanity and all souls the simplest and most profound practical tool to do soul self-healing. The wave of this Divine Soul Song's frequency and vibration can remove all blockages to heal your physical, emotional, mental, and spiritual bodies and transform your relationships, finances, and every aspect of your life.

With the second line, *Lu La Lu La La Li,* which means *I love all humanity,* the Divine gives humanity and all souls the simplest and most profound practical tool to offer service to others, to the world, and to all universes. As I mentioned in the first section of this book on the Soul Power Series, the Divine shared the Universal Law of Universal Service with me in 2003. The essence of this divine law is that the purpose of life is to serve. There are two kinds of service: good service—which includes universal love, forgiveness, peace, healing, blessing, harmony, and enlightenment—and bad service, which includes killing, harming, taking advantage of others, cheating, stealing, greed, selfishness, and so on. Give good service to humanity and the world, receive divine blessings. Give bad service to humanity and the world, learn all kinds of lessons in your life.

The second line, *Lu La Lu La La Li, I love all humanity,* is also a sacred divine treasure to clear your bad karma. Your bad karma is the spiritual blockages that are the root blockages for every aspect of your life. When you sing or chant *Lu La Lu La La Li, I love all humanity,* divine love, forgiveness, compassion, and light from this Divine Soul Song are offering divine service to humanity and all souls. This service is recorded in your Akashic

Records. Divine virtue is given to you at the moment you are singing or chanting. This good virtue, or good karma, will help to clear your bad karma, which is your spiritual debt.

To serve is to make others healthier and happier. To serve is to create divine love, peace, and harmony for you, humanity, Mother Earth, and all universes. When you serve, do not expect anything in return. Just serve. Serve unconditionally. The Divine and the Soul World will know about and reward your service by giving you divine virtue. The moment you sing or chant this Divine Soul Song, you are receiving divine virtue in your Akashic Records. That follows one of the most important spiritual laws and principles created by the Divine. Therefore, to serve is to transform every aspect of your life, including health, relationships, and finances. The Divine and the Soul World will not let you serve for nothing. They will give you benefits many times greater than the service you offer.

In summary, the benefits of singing or chanting this and any Divine Soul Song are to:

- make yourself and others healthier and happier
- heal your physical, emotional, mental, and spiritual bodies
- heal others, humanity, Mother Earth, and all universes
- purify your soul, heart, mind, and body to enlighten your soul, heart, mind, and body
- purify others, humanity, Mother Earth, and all universes to enlighten them
- receive divine virtue to clear your bad karma and uplift your spiritual standing to bless every aspect of your life

- spread divine love, forgiveness, compassion, and light to humanity, Mother Earth, and all universes to transform the consciousness of humanity and all souls to divine consciousness
- create love, peace, and harmony for humanity, Mother Earth, and all universes

Sing or chant a little, receive a little blessing from the Divine and the universe.

Sing or chant more, receive more blessing.

Sing or chant as much as you can, receive unlimited blessings.

The Divine also gave the second line of this Divine Soul Song, *Lu La Lu La La Li, I love all humanity,* to give you and humanity the golden key to unlock the gate of life. When you realize and understand this, it is like suddenly finding a gold mine after searching for many years without success. *I love all humanity* is a divine one-sentence secret to transform all life. It may be too simple to believe, but it is more valuable than any gold mine. It is so powerful that singing or chanting this one sentence could clear your spiritual debt accumulated from all your past lives and your present life. It may take many years to clear your spiritual debt accumulated from your hundreds or thousands of lifetimes in this way, but the value and benefits are immeasurable and unimaginable.

The third line, *Lu La Lu La Li Lu La,* which means *Join hearts and souls together,* is a divine calling. Mother Earth is in a transition period. More and more, we are seeing natural disasters, serious illnesses—including cancer, AIDS, depression, and new diseases—wars, threats of nuclear weapons, conflicts between religions and nations, economic collapse, and more. At this critical historic moment, the Divine is calling all humanity, all nations, all souls, and all universes to join hearts and souls together as one.

The Divine is also calling us to transform all consciousnesses to one. This "one" means divine consciousness within the Divine's heart and soul. All humanity is one. All souls are one. All universes are one. The Divine is one. The Divine is within every human being. The Divine is within everything in all universes. The Divine is within all souls. Open the hearts and souls of everyone and everything and awaken and transform their consciousnesses to join with the Divine as one. This is the essence of this third line.

The fourth and fifth lines, *Lu La Li Lu La,* or *Love, peace and harmony,* are the same line repeated to emphasize love, peace, and harmony. The ultimate goal of the Divine Mission *is* love, peace, and harmony. The Divine desires and intends to create love, peace, and harmony for humanity, Mother Earth, and all universes.

The Soul Light Era started on August 8, 2003. It will last fifteen thousand years. The Divine Mission for these fifteen thousand years is to create love, peace, and harmony for humanity, Mother Earth, and all universes. Accomplishing this mission will require a great process of purification, healing, transformation, and enlightenment for all humanity and all souls. The Divine has decided the direction and the goal. The Divine is leading us to join hearts and souls to achieve this goal. We *will* be successful. Love, peace, and harmony for humanity, Mother Earth, and all universes *will* appear, shine, vibrate, radiate, and flourish in humanity, Mother Earth, and all universes.

Hao!

Thank you. Thank you. Thank you.

HOW I RECEIVED THIS FIRST DIVINE SOUL SONG

On Saturday, September 10, 2005, I visited the redwoods in
Marin County, California, with three of my students. One of
them asked me, "Master Sha, could you ask the Divine for a song
for the Divine Mission?" I replied, "Of course! I am delighted to
ask for a song from the Divine." I raised my arm to Heaven and
said, "Dear Divine, could you give me a Soul Song for our mission?" Instantly, a beam of rainbow light shot down from the
Divine's heart and went through my body from head to toe. I
opened my mouth and this Divine Soul Language flowed out:

> *Lu La Lu La Li*
> *Lu La Lu La La Li*
> *Lu La Lu La Li Lu La*
> *Lu La Li Lu La*
> *Lu La Li Lu La*

I had never heard "Lu La Lu La Li" before. I did not know
what this Soul Language meant, but I knew how to translate it. I
immediately asked the Divine for a translation, which I was given
in Chinese:

> *Wo ai wo xin he ling*
> *Wo ai quan ren lei*
> *Wan ling rong he mu shi sheng*
> *Xiang ai ping an he xie*
> *Xiang ai ping an he xie*

"Wo" (pronounced *waw*) means I. "Ai" (pronounced *eye*)
means *love*. "Xin" (pronounced *sheen*) means *heart*. "He" (pro-

nounced *huh*) means *and.* "Ling" (rhymes with *sing*) means *soul.* So "Wo ai wo xin he ling" means *I love my heart and soul.*

"Quan" (pronounced *chwahn*) means *all.* "Ren lei" (pronounced *run lay*) means *humanity.* So "Wo ai quan ren lei" means *I love all humanity.*

"Wan ling" (pronounced *wahn ling*) means *ten thousand souls,* which represents and means *all souls.* "Rong he" (pronounced *rong huh*) means *join together.* "Mu" (pronounced *moo*) means *harmony.* "Shi" (pronounced *shr*) means *world.* "Sheng" (pronounced *shung*) means *produces.* So "Wan ling rong he mu shi sheng" means *All souls join together to produce a harmonized world.*

"Xiang ai" (pronounced *shyahng eye*) means *love.* "Ping an" (pronounced *ping ahn*) means *peace.* "He xie" (pronounced *huh shyeh*) means *harmony.* So "Xiang ai ping an he xie" means exactly *Love, peace and harmony.*

Then I asked the Divine to give me a melody for these lyrics. I received it instantly. The melody of this Divine Soul Song is beautiful and easy to learn. See figure 2 in the insert. Listen to the excerpt of *Love, Peace and Harmony* on the first track of the enclosed audio CD. Remember, though, that you can sing or simply chant the words to any Divine Soul Song with the same power and benefits.

To better fit the melody, the lyrics of this Divine Soul Song in English are:

> *I love my heart and soul*
> *I love all humanity*
> *Join hearts and souls together*
> *Love, peace and harmony*
> *Love, peace and harmony*

I was so excited to sing with my three students. As we were singing, a little girl about two or three years old walked by. She was fascinated by this first Divine Soul Song that I received. She listened with full attention until we finished singing. Then she broke out into a big smile and raised both arms above her head, waving them and making a very happy sound—*Yaaaay!!!* A few minutes later she and her mother had walked a couple of hundred feet away. My students and I continued to sing with great joy. The girl was walking farther and farther away. Suddenly, she stopped, turned around to face us, and raised both hands again, waving both arms, and screamed *Yaaaay!!!* delightedly again.

My students and I sang together for more than an hour. We left the redwoods and went to a beach on the ocean. We were singing the whole time. Hungry, we finally went into town to have dinner at a crowded and popular restaurant. I couldn't stop singing. Three waitresses stopped their work and came to our table to listen. They stood there for a few minutes just listening, without moving or speaking. Finally, they asked me, "What are you singing?" I explained, "I am singing a Soul Song." They said, "It is beautiful! We never heard of Soul Song before. We enjoyed it a lot."

This story shares how I received my first Divine Soul Song from the Divine. From that moment, I have taught this Soul Song in every workshop and class I have held worldwide. Wherever I go, I sing this Divine Soul Song. Wherever I teach, I introduce this Divine Soul Song. Wherever I have the opportunity, I share this Divine Soul Song.

The more I teach and sing this Divine Soul Song, the more divine power people and I have experienced. I have realized that this Divine Soul Song is one of the most powerful divine soul treasures to heal, rejuvenate, and transform you, humanity, Mother Earth, and all universes. Therefore, on March 2, 2008, I asked the Divine, "Dear Divine, I was so honored to receive your first Divine Soul Song, *Lu La Li Lu La, Love, Peace and Harmony.* Could you literally download your soul treasure of a divine soul of this song to all humanity and all souls?"

The Divine replied, "Dear my son and my servant, Zhi Gang, I am honored and pleased to offer my Divine Soul Download of my Divine Soul Song *Lu La Li Lu La, Love, Peace and Harmony* to all humanity and all souls."

I bowed to the floor one thousand times to show total gratitude to the Divine. Then in my regular Sunday Divine Blessings teleconference, I offered the Divine Soul Download of this Divine Soul Song to all humanity and all souls. You can invoke this Divine Soul Song Download given to your soul anytime, anywhere to receive divine healing, blessing, and life transformation. In the next section, I will lead you to apply this Divine Soul Download in three practices for healing, blessing, and life transformation.

APPLY THE DIVINE SOUL SONG *LOVE, PEACE AND HARMONY* TO HEAL, REJUVENATE, AND TRANSFORM YOU, HUMANITY, MOTHER EARTH, AND ALL UNIVERSES

This first Divine Soul Song, *Lu La Li Lu La, Love, Peace and Harmony,* carries divine frequency, vibration, and power to heal and transform all lives. You may wonder, "Does this Divine Soul Song really have the power to do this?" My answer is straightforward: *Yes, of course!* This Divine Soul Song has power beyond words and thought.

Let me lead you step by step to apply this Divine Soul Song

treasure to offer healing and transformation. In the previous section, I explained that I offered a Divine Soul Download of this Divine Soul Song to all humanity and all souls. Specifically, in March 2008, the Divine offered the soul of the Divine Soul Song *Love, Peace and Harmony* as a Soul Transplant gift to all humanity and all souls. A Divine Soul Song itself carries divine power. The Divine Soul Transplant of the Divine Soul Song *Lu La Li Lu La, Love, Peace and Harmony* is a new divine soul. It is a permanent divine treasure that every human being and every soul has. This divine soul is a bright golden light ball. When you invoke this treasure, it is just like turning on a switch for this light ball. This divine soul will shine, vibrate, rotate, and radiate. If you do not invoke it, this divine light ball will be switched off.

The first practice will show you how to receive divine healing from the Divine Soul Song *Lu La Li Lu La, Love, Peace and Harmony* and the Divine Soul Download of the Divine Soul Song *Lu La Li Lu La, Love, Peace and Harmony*. This is the first Divine Soul Download to be applied in this book. Let's practice now!

> *Dear soul, mind, and body of the Divine Soul Song*
>     Lu La Li Lu La, Love, Peace and Harmony *and*
> *Dear divine soul of the Divine Soul Song* Lu La Li Lu
>     La, Love, Peace and Harmony *downloaded permanently to my soul,*
> *I love you, honor you, and appreciate you.*
> *Please turn on to give me a divine healing for* _____
>     (request healing for your physical, emotional,
>     mental, or spiritual bodies).
> *I am very grateful.*
> *Thank you.*

Then sing or chant the words to the Divine Soul Song *Love, Peace and Harmony* aloud or silently for at least three minutes:

> *Lu La Lu La Li*
> *Lu La Lu La La Li*
> *Lu La Lu La Li Lu La*
> *Lu La Li Lu La*
> *Lu La Li Lu La*
>
> *I love my heart and soul*
> *I love all humanity*
> *Join hearts and souls together*
> *Love, peace and harmony*
> *Love, peace and harmony . . .*

The moment you begin to sing the Divine Soul Song *Lu La Li Lu La, Love, Peace and Harmony*, it will vibrate. At the same time, the Divine Soul Download of the Divine Soul Song *Lu La Li Lu La, Love, Peace and Harmony* will resonate together with this vibration to serve your request.

> *Hao! Hao! Hao!*
> *Thank you. Thank you. Thank you.*

Generally speaking, sing for three to five minutes per time, three to five times per day. The more you practice, the better. You may sing or chant the words aloud or silently. For chronic or life-threatening conditions, sing or chant for a total of at least two hours each day. You can sing or chant three, seven, fifteen, or twenty times a day. It doesn't matter. Just make sure your total practice time is at least two hours. There are no time limits. You could receive remarkable healing results.

The second practice is to bless your relationships. Do it with me now:

> *Dear soul, mind, and body of* _____ (name the person with whom you would like to receive a relationship blessing),
> *I love you, honor you, and appreciate you.*
> *Dear soul, mind, and body of the Divine Soul Song* Lu La Li Lu La, Love, Peace and Harmony *and*
> *Dear divine soul of the Divine Soul Song* Lu La Li Lu La, Love, Peace and Harmony *downloaded permanently to my soul and* _____*'s* (name the person again) *soul,*
> *I love you, honor you, and appreciate you.*
> *Please turn on to bless my relationship with* _____ (name the person again).
> *I am very grateful.*
> *Thank you.*

Then sing or chant the words to this Divine Soul Song:

> *Lu La Lu La Li*
> *Lu La Lu La La Li*
> *Lu La Lu La Li Lu La*
> *Lu La Li Lu La*
> *Lu La Li Lu La*
>
> *I love my heart and soul*
> *I love all humanity*

*Join hearts and souls together*
*Love, peace and harmony*
*Love, peace and harmony*

Again, sing or chant the words for three to five minutes per time, three to five times per day—the more and the longer, the better. There are no time limits. You could receive a remarkable blessing for your relationship.

*Hao! Hao! Hao!*
*Thank you. Thank you. Thank you.*

How does singing or chanting this Divine Soul Song work to bless your relationship? Relationship blockages can occur at the levels of soul, mind, and body. The Divine Soul Song and the Divine Soul Transplant of the Divine Soul Song carry divine frequency with divine love, forgiveness, compassion, and light. When you sing or chant, blockages in the relationship at soul, mind, and body levels can be removed.

The third practice is to bless your business and finances. Follow me now to do this practice:

*Dear soul, mind, and body of my finances and*
*Dear soul, mind, and body of _____ (name your*
    *business if you have one),*
*I love you, honor you, and appreciate you.*
*Dear soul, mind, and body of the Divine Soul Song*
    *Lu La Li Lu La, Love, Peace and Harmony and*
*Dear divine soul of the Divine Soul Song Lu La Li Lu*
    *La, Love, Peace and Harmony given to my soul,*

*the soul of my business* (if you have one), *and the*
*soul of my finances,*
*I love you, honor you, and appreciate you.*
*Please turn on to bless my business and finances.*
*I am very grateful.*
*Thank you.*

Then sing or chant the words to this Divine Soul Song:

*Lu La Lu La Li*
*Lu La Lu La La Li*
*Lu La Lu La Li Lu La*
*Lu La Li Lu La*
*Lu La Li Lu La*

*I love my heart and soul*
*I love all humanity*
*Join hearts and souls together*
*Love, peace and harmony*
*Love, peace and harmony*

Again, sing or chant for three to five minutes per time, three to five times per day—the more, the better. There are no time limits. You could receive remarkable blessing for your finances.

*Hao! Hao! Hao!*
*Thank you. Thank you. Thank you.*

How does singing or chanting this Divine Soul Song work to bless your finances? Financial challenges, such as blockages in finding a job and blockages in developing a successful business, are due to soul blockages, which are karma, and mind blockages, which are energy blockages. All Divine Soul Songs and all Divine Soul Transplants of Divine Soul Songs carry divine frequency with divine love, forgiveness, compassion, and light that can remove soul blockages, energy blockages, and other blockages, such as in relationships or technology, to bless your finances.

You can also apply this and any Divine Soul Song to offer healing to humanity, Mother Earth, and all universes. I will show you how later in this chapter.

## GO INTO THE DIVINE CONDITION

When you sing or chant the words to a Divine Soul Song, the best practice is to *go into the divine condition*. What does "go into the divine condition" mean? It means your heart is the Divine's heart. Your mind is the Divine's mind. Your body is the Divine's body. You are totally aligned with divine consciousness. You are completely aligned with the Divine.

When you go into the divine condition as you sing or chant a Divine Soul Song, the divine frequency and vibration of the Divine Soul Song are transforming your frequency and vibration. Every system, every organ, every cell, and every DNA and RNA of your body is receiving divine transformation. As we are doing in every practice in this book, first say *hello* and request the healing, rejuvenation, and specific life transformation you wish to receive. However, when you start to sing or chant, do not think of your request anymore. Forget yourself. You are in the divine condition. The Divine is healing, rejuvenating, and transforming your life. Sing or chant from the bottom of your heart. Sing and chant with total gratitude and honor. As you do this, the Divine is healing, blessing, and transforming you on the spot.

If you understand this, then your singing or chanting *is* in the divine condition. You will receive benefits so quickly that it will be beyond your comprehension. In many cases, divine results are instant.

Soul is the boss for life. Soul is the boss for a human being. Soul is the boss for every aspect of life. Divine Soul Songs can transform the soul of your body and the souls of every aspect of your life. When your soul is transformed, your mind and body will be transformed. Every aspect of your life will be transformed. Soul transformation can be instant. Transformation of every aspect of your life will follow very quickly. Therefore, singing or chanting the words to Divine Soul Songs could bring you remarkable, surprising, and even shocking results. You may be wondering, "Can Divine Soul Songs really work this fast?" The answer is *yes*. The speed with which Divine Soul Songs can transform your life cannot be defined or expressed by any thought or any imagining.

Therefore, to *go into the divine condition* when you sing and chant is a vital principle for divine transformation, which includes divine healing, divine rejuvenation, divine transformation of relationships, divine transformation of finances, and more. *Go into the divine condition* to sing Divine Soul Songs is vital wisdom for this book. To receive the greatest benefits, I wish that you and every other reader will remember and follow this principle when singing or chanting Divine Soul Songs.

## APPLY THE DIVINE SOUL SONG *LOVE, PEACE AND HARMONY* TO REMOVE SELFISHNESS AND GREED

In your spiritual journey, one of the most important issues is to purify your soul, heart, mind, and body. The key purification is to remove selfishness. This is directly related with service. How much do you want to serve? Do you want to serve a little because you have no time, because you only can serve so much? Do you want to serve more? Do you want to serve unconditionally?

The Divine's calling is to serve humanity unconditionally, which means to serve without asking for anything in return. This is easy to say. It is difficult to do. Think about Jesus, Mary, Shi Jia Mo Ni Fuo, Guan Yin, A Mi Tuo Fuo, and many other great teachers. They have served for centuries without asking for anything in return. Therefore, they are spiritual fathers and mothers for humanity. As unconditional universal servants, they are great examples for spiritual beings.

To serve unconditionally is to serve selflessly. To reach this condition is a major purification process for every spiritual being. This is a vital and most important process to advance your spiritual journey. The Divine Soul Song *Lu La Li Lu La, Love, Peace and Harmony* can help you purify your soul, heart, mind and body in order to remove selfishness. Therefore, singing this and other Divine Soul Songs is a very important spiritual purification practice in order to fulfill your spiritual journey.

Let's do it together now! *Really* sing or chant the words for three minutes with me to purify our souls, hearts, minds, and bodies.

> *Dear soul, mind, and body of the Divine Soul Song*
>     Lu La Li Lu La, Love, Peace and Harmony,
> *We love you, honor you, and appreciate you.*
> *Please purify our souls, hearts, minds, and bodies to re-*
>     *move all selfishness.*
> *We are very grateful.*
> *Thank you. Thank you. Thank you.*

Then go into the divine condition and sing or chant the words to this Divine Soul Song for three minutes:

> *Lu La Lu La Li*
> *Lu La Lu La La Li*
> *Lu La Lu La Li Lu La*
> *Lu La Li Lu La*
> *Lu La Li Lu La*
>
> *I love my heart and soul*
> *I love all humanity*
> *Join hearts and souls together*
> *Love, peace and harmony*
> *Love, peace and harmony*

The Divine Soul Song *Love, Peace and Harmony* will purify our souls, hearts, minds, and bodies. Our souls, hearts, minds, and bodies will open. We could feel very honored to be a servant of humanity. The more we sing or chant, the further we can purify our souls, hearts, minds, and bodies. There is no time limit. Ancient spiritual practitioners very often chanted mantras for hours at a time. The longer we sing or chant, the longer divine frequency and vibration are transforming the frequency and vibration of our souls, hearts, minds, and bodies. The more we sing or chant, the purer we become.

> *Hao! Hao! Hao!*
> *Thank you. Thank you. Thank you.*

Next let us apply the Divine Soul Song *Love, Peace and Harmony* to remove greed.

Millions of people do business. Millions of people desire

wealth. Many courses and workshops in the world teach people how to become millionaires. I honor every book, every workshop, and every teaching.

I want to ask about the desire and intention to become a millionaire. What exactly will you do when you are a millionaire? Are you clear in your soul, heart, and mind why you want to become a millionaire? How and where will you spend your money when you are a millionaire? Of course, you have the right to spend your money wherever you choose. I am not interfering with how you spend money. I want to present these questions to offer some spiritual guidance.

I personally believe financial abundance is related to service. I deeply believe in karma and the Akashic Records. If you have great financial abundance in this life, it is due to the great service you have given in past lives and in this life. Financial abundance is Heaven's reward. Your own physical efforts and your physical team's efforts are very important for financial abundance. In an organization, proper planning, marketing, organizing, controlling, managing, harmonizing, and more are very important for financial abundance. But financial abundance requires the support of *both* the yin (spiritual) world and the yang (physical) world. The yang world offers its efforts. The yin world offers support and blessings from Heaven and the Divine. Great success cannot be attained by anyone or any organization without the support of both the yin and the yang aspects.

If you attain great financial abundance, you have received blessings from the both the yin and the yang teams. If you continue to serve humanity with love, care, compassion, generosity, and kindness, you will continue to flourish. If you become selfish, greedy, or mean, challenges and blockages could come.

There is a renowned spiritual statement:

## Ren zai zuo. Tian zai kan.

"Ren" (pronounced *run*) means *human being*. "Zai" (pronounced *zye*) means *is*. "Zuo" (pronounced *zwaw*) means *doing* or *working*. "Tian" (pronounced *tyen*) means *Heaven*. "Kan" (pronounced *kahn*) means *watching* or *observing*.

This statement means: Whatever a person does, Heaven is watching. I very often share another spiritual wisdom that offers a similar teaching:

**If you do not want others to know, do not do it.**

You can hide nothing from the Divine and from the spiritual world. Every action, behavior, and thought is recorded in the Akashic Records.

The Divine made a spiritual law, the Universal Law of Universal Service that I shared earlier:

> *Serve a little, receive a little blessing.*
> *Serve more, receive more blessing.*
> *Serve unconditionally, receive unlimited blessing.*

After you receive a financial blessing, two realizations are very important for you. The first realization is that Heaven and the Divine have rewarded you for your efforts in past lives and in this life. The second realization is to remind you that this financial blessing is a beginning. There could be ten, twenty, even hundreds of times more blessings on the way. Do not forget the spiritual principle: Always serve humanity with love, care, compassion, and generosity. If you do this, you can keep and even increase your wealth more and more. If you turn to selfishness and greed,

Heaven can limit, reduce, and even end your abundance in an instant. I wish you and every reader will receive the essence of this spiritual sharing and teaching.

Now join me in a Divine Soul Song practice to remove and prevent greed:

> *Dear soul, mind, and body of the Divine Soul Song*
> 　　Lu La Li Lu La, Love, Peace and Harmony,
> *We love you, honor you, and appreciate you.*
> *Please purify our souls, hearts, minds, and bodies to re-*
> 　　*move all greed and to prevent greed from returning.*
> *We are very grateful.*
> *Thank you. Thank you. Thank you.*

Then sing or chant the words to this Divine Soul Song with me for three minutes:

> *Lu La Lu La Li*
> *Lu La Lu La La Li*
> *Lu La Lu La Li Lu La*
> *Lu La Li Lu La*
> *Lu La Li Lu La*
>
> *I love my heart and soul*
> *I love all humanity*
> *Join hearts and souls together*
> *Love, peace and harmony*
> *Love, peace and harmony*

After three minutes, close the practice:

*Hao! Hao! Hao!*
*Thank you. Thank you. Thank you.*

This practice can purify your soul, heart, and mind to remove your greed if you have it and even prevent greedy thoughts if you do not have it. The Divine's heart, love, and light can totally transform your greed. Therefore, every time I ask you to practice with me for three minutes, do it! Do not read on. Put the book down and spend three minutes with me. Remember, you are in a workshop with me. We are practicing purification to remove and prevent greed. This is very important for our spiritual journeys.

There is no time limit for doing this practice or for singing or chanting this Divine Soul Song. The longer you sing, the better. The benefits of this blessing to purify, transform, and enlighten our souls, hearts, minds, and bodies are unlimited.

### The Power and Significance of the Divine Soul Song
### *God Gives His Heart to Me*

On November 14, 2006, I received the second major Divine Soul Song: *God Gives His Heart to Me.* We were driving to Mt. Shasta, California, where I would lead a Soul Healing and Enlightenment retreat. Suddenly the Divine spoke to me and gave me the words of this Divine Soul Song in Soul Language:

*Lu la lu la la li*
*Lu la lu la la li*
*Lu la lu la li*
*Lu la lu la li*

Then the Divine gave me the melody. See figure 4 in the insert.

The English translation of the lyrics is:

> *God gives his heart to me*
> *God gives his love to me*
> *My heart melds with his heart*
> *My love melds with his love*

For your reference, the Chinese translation of the lyrics is:

> *Shang di gei wo ta di xin*
> *Shang di gei wo ta di ai*
> *Wo di xin rong yu ta di xin*
> *Wo di ai rong yu ta di ai*

"Shang di," pronounced *shahng dee,* means *God.* "Gei wo," pronounced *gay waw,* means *gives me.* "Ta di," pronounced *tah dee,* means *his.* "Xin," pronounced *sheen,* means *heart.* "Ai," pronounced *eye,* means *love.* "Wo di," pronounced *waw dee,* means *my.* "Rong yu," pronounced *rawng yü,* means *melds with.*

A Divine Soul Song is a divine mantra. It carries divine power for healing and transformation of every aspect of life. The first line of this Divine Soul Song, *God gives his heart to me,* means God offers his love, forgiveness, compassion, and light from his heart to our hearts and to every aspect of our lives. God is an unconditional servant.

The second line, *God gives his love to me,* means God gives his love to every aspect of our lives to transform them. God's love can heal, prevent sickness, rejuvenate, prolong life, and transform relationships, finances, and anything.

The third line, *My heart melds with his heart,* means God and I are one. God and you are one. Heart touches heart. Heart melds with heart. God's heart has unlimited power. Our hearts have unlimited power also. It is very important to understand this, but of course we realize that the frequency of God's heart and the frequencies of our hearts are very different. To transform the frequencies of our hearts to the frequency of God's heart takes great time and effort. Singing or chanting the words to this Divine Soul Song is one of the best ways to transform the frequencies of our hearts.

Every human being has a different spiritual standing. Every human being's heart has a different frequency. In order to transform our heart frequency to the frequency of God's heart, it takes different amounts of time and effort for different individuals, but in theory and in practice, we *can* transform our heart frequency to God's heart frequency. Therefore, remember my teaching in every book of the Soul Power Series:

**When you chant a mantra and when you sing a Divine Soul Song, there is no time limit—the longer, the better.**

The true secret is that it takes time to transform the frequencies of our hearts to the frequency of God's heart.

The fourth and final line, *My love melds with his love,* means God's love power can become our love power. My heart and God's heart are one. Your heart and God's heart are one. My love and God's love are one. Your love and God's love are one. But we must realize that the purity of our hearts is far from the purity of God's heart. The unconditional service—which includes unconditional love, forgiveness, peace, healing, blessing, harmony, and enlightenment—in our hearts is far from the unconditional service in God's heart. To attain the power of divine love, it again takes time to purify our hearts and to truly become a total GOLD unconditional universal servant.

Soul touches soul. Our souls are touched by God's soul. Soul melds with soul. Our souls meld with God's soul. This is the ultimate goal and destiny of our spiritual journeys.

To sing or chant

> *Lu la lu la la li*
> *Lu la lu la la li*
> *Lu la lu la li*
> *Lu la lu la li*

and

> *God gives his heart to me*
> *God gives his love to me*
> *My heart melds with his heart*
> *My love melds with his love*

is literally to transform the frequencies of our hearts to the frequency of the Divine's heart; to transform the purity of our love to the purity of the Divine's love; and to make a commitment to be a total GOLD unconditional universal servant from our hearts and souls just like the Divine.

- To sing a Divine Soul Song is to offer and receive divine healing.
- To sing a Divine Soul Song is to offer and receive divine prevention of sickness.
- To sing a Divine Soul Song is to offer and receive divine rejuvenation.

- To sing a Divine Soul Song is to prolong life.
- To sing a Divine Soul Song is to transform relationships.
- To sing a Divine Soul Song is to transform finances.
- To sing a Divine Soul Song is to purify soul, heart, mind, and body.
- To sing a Divine Soul Song is to transform our frequencies to divine frequency.
- To sing a Divine Soul Song is to transform our service to divine service.
- To sing a Divine Soul Song is to offer and receive divine enlightenment of soul, heart, mind, and body.
- To sing a Divine Soul Song is to offer healing, prevention of sickness, rejuvenation, prolongation of life, transformation, purification, and enlightenment to yourself and others, including all humanity, Mother Earth, and all universes.

Even if you do not know the melody of a Divine Soul Song, you can chant the words repeatedly. You will receive the same benefits.

✻

I am honored to present once more in this book the Divine Soul Song I received in July 2008 in Frankfurt, Germany. This new Divine Soul Song absolutely and perfectly expresses the power and significance of the Divine Soul Song *Love, Peace and Harmony*, the Divine Soul Song *God Gives His Heart to Me*, and every other Divine Soul Song for healing and transforming you, humanity, Mother Earth, and all universes. It is named "Divine

Soul Song for World Soul Healing, Peace and Enlightenment"
(see figure 3 in the insert):

*Chanting Chanting Chanting*
*Divine chanting is healing*
*Chanting Chanting Chanting*
*Divine chanting is rejuvenating*
*Singing Singing Singing*
*Divine singing is transforming*
*Singing Singing Singing*
*Divine singing is enlightening*

*Humanity is waiting for divine chanting*
*All souls are waiting for divine singing*
*Divine chanting removes all blockages*
*Divine singing brings inner joy*

*Divine is chanting and singing*
*Humanity and all souls are nourishing*
*Humanity and all souls are chanting and singing*
*World love, peace and harmony are coming*

*World love, peace and harmony are coming*

*World love, peace and harmony are coming*

Earlier I shared one of the most secret and sacred Buddhist
teachings:

**To chant *A Mi Tuo Fuo* is to become a buddha.**

To become a buddha is the highest enlightenment and great-est achievement in Buddhist teaching.

To sing a Divine Soul Song and to chant a divine mantra are to reach the Divine and to become divine. Remember I just shared the significance, possibility, and reality that *My heart melds with the Divine's heart, My love melds with the Divine's love.* In fact, our souls, hearts, minds, and bodies *can* be transformed to the Divine's soul, heart, mind, and body.

To transform and enlighten our hearts to the Divine's heart, to transform and enlighten our love to the Divine's love takes a long time practicing and serving. It could take hundreds and thousands of lifetimes to achieve this. Imagine—to totally trans-form and enlighten our souls, hearts, minds, and bodies to the Divine's soul, heart, mind, and body takes even more time and effort. But a totally devoted spiritual being *can* achieve this.

The Divine has directed us to create love, peace, and har-mony for humanity, Mother Earth, and all universes. The Divine is also giving us the Divine's practical treasures, which include Divine Soul Songs, to transform and enlighten our souls, hearts, minds, and bodies to the Divine's soul, heart, mind, and body. The Divine and I are one. The Divine and you are one. The Di-vine and humanity are one. The Divine and Mother Earth and all universes are one. This Divine Oneness of all souls and all universes is a divine calling to you, humanity, and all souls.

Divine Oneness is to transform the consciousness of human-ity and all souls in all universes to divine consciousness.

Divine Oneness is to transform and enlighten our souls, hearts, minds, and bodies and the souls, hearts, minds, and bod-ies of humanity, Mother Earth, and all souls in all universes to divine souls, hearts, minds, and bodies.

We are responding to this calling for Divine Oneness.

We want to achieve this Divine Oneness.

We *can* achieve it.

We have Divine Soul Songs to achieve it.

We must practice hard to achieve it.

We *will* achieve it.

Humanity *will* achieve it.

Mother Earth *will* achieve it.

All souls in all universes *will* achieve it.

Divine Oneness will flourish for humanity, Mother Earth, and all universes.

Hao!

Thank you. Thank you. Thank you.

HOW I RECEIVED THIS SECOND DIVINE SOUL SONG

On November 14, 2006, as I was being driven from San Francisco to Mt. Shasta for a Soul Healing and Enlightenment retreat, suddenly the Divine said to me:

> *Zhi Gang,*
> *I am ready to pass a second major Divine Soul Song to you. This Divine Soul Song is another major divine treasure for healing, transforming, and enlightening humanity and all souls.*

The Divine continued:

> *I gave you my first Divine Soul Song a little more than a year ago. You have shared it with thousands of students worldwide, and you shared it with the thousands of people you met in your worldwide Soul Mind Body Medicine*

*book tour. You created more than one hundred forty of your own events worldwide in six months. You listened to me when I told you to do this. You showed your total commitment to listen to what I told you to do. In every event you are delighted to sing and teach my first Soul Song,* Lu La Li Lu La, Love, Peace and Harmony. *That Soul Song has deeply touched people worldwide. I am very happy. I appreciate your total GOLD commitment to serve humanity. I have seen the frequency and the vibration of this Soul Song deeply transform souls, hearts, minds, and bodies.*

*Now I am going to give you my second major Soul Song, which is named* God Gives His Heart to Me. *You can start to share this Soul Song in your coming Soul Healing and Enlightenment retreat. This Soul Song is another of my major divine treasures for transformation and enlightenment.*

Then the Divine gave me the words of this new Divine Soul Song:

> *Lu la lu la la li*
> *Lu la lu la la li*
> *Lu la lu la li*
> *Lu la lu la li*
>
> *God gives his heart to me*
> *God gives his love to me*
> *My heart melds with his heart*
> *My love melds with his love*

I was profoundly moved and touched by the Divine's generosity and love. I responded to the Divine:

> *Dear Divine,*
> *I am extremely honored to receive your second major Soul Song. I am profoundly touched by your love and light. I am privileged to be your servant and a servant of humanity. I love Soul Songs from the bottom of my heart. I am so happy to reveal and share your second Soul Song with humanity and all souls. Please give me the melody for this song.*

Instantly, the Divine sang his Soul Song to me (figure 4 in the insert). I was following along as I listened. The melody was so beautiful. When I sang it, tears filled my eyes. Even now, every time I sing this Divine Soul Song, tears are in my eyes. The divine love within this Soul Song is inexpressible in words alone. Track 2 of the enclosed audio CD is a sample of this Divine Soul Song.

A short while later I gave this melody to Mr. Jun Yen Jiang, a renowned music composer in Taiwan, so that he could create an arrangement of this Divine Soul Song for an audio CD. Mr. Jiang is a Divine Soul Music Composer. I offered a Divine Soul Transplant of Divine Music Composer to his soul in 2005. I trained him to open his Soul Language and sing his Soul Song. Through his Divine Soul Music Composer channel, he has received many exquisite pieces of Divine Soul Music from Heaven. People worldwide love his Divine Soul Music CDs.

Mr. Jiang told me, "Master Sha, when you sang *God Gives His Heart to Me* in the recording studio, I was moved to tears. Every time I listen to the CD we created, I am still moved to tears." I have exactly the same response when I listen to this CD and when I sing this Divine Soul Song. Every time, the unconditional love and compassion within this Divine Soul Song deeply touch and move my heart and soul.

> *God gives his heart to me*
> *God gives his love to me*
> *My heart melds with his heart*
> *My love melds with his love*

Hao!
Thank you. Thank you. Thank you.

APPLY THE DIVINE SOUL SONG *GOD GIVES HIS HEART TO ME* TO HEAL, REJUVENATE, AND TRANSFORM YOU, HUMANITY, MOTHER EARTH, AND ALL UNIVERSES

The power of Divine Soul Songs has no limit. Therefore, the applications of Divine Soul Songs have no limit. In this section I will lead you in practices to apply the Divine Soul Song *God Gives His Heart to Me* to heal and transform life.

The first practice is to apply this Divine Soul Song to purify your heart.

Purifying the heart is vital to advancing on your spiritual journey. Five thousand years ago traditional Chinese medicine stated: *The heart houses the soul and the mind.* Purifying the heart will benefit your soul and mind. People often say things like *she has a kind heart* or *he has a compassionate heart* or *she has such a peaceful heart.* Sometimes people say they are so hurt in their hearts or their hearts ache. The heart represents one's behavior. The heart represents one's thoughts. The heart represents one's spirit.

Therefore, transforming the heart is directly related to transforming one's behavior, one's thoughts, and one's soul. This second Divine Soul Song has unimaginable power to transform your heart. Let's do it now!

> *Dear soul, mind, and body of the Divine Soul Song*
>    Lu La Lu La La Li, God Gives His Heart to Me,
> *I love you, honor you, and appreciate you.*
> *Please purify my heart.*
> *I am very grateful.*
> *Thank you. Thank you. Thank you.*

Then sing or chant the words of the Divine Soul Song *God Gives His Heart to Me* for at least three minutes:

> *Lu la lu la la li*
> *Lu la lu la la li*
> *Lu la lu la li*
> *Lu la lu la li*
>
> *God gives his heart to me*
> *God gives his love to me*
> *My heart melds with his heart*
> *My love melds with his love*

Close the practice in the usual way:

*Hao! Hao! Hao!*
*Thank you. Thank you. Thank you.*

Generally speaking, sing for three to five minutes per time, three to five times per day—the more, the better.

The second practice is to apply this Divine Soul Song to purify your soul.

Soul is the boss of a human being. As I taught in *The Power of Soul*,[5] the authoritative book of my Soul Power Series, and as I will further explain in chapter 3 of this book, a human being's soul could reside in seven areas of the body. I name them the seven soul houses. They correspond closely to the seven principal chakras found in ancient Indian teachings such as Hinduism. To uplift its standing higher and higher, a soul needs more and more purification. Purification is unlimited. No one can ever claim to have a completely pure soul. You may have a very pure soul, but your soul can always be purified further. The Divine's love and heart can purify our souls further and further.

This is the way to apply the Divine Soul Song *God Gives His Heart to Me* to purify your soul:

> *Dear soul, mind, and body of the Divine Soul Song*
> *Lu La Lu La La Li, God Gives His Heart to Me,*
> *I love you, honor you, and appreciate you.*
> *Please purify my soul.*
> *I am very grateful.*
> *Thank you. Thank you. Thank you.*

---

5. Zhi Gang Sha, 2009, *The Power of Soul: The Way to Heal, Rejuvenate, Transform, and Enlighten All Life*, New York/Toronto: Atria Books/Heaven's Library.

Then sing or chant the words of this Divine Soul Song for at least three minutes:

> *Lu la lu la la li*
> *Lu la lu la la li*
> *Lu la lu la li*
> *Lu la lu la li*
>
> *God gives his heart to me*
> *God gives his love to me*
> *My heart melds with his heart*
> *My love melds with his love*

Again, sing for three to five minutes per time, three to five times per day—the more, the better. Close the practice in the usual way.

The third practice is to apply this Divine Soul Song to heal your physical body.

Love is and has always been the most important teaching for all spiritual groups and all spiritual beings throughout history. This spiritual teaching from all different sources can be summarized in one sentence:

**Love melts all blockages and transforms all life.**

There are different kinds of love. A mother gives love to her children. Family members and friends give love to each other. Spiritual beings give love to each other. What is important to understand is that *true love is unconditional love*. Unconditional love is love that is given without asking for or expecting anything in return. The sun gives light and heat to Mother Earth and all the planets of our solar system. This is the unconditional service and unconditional love of the sun. The moon also gives her light to Mother Earth and the solar system. This is her unconditional service and unconditional love. The sun and the moon do not ask for anything in return. They just give. Billions of people pray to the Divine. The Divine has answered countless prayers. The Divine does not ask for anything in return. The Divine just gives. This is unconditional love.

Unconditional love is the only love that can melt all blockages and transform all life. Conditional love has limited power. Unconditional love has unlimited power. The Divine Soul Song *God Gives His Heart to Me* is the Divine's offering of unconditional love to you, humanity, Mother Earth, and all universes. That is why this Divine Soul Song has unlimited power.

To fully understand this, you must really practice. You must chant three minutes per time, and even more and even longer because you understand that the Divine is giving us the Divine's unconditional love through this Soul Song. We are honored to practice and receive it.

Let us practice now to heal our physical bodies:

> *Dear soul, mind, and body of the Divine Soul Song*
>    Lu La Lu La La Li, God Gives His Heart to Me,
> *I love you, honor you, and appreciate you.*
> *Please give me a divine healing for* _____ (request
>    healing for any condition at the level of the
>    systems, organs, or cells).
> *I am very grateful.*
> *Thank you. Thank you. Thank you.*

Then sing or chant the words of this Divine Soul Song for at least three minutes:

*Lu la lu la la li*
*Lu la lu la la li*
*Lu la lu la li*
*Lu la lu la li*

*God gives his heart to me*
*God gives his love to me*
*My heart melds with his heart*
*My love melds with his love*

After singing, close in the usual way.

Generally speaking, sing for three to five minutes per time, three to five times per day—the more, the better. For chronic or life-threatening conditions, sing or chant for a total of two hours or more each day. You can sing or chant three, seven, eleven, or twenty times a day. Just make sure your total practice time is at least two hours. There are no time limits. You could receive remarkable healing results.

The fourth practice is to apply this Divine Soul Song to heal your emotional body.

Five thousand years ago the ancient masters of traditional Chinese medicine shared the wisdom that the physical body is directly connected with the emotional body. They found, for example, that the liver in the physical body directly connects with the emotional body of anger. When you have a sickness of the liver, such as hepatitis B or C, cirrhosis, or liver cancer, you can easily become angry. On the other hand, if you are often angry in your emotional body, it could affect the physical condition of the liver. *The liver connects with anger.*

Traditional Chinese medicine wisdom further teaches that the heart connects with depression and anxiety in the emotional body. If you have a physical sickness of the heart, such as blocked heart arteries or an irregular heartbeat, these physical blockages can easily cause depression and anxiety. One the other hand, if you suffer from depression and anxiety in your emotional body, it could affect the physical condition of the heart. *The heart connects with depression and anxiety.*

The spleen connects with worry in the emotional body. In traditional Chinese medicine, the spleen is in charge of transportation and transformation of food and bodily fluids. This means the spleen is in charge of digestion and absorption. This wisdom has guided traditional Chinese medicine for five thousand years in dealing with digestive system issues. There is another wisdom from traditional Chinese medicine that I would like to share. Another key function of the spleen is to keep blood within the blood vessels. People who suffer from chronic bleeding of any kind, whether in the gums, nose, vagina, or skin, have a spleen dysfunction. The practical treasure in traditional Chinese medicine to stop chronic bleeding is to adjust the function of the spleen by using herbs or acupuncture. *The spleen connects with worry.*

The lungs connect with grief and sadness in the emotional body. When one suffers from asthma, breathing difficulties, or other chronic lung conditions in the physical body, it can easily cause grief. On the other hand, when people lose their loved ones, they have great sadness. This will affect their lungs. They could catch a cold easily because *the lungs connect with grief.*

The kidneys connect with fear in the emotional body. If you suffer from kidney failure, impaired kidney function, stones, inflammation, tumors, or cancer in the kidneys, you could easily be fearful. On the other hand, if you suffer from fear, it could affect the physical condition of the kidneys. Some people were really frightened by something when they were children. This could affect the health of their kidneys for a long time. *The kidneys connect with fear.*

In summary, the physical body and the emotional body are closely related. This connection was revealed five thousand years ago in traditional Chinese medicine. Use this wisdom to apply the healing principles of traditional Chinese medicine, which have had profound results.

Practice with me now to heal our emotional bodies:

> *Dear soul, mind, and body of the Divine Soul Song*
>     Lu La Lu La La Li, God Gives His Heart to Me,
> *I love you, honor you, and appreciate you.*
> *Please give me a divine healing to balance all of my*
>     *emotions.*
> *I am very grateful.*
> *Thank you. Thank you. Thank you.*

Then sing or chant the words of this Divine Soul Song for three to five minutes:

> *Lu la lu la la li*
> *Lu la lu la la li*
> *Lu la lu la li*
> *Lu la lu la li*
>
> *God gives his heart to me*
> *God gives his love to me*
> *My heart melds with his heart*
> *My love melds with his love*

Then close:

> *Hao! Hao! Hao!*
> *Thank you. Thank you. Thank you.*

The fifth practice is to apply this Divine Soul Song to heal others.

When you sing or chant the words of a Divine Soul Song, you can sing or chant aloud or silently. Singing or chanting aloud vibrates the bigger cells and spaces in the body. Singing or chanting silently vibrates the smaller cells and spaces in the body. Most important is to sing or chant from your heart. When you chant from your heart, the Divine Soul Song will carry power beyond comprehension.

Let me share a story about practicing from your heart. When I taught a workshop in Toronto in June 2005, there was one student who had suffered from serious arthritis for more than fifteen years. I told her, "Use your heart to give love to both of your knees for seven minutes. Just say 'I love my knees. Heal my knees.' repeatedly and tap your knees gently with your fingertips." She followed my instructions. After seven minutes she stood up and walked. She cried and cried. She said she had not experienced such relief in fifteen years. That left a deep impression on me. She healed herself by applying love for a few minutes. She received such good results. I did not give her any healing at all. She just applied love. Love has power beyond words and thought.

Now let us apply the Divine Soul Song *God Gives His Heart to Me* to offer healing to others. Do it with me. Do not skip this practice. You will understand more and more the power of singing and chanting Divine Soul Songs.

> *Dear soul, mind, and body of the Divine Soul Song*
> Lu La Lu La La Li, God Gives His Heart to Me,
> *I love you, honor you, and appreciate you.*
> *Please give a divine healing to _____ for _____*
> (name the person or persons and make requests
> for their healing).
> *I am very grateful.*
> *Thank you. Thank you. Thank you.*

Then sing or chant the words of this Divine Soul Song for at least three minutes:

> *Lu la lu la la li*
> *Lu la lu la la li*
> *Lu la lu la li*
> *Lu la lu la li*
>
> *God gives his heart to me*
> *God gives his love to me*
> *My heart melds with his heart*
> *My love melds with his love*

Generally speaking, sing for three to five minutes per time, three to five times per day—the more, the better. For chronic or life-threatening conditions, chant for a total of at least two hours each day. Close each practice in the usual way.

The sixth practice is to apply this Divine Soul Song to heal your pets:

> *Dear soul, mind, and body of the Divine Soul Song*
> Lu La Lu La La Li, God Gives His Heart to Me,

*I love you, honor you, and appreciate you.*
*Please give a divine healing to _____ (name your*
    pet) *for* _____ (request any healing for your
    pet's physical, emotional, mental, or spiritual
    bodies).
*I am very grateful.*
*Thank you. Thank you. Thank you.*

Then sing or chant the words of this Divine Soul Song for at
least three minutes, the longer, the better:

*Lu la lu la la li*
*Lu la lu la la li*
*Lu la lu la li*
*Lu la lu la li*

*God gives his heart to me*
*God gives his love to me*
*My heart melds with his heart*
*My love melds with his love*

Follow the same practice principles stated before.

The seventh practice is to apply this Divine Soul Song to
boost your energy, stamina, vitality, and immunity:

*Dear soul, mind, and body of the Divine Soul Song*
    *Lu La Lu La La Li, God Gives His Heart to Me,*
*I love you, honor you, and appreciate you.*
*Please boost my energy, stamina, vitality, and immu-*
    *nity.*

*I am very grateful.*
*Thank you. Thank you. Thank you.*

Then sing or chant the words of this Divine Soul Song for at least three minutes, the longer, the better:

*Lu la lu la la li*
*Lu la lu la la li*
*Lu la lu la li*
*Lu la lu la li*

*God gives his heart to me*
*God gives his love to me*
*My heart melds with his heart*
*My love melds with his love*

Follow the same practice principles stated before.

APPLY THE DIVINE SOUL SONG *GOD GIVES HIS HEART TO ME*
TO REMOVE MIND-SETS, EGO, AND ATTACHMENT

It is very important to know that some of the biggest blockages to advancing on your spiritual journey are your mind-sets. You may have your own belief system. You may have your own ways of looking at things. You may analyze things a lot to figure out what you think is right. You may think something has to be a certain way and not another way. Mind-sets are one of the major blockages on your spiritual journey. A spiritual being must learn from the Divine. A spiritual being must learn divine creation, divine manifestation, and divine flexibility. With the Divine the "impossible" can become possible. Therefore, transforming mind-sets is vital for your spiritual journey.

For example, experiencing soul enlightenment and other spiritual "aha" moments could be beyond any experience, expectation, and imagination that you have ever had. Open your heart and soul. Be in the moment. Trust divine creation and manifestation. Do not be stuck on having a hard time believing in divine possibility. Do not be stuck on a fixed way of doing things. Do not believe that you do not have the power to change something. Transform your mind-sets to become more creative and flexible. I believe every one of you would like to do this. This transformation is very important for advancing on your spiritual journey.

The Divine Soul Song *God Gives His Heart to Me* is a divine treasure to transform mind-sets. Let's apply this Divine Soul Song to do it!

> *Dear soul, mind, and body of the Divine Soul Song*
>      Lu La Lu La La Li, God Gives His Heart to Me,
> *I love you, honor you, and appreciate you.*
> *Please transform my mind-sets.*
> *Let them be filled with divine love, light, creativity,*
>      *and flexibility.*
> *I am very grateful.*
> *Thank you. Thank you. Thank you.*

Then sing or chant the words of the Divine Soul Song *God Gives His Heart to Me*:

> *Lu la lu la la li*
> *Lu la lu la la li*

*Lu la lu la li*
*Lu la lu la li*

*God gives his heart to me*
*God gives his love to me*
*My heart melds with his heart*
*My love melds with his love*

After three minutes (or more) close the practice in the usual way:

*Hao! Hao! Hao!*
*Thank you. Thank you. Thank you.*

This Divine Soul Song tells us that if your heart melds with the Divine's heart and your love melds with the Divine's love, you carry the power of the Divine's heart and the Divine's love. The Divine's heart and love can transform your mind-sets and every aspect of your life.

There is no time limit for this practice. The more you sing or chant, the more your mind-sets will be transformed.

※

The next practice is to transform and remove ego.

On one's spiritual journey, ego is another major blockage. I have taught thousands of spiritual seekers in the last few years. I trained them to open their spiritual channels. When they can talk with the Divine to receive divine guidance, and when they can offer divine healing with great results, it is easy for them to have ego because they feel they are special.

In the physical world, the most successful people in every profession generally have worked hard to attain their success.

They have done serious study, research, practice, creation, and manifestation. They then make major contributions in their fields and receive great respect from society and from people worldwide. Such people could also think they are special and easily gain ego if they do not have a pure soul, heart, and mind. When you are successful, it is easy to have ego. Ego is a very common issue for humanity.

In fact successful people *are* special. But if you have achieved success in any aspect of your profession or life, do not forget that the path to your success has received guidance from the spiritual world and blessings from Heaven and the Divine. Remember also all the people who worked with you and all the people around you. Their support and their contributions also helped make you successful.

Think about it. Without the inspiration and blessings from the spiritual world, Heaven, and the Divine, without the support and contributions from the people you work with, could you have attained the success you have? If you have total gratitude to Heaven and to all the teachers and other people who prepared you in every aspect of your life to become special, then you will feel humble.

What you have achieved is special, but it could be much better. There are countless wisdoms and unlimited abilities in the universe. Regardless of how successful you are, you definitely can do much better. If you hold this kind of attitude with humbleness and gratitude, you will prevent ego and remove the ego you have.

Think about five thousand years of recorded history. Every path of human life has developed step by step up to now. Science is still developing. Human wisdom is still developing. Human intelligence is still developing. Human abilities to create and manifest are developing. Every aspect of life is developing and can develop further. Ego will block your development. Removing ego is vital for improving every aspect of your life. When you have ego on your spiritual journey, the uplifting of your spiritual standing will be blocked. Your progress in gaining higher spiritual abilities will also be blocked.

I would like to share some insights from my experiences over the last several years. In 2003, the Divine chose me to download divine souls to humanity. I have transmitted countless divine souls for divine bodily systems, organs, and cells. Divine Soul Downloads or Soul Transplants are divine creation on the spot. According to the divine teaching that I have shared previously in the books of my Soul Power Series, when a person has a sickness in a bodily system, organ, or cells, the soul of the system, organ, or cells is sick. A Divine Soul Transplant replaces this original soul with a new divine soul. The original soul will return to Heaven. The Divine creates new divine souls for systems, organs, or cells and instantly transmits them to recipients. These new souls are created from the Divine's heart or the Divine's soul. I have offered Divine Soul Downloads for healing for six years. In that time, we have received thousands of moving stories of heart-touching healing, including healing for many chronic or life-threatening conditions.

The Divine has also transmitted Divine Healer souls. I have offered Divine Healer souls to more than seven hundred people on Mother Earth. These seven hundred Divine Healers have created thousands and thousands of heart-touching healing stories. Most of them do not have a healing background, but they do have pure hearts. They have love, care, and compassion. They want to remove people's suffering. They made a commitment to serve.

To become a Divine Healer, one must first apply. If the Divine approves the application, one can receive a Divine Soul Download of a Divine Healer soul, followed by training to be certified as a Divine Healer. When a Divine Healer offers healing, the Divine Healer soul downloaded to him or her will come out from the healer's soul, mind, and body and go to the recipient of the healing. This Divine Healer soul can subdivide to serve more than one recipient, even hundreds and thousands of recipients. The Divine Healer soul can offer a divine healing to remove blockages at the levels of soul, mind, and body. The Divine Healer Soul Download is divine creation of a Divine Healer in the moment. The moment the Divine gives you this download is the moment you carry the power of a Divine Healer. Words cannot fully explain how special a Divine Soul Download of a Divine Healer soul is.

The Divine has also downloaded many Divine Occupation souls to create Divine Artists, Divine Chiropractors, Divine Music Composers, Divine Business Entrepreneurs, and many other divine professionals. Again, the Divine created these new divine professional souls on the spot. These souls carry the divine wisdom, creation, and manifestation abilities of that profession or occupation. These divine abilities will guide the recipient to do a much better job in his or her profession or occupation. The people who have received Divine Occupation souls have reported many heart-touching stories. The Divine has once again demonstrated divine creation and manifestation abilities on the spot.

Let me share one specific example.

In February 2008, I was teaching and healing in Frankfurt, Germany. I offered Divine Soul Transplants of Divine Occupations to create divine professionals. I asked for someone in the audience who would be willing to receive one of these Divine

Soul Transplants as a demonstration. A female opera singer volunteered. I asked her to sing an aria for us. Her singing was beautiful and powerful. Everyone gave her a big round of applause. Then I asked her to close her eyes and prepare to receive a Divine Soul Transplant of a Divine Opera Singer soul. I raised my right hand to Heaven and said, "Dear Divine, I request a Divine Soul Transplant of Divine Opera Singer to her." The Divine instantly responded to my request and downloaded a Divine Opera Singer soul to her.

She began to sing the same aria again, but this time I knew her singing was from her new Divine Opera Singer soul. The vibration was obviously different and much more powerful. The wave of her sound swept over all two hundred of us in the room. When she finished, people cheered wildly. Many of them wanted to receive their own Divine Soul Transplant for Divine Occupation immediately.

I honor all professionals. The Divine creates *divine* professionals by transmitting the Divine's souls for that profession. This is not a physical professional. It is divine creation and divine presence with divine wisdom, divine creativity, and divine manifestation abilities.

I share this experience to inspire you to think about what the Divine can do. What the Divine can do is beyond our imagination. Whatever we can imagine, the Divine can do. What we cannot imagine or even think about, the Divine can also do. The Divine is the creator of the universe. Divine creation and manifestation abilities are beyond any words, any thoughts, and any imaginings.

If you are a spiritual being, think about what the Divine can do. Think about divine creation and manifestation. Then think about what we can do. What the Divine can do is an ocean.

What we can do is like one drop of water in the ocean. Humbleness will be produced in your heart right away. What reason do we have to show any ego? Our success has been supported and nurtured by many, many people. Our success is given by the Divine. Our success is blessed by Heaven. What happens in our lives comes from the creation and manifestation of the Divine. When you can understand and appreciate this, it will really help you remove ego.

Ego comes from impurities of your soul, heart, and mind. To purify your soul, heart, and mind is to remove ego. The Divine Soul Song *Lu La Lu La La Li, God Gives His Heart to Me* is a powerful divine treasure to remove your ego. The divine frequency and vibration with divine love, forgiveness, compassion, and light within this Soul Song could transform your ego very quickly.

Practice it.

Benefit from it.

Remove your ego as soon as possible.

Join me now in applying this Divine Soul Song to remove ego:

> *Dear soul, mind, and body of the Divine Soul Song*
>     Lu La Lu La La Li, God Gives His Heart to Me,
> *I love you, honor you, and appreciate you.*
> *Please purify my soul, heart, mind, and body to remove ego and prevent ego.*
> *I am very grateful.*
> *Thank you. Thank you. Thank you.*

Then sing or chant the words of this Divine Soul Song for at least three minutes:

*Lu la lu la la li*
*Lu la lu la la li*
*Lu la lu la li*
*Lu la lu la li*

*God gives his heart to me*
*God gives his love to me*
*My heart melds with his heart*
*My love melds with his love*

After singing, close in the usual way.

How does this practice work?

Every line you sing, the Divine's heart and the Divine's love are purifying your soul, heart, mind, and body. Every line you sing, divine frequency and divine vibration are transforming your frequency and vibration. Your thoughts, behavior, and activities will be transformed by the Divine's heart and love. Ego will be removed. The bigger your ego, the more you need to sing or chant.

A divine treasure to remove your ego is in front of your eyes. Sing or chant. Apply the divine treasure to transform your ego. If you do not practice, you will not receive the benefits of soul transformation of your ego.

Millions of people worldwide desire life transformation. They want to transform their relationships and finances. They want to transform their health. They want to be happier. This book delivers divine treasures to transform every aspect of your life. Be aware of these treasures. Grab these treasures. Do not ignore them. Really practice with them. The benefits could totally shock you.

I always repeat this ancient statement: *If you want to know if a pear is sweet, taste it.* If you want to know whether Divine Soul Songs are powerful for transforming your life, experience them. It is not difficult to understand. A Divine Soul Song carries divine frequency and vibration. Divine love, forgiveness, compassion, and light can remove blockages in any aspect of your life. Divine treasures are waiting for you to use them. Just do it! Life transformation will follow. If you do not do it, you will not receive the results that you could receive easily.

For thousands of years, singing or chanting has been one of the most powerful spiritual practices for life transformation. Singing or chanting a Divine Soul Song is *divine* singing or chanting. It carries divine power. It really is very simple. It may be too simple to believe. But in the last several years, thousands of heart-touching and moving stories have convinced me deeply that divine treasures are beyond any words, any thoughts, any imagination, and any comprehension.

Realize the power of divine treasures. What you need to do is use them. Only by using them will you receive their benefits. I wish you will receive all kinds of benefits by applying Divine Soul Songs to transform every aspect of your life.

❋

A third major blockage on one's spiritual journey is attachment. Attachment is karma-related. For example, you meet a person you love deeply. Later, for whatever reason, you separate. Your heart could be bothered for the rest of your life because of your deep attachment to that person. To transform this hurt, first understand that you may be deeply attached because you have been together for many lifetimes. This deep soul connection spanning many lifetimes is very difficult to forget in this lifetime. Your soul has strong memories. Your soul connects with and affects your subconscious mind. Therefore, you have strong feelings and thoughts about that person. This is not unusual at all.

Many people very much like things that are not healthy for them. Yet it is very difficult for them to change. You may like something very much but find it very hard to change. This kind of special liking for something or someone usually has a spiritual reason from many lifetimes. Therefore, when you especially like something, do not think it is a simple liking. It could be related to your experiences in many lifetimes.

In one's spiritual journey, to remove attachment is very important. When you make a commitment to serve humanity totally, when you reach advanced soul enlightenment, and when you give your heart to the Divine, you could remove attachment completely because you realize deeply that the purpose of life is to serve, to make others healthier and happier, and to create love, peace, and harmony for humanity, Mother Earth, and all universes. This Divine Mission becomes your mission. It is exactly what you want to do. When you have a total commitment to serve, any attachment will be removed automatically because it is no longer important to you. In order to reach this level, apply Divine Soul Songs to purify your soul, heart, mind, and body. Apply Divine Soul Songs to self-clear the karma that is the root cause of your attachment.

Do not expect to transform your attachment in a few days of practice. It takes time singing Divine Soul Songs to transform. It could take months, even years, of practice to remove attachment completely, but it is very possible to do it. If you use your heart and soul to sing or chant, you could remove attachment very quickly. As I taught earlier in this chapter, go into the divine condition when you practice. When you sing or chant the words

*Lu la lu la la li*
*Lu la lu la la li*
*Lu la lu la li*
*Lu la lu la li*

*God gives his heart to me*
*God gives his love to me*
*My heart melds with his heart*
*My love melds with his love*

going into the divine condition means your heart *becomes* the Divine's heart. Your love *becomes* the Divine's love. If your heart and love become the Divine's heart and love, what kind of attachment can you continue to have? You will not have any attachment because you are in the divine frequency and vibration of the Divine's heart and love. This will completely transform your behavior and attitudes. You could be surprised by how much you change.

Every minute you sing or chant a Divine Soul Song, you are literally transforming your consciousness, your heart, and your soul to be closer to the Divine. Divine Soul Songs carry power that can transform any aspect of your life. If you sing a Divine Soul Song from the bottom of your heart and go into the divine condition, you will not need months or years to remove your attachment. It can happen in weeks or even days. When you go into the divine condition, your transformation will be so fast and so powerful that no words can fully explain it.

To do is to experience. To do is to transform. Join me now in applying the Divine Soul Song *Lu La Lu La La Li, God Gives His Heart to Me* to remove attachment. This Divine Soul Song can remove any attachment from any aspect of life. Here's how to do it:

> *Dear soul, mind, and body of the Divine Soul Song*
>     Lu La Lu La La Li, God Gives His Heart to Me,
> *I love you, honor you, and appreciate you.*
> *Please remove my attachment to* (name the specific
>     attachment[s] you would like to remove).
> *I am very grateful.*
> *Thank you. Thank you. Thank you.*

Then sing or chant the words of the Divine Soul Song *God Gives His Heart to Me*:

> *Lu la lu la la li*
> *Lu la lu la la li*
> *Lu la lu la li*
> *Lu la lu la li*
>
> *God gives his heart to me*
> *God gives his love to me*
> *My heart melds with his heart*
> *My love melds with his love*

After three minutes (or more) close the practice in the usual way:

> *Hao! Hao! Hao!*
> *Thank you. Thank you. Thank you.*

I wish you great success in removing mind-sets, ego, and attachment.

I wish you great success in your spiritual journey.

Hao!

APPLY THE DIVINE SOUL DOWNLOAD OF THE DIVINE SOUL
SONG *GOD GIVES HIS HEART TO ME* TO HEAL AND
TRANSFORM LIFE

At my Soul Healing and Enlightenment retreat in San Francisco on November 8, 2007, I asked the Divine to offer a permanent Divine Soul Transplant of the Divine Soul Song *Lu La Lu La La Li, God Gives His Heart to Me* to all humanity and all souls in the universes. Since that day this priceless treasure has been with your soul. Let me show you how to apply this divine soul treasure to heal and transform life.

This is the way to apply this divine soul to offer healing to humanity:

> *Dear soul, mind, and body of the Divine Soul Transplant of the Divine Soul Song* Lu La Lu La La Li, God Gives His Heart to Me, *on every human being's soul,*
> *I love you, honor you, and appreciate you.*
> *Please turn on to offer a divine healing to all humanity.*
> *I am very grateful.*
> *Thank you. Thank you. Thank you.*

Then chant for three minutes:

*Divine Permanent Soul Song Treasure* Lu La Lu La
   La Li, God Gives His Heart to Me,
*Heal humanity. Thank you, Divine.*
*Divine Permanent Soul Song Treasure* Lu La Lu La
   La Li, God Gives His Heart to Me,
*Heal humanity. Thank you, Divine.*
*Divine Permanent Soul Song Treasure* Lu La Lu La
   La Li, God Gives His Heart to Me,
*Heal humanity. Thank you, Divine.*
*Divine Permanent Soul Song Treasure* Lu La Lu La
   La Li, God Gives His Heart to Me,
*Heal humanity. Thank you, Divine.*

Close the practice in the usual way.

Chant three to five times per day. The more you chant, the better.

This is a very important practice. The very first sentence of this book, in the beginning section on the Soul Power Series, is: *The purpose of life is to serve.* To do this practice is to offer a major divine service to humanity. To serve is to transform. To serve is the best way to transform your life. As you chant in this practice, the Divine and the Akashic Records are pouring divine flowers, which are divine virtue, to your book in the Akashic Records. This divine virtue rewards you for your service and can transform every aspect of your life beyond your comprehension. This is so simple it could be very difficult to understand the profound benefits for transforming your life.

## To serve is to transform all life.

This is a one-sentence secret to transform all life. You will understand this one-sentence secret more and more deeply on your spiritual journey. One year from now you will understand this one-sentence secret more deeply than you do now. Five years from now you will understand the value of this secret even further and twenty years from now, further still.

Why? Because this is the fourth Universal Law made by the Divine for all souls in all universes. I explained this Universal Law and how I received it in the "Soul Power Series" section of this book. In the next chapter I will explain it further.

Earlier in this chapter I led you to do many practices applying the Divine Soul Song *God Gives His Heart to Me* to transform any aspect of life. The Divine Soul Transplant of the Divine Soul Song *God Gives His Heart to Me* is another divine soul treasure that can transform any aspect of life. Let us do a few practices to experience the power of the Divine Soul Transplant of the Divine Soul Song *God Gives His Heart to Me*.

For example, you may have just finished a meal. You may have some problems with digestion and absorption. The Divine Soul Transplant of the Divine Soul Song *God Gives His Heart to Me* can help you digest and absorb. It can help you heal your digestive system.

This is the way to do it by applying this Divine Soul Transplant:

> *Dear soul, mind, and body of the Divine Soul Transplant of the Divine Soul Song* Lu La Lu La La Li, God Gives His Heart to Me *downloaded to my soul,*
> *I love you, honor you, and appreciate you.*
> *Please turn on to help me digest and absorb food and to offer a divine healing to my digestive system issue.* (If you do not have a digestive system issue,

ask for divine rejuvenation of your digestive
system.)
*I am very grateful.*
*Thank you. Thank you. Thank you.*

Then chant for three minutes:

*Divine Permanent Soul Song Treasure* Lu La Lu La
La Li, God Gives His Heart to Me,
*Heal my digestive system and help me digest and absorb food well.*
*Thank you, Divine.*
*Divine Permanent Soul Song Treasure* Lu La Lu La
La Li, God Gives His Heart to Me,
*Heal my digestive system and help me digest and absorb food well.*
*Thank you, Divine.*
*Divine Permanent Soul Song Treasure* Lu La Lu La
La Li, God Gives His Heart to Me,
*Heal my digestive system and help me digest and absorb food well.*
*Thank you, Divine.*
*Divine Permanent Soul Song Treasure* Lu La Lu La
La Li, God Gives His Heart to Me,
*Heal my digestive system and help me digest and absorb food well.*
*Thank you, Divine.*

Chant for three minutes. Then close the practice in the
usual way.
Do you feel better? If you chant longer, you could heal your

digestive system very quickly. There is no time limit for this practice. The longer you chant, the better.

Here is another application of this Divine Soul Transplant for a very common and practical situation: tiredness. If you are tired, which happens often in a human's life, sit down right away and practice like this:

> *Dear soul, mind, and body of the Divine Soul Transplant of the Divine Soul Song* Lu La Lu La La Li, God Gives His Heart to Me *downloaded to my soul,*
> *I love you, honor you, and appreciate you.*
> *Please turn on to give me a divine blessing to boost my energy.*
> *I am very grateful.*
> *Thank you. Thank you. Thank you.*

Then chant for three minutes:

> *Divine Permanent Soul Song Treasure* Lu La Lu La La Li, God Gives His Heart to Me,
> *Boost my energy. Thank you, Divine.*
> *Divine Permanent Soul Song Treasure* Lu La Lu La La Li, God Gives His Heart to Me,
> *Boost my energy. Thank you, Divine.*
> *Divine Permanent Soul Song Treasure* Lu La Lu La La Li, God Gives His Heart to Me,
> *Boost my energy. Thank you, Divine.*
> *Divine Permanent Soul Song Treasure* Lu La Lu La La Li, God Gives His Heart to Me,
> *Boost my energy. Thank you, Divine.*

After three minutes close the practice:

> *Hao! Hao! Hao!*
> *Thank you. Thank you. Thank you.*

Here is another very practical example:

You are studying or working. Suddenly you cannot think clearly. You feel heavy and sluggish in your mind. This is the way to apply this Divine Soul Transplant to clear your mind:

> *Dear soul, mind, and body of the Divine Soul Trans-*
>     *plant of the Divine Soul Song* Lu La Lu La La Li,
>     God Gives His Heart to Me *downloaded to my*
>     *soul,*
> *I love you, honor you, and appreciate you.*
> *Please turn on to clear my mind.*
> *Remove the heaviness in my head.*
> *I am very grateful.*
> *Thank you. Thank you. Thank you.*

Then chant for three minutes:

> *Divine Permanent Soul Song Treasure* Lu La Lu La
>     La Li, God Gives His Heart to Me,
> *Clear my mind and head. Thank you, Divine.*
> *Divine Permanent Soul Song Treasure* Lu La Lu La
>     La Li, God Gives His Heart to Me,
> *Clear my mind and head. Thank you, Divine.*
> *Divine Permanent Soul Song Treasure* Lu La Lu La
>     La Li, God Gives His Heart to Me,
> *Clear my mind and head. Thank you, Divine.*

> *Divine Permanent Soul Song Treasure* Lu La Lu La
>    La Li, God Gives His Heart to Me,
> *Clear my mind and head. Thank you, Divine.*

Close the practice in the usual way.

Here is one more practical example:

You are upset by someone or something. You may be a little irritated. You may be very angry. This happens in life a lot! Do not be upset. Pause for a moment. Apply this Divine Soul Transplant to balance your emotions:

> *Dear soul, mind, and body of the Divine Soul Trans-*
>    *plant of the Divine Soul Song* Lu La Lu La La Li,
>    God Gives His Heart to Me *downloaded to my*
>    *soul,*
> *I love you, honor you, and appreciate you.*
> *Please turn on to bless me to remove my anger or irri-*
>    *tation.*
> *Please apply love and forgiveness to transform my*
>    *emotions.*
> *I am very grateful.*
> *Thank you. Thank you. Thank you.*

Then chant for three minutes:

> *Divine Permanent Soul Song Treasure* Lu La Lu La
>    La Li, God Gives His Heart to Me,
> *Remove my irritation and anger. Let me love and*
>    *forgive.*
> *Thank you, Divine.*

*Divine Permanent Soul Song Treasure* Lu La Lu La
La Li, God Gives His Heart to Me,
*Remove my irritation and anger. Let me love and*
*forgive.*
*Thank you, Divine.*
*Divine Permanent Soul Song Treasure* Lu La Lu La
La Li, God Gives His Heart to Me,
*Remove my irritation and anger. Let me love and*
*forgive.*
*Thank you, Divine.*
*Divine Permanent Soul Song Treasure* Lu La Lu La
La Li, God Gives His Heart to Me,
*Remove my irritation and anger. Let me love and*
*forgive.*
*Thank you, Divine.*

Close after chanting for at least three minutes.

I just led you in a few practices for some very common issues that could arise in your life almost every day. Remember, when you are tired, when you cannot think properly, or when you are upset, pause for a moment. Connect with the permanent Divine Soul Transplant of the Divine Soul Song *God Gives His Heart to Me* that you have on your soul. You *have* this divine treasure already. Use it! Turn it on. Spend three minutes to receive its healing and blessing. You could receive life transformation instantly. Your tiredness, inability to think clearly, and irritation and anger are just like locks keeping you imprisoned. To open these locks, you need a key. The Divine Soul Transplant of the Divine Soul Song *God Gives His Heart to Me* is the key to these and many other locks. Use this divine golden key to unlock them and free your soul, heart, mind, and body.

Tao (pronounced *dow*, rhymes with *cow*) is "the Way," the laws and principles of the universe. Tao can appear in every aspect of your life. Tao is in walking. Tao is in eating. Tao is in sleeping. Tao is in writing. Tao is in singing. Tao is in dancing. Tao is in thinking. Tao is in every movement of universe. I use these last few examples to share with you and all humanity that:

**To transform life is to transform every aspect of life.**

When you have negative or unhealthy thoughts, transform them right away with this divine soul treasure:

> *Dear soul, mind, and body of the Divine Soul Transplant of the Divine Soul Song* Lu La Lu La La Li, God Gives His Heart to Me *downloaded to my soul,*
> *I love you, honor you, and appreciate you.*
> *Please turn on to transform my unhealthy thoughts.*
> *I am very grateful.*
> *Thank you. Thank you. Thank you.*

Then chant as I have taught you in the preceding practices.

When you are confused, turn on this divine soul treasure to transform your confusion.

When you are hurt by someone, turn on this divine soul treasure to transform the hurt and forgive.

You can apply this divine soul treasure to transform every aspect of your life.

This divine soul treasure can not only transform your life, it can transform the lives of others. You can apply this divine soul treasure to transform your loved ones' lives. When you apply this soul treasure to transform the lives of others, that person does not have to be with you because this is *soul transformation*. Apply the divine soul treasure to give a healing or blessing to your loved ones. This is soul healing and soul transformation. If the soul is healed, healing of the mind and body will follow. If the soul is transformed, transformation of every aspect of life will follow.

The key teaching I want to share with you is to apply any Divine Soul Song and any divine soul treasure to transform your life anytime, anywhere. Tao is within every aspect of life. If you disalign with the Tao, you can apply Divine Soul Songs and other divine soul treasures to align with the Tao right away. You do not need to wait. You can do soul transformation instantly.

SOUL TRANSFORMATION FOR PAST, PRESENT, AND FUTURE

Soul transformation is beyond people's comprehension. Soul transformation is not limited by time or space. Soul transformation can apply to events that happened in the past. For example, suppose you had a big conflict with somebody three years ago. Connect with that event. Sing a Divine Soul Song to transform the soul of the event and the soul of your relationship with the other person:

> *Dear soul, mind, and body of the Divine Soul Song*
>     Lu La Lu La La Li, God Gives His Heart to Me,
> *I love you, honor you, and appreciate you.*
> *Please transform the conflict that I had with* _____
>     (name the person) *three years ago.*
> *Please offer divine love, forgiveness, and light to heal*
>     *our conflict and bless our relationship.*

*I am very grateful.*
*Thank you. Thank you. Thank you.*

Then sing or chant the words of the Divine Soul Song *God Gives His Heart to Me* for at least three minutes:

*Lu la lu la la li*
*Lu la lu la la li*
*Lu la lu la li*
*Lu la lu la li*

*God gives his heart to me*
*God gives his love to me*
*My heart melds with his heart*
*My love melds with his love*

Close the practice in the usual way:

*Hao! Hao! Hao!*
*Thank you. Thank you. Thank you.*

The conflict happened three years ago. You may think that things have passed already. But on the advanced spiritual level, there is no past, no future. *Now is then. Then is now.* The message and the blockage from that unpleasant event three years ago are still there. Use the Divine Soul Song *God Gives His Heart to Me* to transform the event. The blockage from three years ago could be removed. It will bless your life *now.*

Soul transformation can be applied to past events and past lives. Soul transformation can be applied to every aspect of your present life. Soul transformation can apply to future events and future lives.

Let me give you an example. Suppose you are planning and organizing a big event next year. There could be many blockages and problems for you and the event. You may or may not know about the blockages. You may or may not be able to foresee them. It doesn't matter. You can ask the Divine Soul Transplant of the Divine Soul Song *God Gives His Heart to Me* to transform the future problems that are supposed to come or that may come. Here is how to do it:

> *Dear soul, mind, and body of the Divine Soul Transplant of the Divine Soul Song* Lu La Lu La La Li,
> God Gives His Heart to Me *downloaded to my soul and the soul of the event next year,*
> *I love you, honor you, and appreciate you.*
> *Please turn on to bless the event next year.*
> *Please remove all blockages to the success of the event.*
> *Let as many people as possible benefit fully from a successful event.*
> *I am very grateful.*
> *Thank you. Thank you. Thank you.*

Then chant for three minutes:

> *Divine Permanent Soul Song Treasure* Lu La Lu La
>     La Li, God Gives His Heart to Me,
> *Bless the event. Thank you, Divine.*
> *Divine Permanent Soul Song Treasure* Lu La Lu La
>     La Li, God Gives His Heart to Me,
> *Bless the event. Thank you, Divine.*

> *Divine Permanent Soul Song Treasure* Lu La Lu La
>     La Li, God Gives His Heart to Me,
> *Bless the event. Thank you, Divine.*
> *Divine Permanent Soul Song Treasure* Lu La Lu La
>     La Li, God Gives His Heart to Me,
> *Bless the event. Thank you, Divine.*

Do this soul transformation practice a few times a day in the months, weeks, and days leading up to the event. If you do soul transformation in this way, potential problems could be removed.

From the first example, you understand how past unpleasant events carry negative messages. We can offer transformation to this negativity today. Future unpleasant events also carry a message and a blockage today. For example, you may not be emotionally unbalanced today, but you could be tomorrow or next week. Ask the divine soul treasure to balance your emotions for tomorrow, for next week, and for next month. Your emotional imbalances for tomorrow, next week, and next month could be removed now. This is soul transformation for the future.

In summary, at the soul level there is no past, present, or future. There is no difference. Soul time is beyond quantum time. We *are* in the present time, but we can do soul transformation for the past. We can do soul transformation for the present. We can do soul transformation for the future. This practical wisdom is a treasure for you and all humanity to learn how to apply soul transformation to benefit every aspect of your lives—past, present, and future. Apply it. Benefit from it. The Divine Soul Transplant of the Divine Soul Song *God Gives His Heart to Me* can help you do it.

## The Power and Significance of the
## Divine Soul Song of Compassion

In May 2007 the Divine gave me the Divine's third major Divine Soul Song, the Divine Soul Song of Compassion. Compassion boosts energy, stamina, vitality, and immunity for healing and rejuvenation. Compassion transforms all lives. Divine compassion carries divine power to heal, rejuvenate, and transform all life.

Shi Jia Mo Ni Fuo, the founder of Buddhism, was asked by Ar Nan, one of his closest disciples, "Is it correct to say that loving kindness and compassion are a part of our practice?" Shi Jia Mo Ni Fuo replied, "No. It would be correct to say that loving kindness and compassion are *all* of our practice." Compassion is very important in all spiritual teachings and traditions.

TEACHINGS AND BLESSINGS OF COMPASSION
I HAVE RECEIVED

Millions of people worldwide know the Bodhisattva of Compassion, Guan Shi Yin Pusa, or Guan Yin. "Guan" literally means *listen, hear,* and *observe.* "Shi" means *world.* "Yin" means *voice.* "Pusa" means *bodhisattva.* Guan Shi Yin is a divine pure soul servant who hears the voices of suffering of all humanity in the world and responds with her great compassion and service. Many Buddhist books have recorded the many lives she has saved with the power of her divine compassion. In the West, people call her the Goddess of Mercy. Her new name in the Soul Light Era is Ling Hui Sheng Shi, pronounced *ling hway shung shr.* "Ling" means *soul.* "Hui" means *intelligence.* "Sheng" means *saint.* "Shi" means *servant.* Ling Hui Sheng Shi is a saint servant with great soul intelligence.

When Guan Yin was a human being on Mother Earth, she met her spiritual master, Qian Guang Wang Jing Zhu Ru Lai (pronounced *chyen gwahng wahng jing joo roo lye*). Her teacher blessed her by teaching her the Big Compassion mantra *Da Bei Zhou,* pronounced *dah bay joe.* ("Da" means *big.* "Bei" means *compassion.* "Zhou" means *mantra.* This ancient mantra has been associated with Guan Yin and has been chanted by Buddhists throughout history.) He explained the power of this mantra to her. After receiving this teaching and practicing the mantra, Guan Yin felt the great power of this mantra and was profoundly moved and touched by it. She bowed to her teacher and made a vow: *I will spread the power and the teaching of Da Bei Zhou forever.* Because of her total sincerity and commitment in making this vow, her teacher transmitted the true power of *Da Bei Zhou* to Guan Yin. This true power is the spiritual power of a thousand hands and a thousand eyes. When Guan Yin gives a spiritual healing or a blessing to transform life, she serves with the very high spiritual power of her thousand hands and thousand eyes.

When I was four years old Guan Yin came to me to teach me *Da Bei Zhou.* I was able to learn it and chant with her. I didn't understand the power of *Da Bei Zhou,* but I followed her soul to chant. I have chanted *Da Bei Zhou* a lot in my life. Even now I very often chant *Da Bei Zhou* in my teleclasses, on radio programs, and in my workshops and Soul Healing and Enlightenment retreats to offer soul healing and blessing.

At age five I caught a serious cold. My parents brought me to see a doctor. He gave me a penicillin injection and then I returned home. My parents went back to work. My grandmother was with me. I suddenly lost consciousness because of an allergic reaction to the penicillin. She was so scared. She ran to my neighbor who was an acupuncturist. He inserted a needle into the Ren Zhong (also called Shui Gou) acupuncture point (right under the nose) to revive me. Afterward, I was very tired and weak. That event has stayed in my memory very clearly to this day. I understood better the suffering of the tired and the weak.

When I was age twelve I saw my aunts, uncles, and family friends suffering from many different illnesses. I was especially touched by those who had asthma. Their breathing difficulties stirred deep compassion in my heart. I wondered, "Why can't someone stop their suffering?" From the bottom of my heart, I wanted to become the one who could help them. A few years later this kind of heartfelt desire led me to study medicine and become a doctor.

From the first grade in elementary school through middle school, high school, and university, I was always selected by my classmates to be their class monitor. My responsibilities and tasks in this position were to give my classmates guidance and inspiration to organize and lead them in their student life. From elementary school to middle school and high school, I always voluntarily sat next to the most difficult student in the class. I always felt in my heart that I wanted to help these students. Now when I recall those times, I realize that this was the compassion that was nurtured by the teaching and training I received at an early age from Guan Yin, other spiritual fathers and mothers, and the Divine. This compassion led me to help those with difficulties. I am so grateful that I was able to offer this service to those students.

In 1973 I graduated from high school. Because of the Cultural Revolution, everyone had to go to the countryside to work on farms. I went to live and work in a village away from my hometown. There I lived with thirty other students in a commune, farming a big area of land. I was chosen as the leader of the commune. We worked so hard as farmers. We did all the manual labor of farmers. Life was hard. Each month, we were given a ration of only three liters of cooking oil for all thirty of us.

As the leader of the student farm commune, I worked extremely hard without enough nutrition or rest. I suffered from serious burnout. I contracted a high fever and went to the hospital, where I was diagnosed with fluid in my lungs. After a two-week stay in the hospital I was healed, but it made me understand further how one suffers when one is seriously ill. I saw many very sick patients in the hospital. I had great compassion for them.

In 1976 China restarted university education. Students across the whole country took national entrance examinations. I passed the examinations and joined one of the first groups of students to enter university when it reopened. My application to study medicine was accepted.

During my five years in medical school, I was again selected by my classmates to be the class monitor. As a monitor, you have to do lots of service for all the classmates. You have to spend many extra hours to take care of lots of issues for the students in the class. I was always very patient and happy to serve my classmates at any opportunity.

We medical students spent our fifth year in practice at a hospital. The most desirable assignment was to stay at the medical university hospital, because as a teaching hospital it had the best doctors and professors. My class of nearly five hundred students was divided into twenty small class groups. Each group had twenty to thirty students. Only two groups could stay at the teaching hospital for their year of practice; the best groups were chosen for this honor. Our group was one of the two in my class to be selected in 1982. For the first four years, our group was a good example for every activity in the university. Love, care, and compassion were always the principles for the classmates in our group. These qualities really helped us to be one of the groups selected by the university to stay in the university hospital. We performed well in every aspect of our school life. Our classmates were so happy to practice in the university teaching hospital. Today seven of the twenty-six students in my group are living and practicing abroad in North America and Europe. For Chinese students of my generation to become successes abroad is a great honor. Following the principles of love, care, and compassion transformed our group's student life and paved the way for the great success of our future service.

To this day I always try to follow the same principles of love, care, and compassion in every aspect of my life. Any time my assistants around me mention someone who is sick or who has some other concern, I instantly offer a divine blessing without being asked to do it. Since I learned *Da Bei Zhou* in childhood, I have practiced compassion throughout my whole life.

Many people thank me for my service. I do not take any credit. I give the credit to all of my teachers in every aspect of my life, including Guan Yin, Shi Jia Mo Ni Fuo, A Mi Tuo Fuo; other spiritual fathers and mothers in Heaven; my physical masters of ancient Chinese arts, including tai chi, qi gong, kung fu, the *I Ching*, and feng shui; my Taoist masters and Buddhist masters; my most beloved spiritual father, Dr. and Master Zhi Chen Guo; all of my teachers from elementary school through medical university; my parents for their love, care, and compassion; and the Divine. All of them have deeply inspired, guided, and blessed my life. I have deeply benefited in every aspect of my life from their teachings and their practice of love, care, and compassion.

The purpose of life is to serve. We cannot serve enough. Love, forgiveness, compassion, and light are vital qualities for service. From my early childhood up to now, compassion has been one of the most important teachings I received from my spiritual fathers and mothers, my parents, my ancestors, and my students. We will carry compassion to humanity and all souls forever.

I have continued to receive teachings and blessings of compassion. In 1998 I was practicing traditional Chinese medicine, qi gong, Zhi Neng Medicine,[6] and spiritual healing in Vancouver, Canada. On the morning of April 4, as I was meditating by chanting *Da Bei Zhou*, Guan Yin and all of the eighty-seven buddhas in *Da Bei Zhou* came and gave me an incredible blessing. Golden and rainbow light shone within my body from head to toe and skin to bone. I became a golden and rainbow light being. My whole body vibrated and shook. I bowed down to Guan Yin and the eighty-seven buddhas of *Da Bei Zhou* and made a vow:

> *Dear Guan Yin and the eighty-seven buddhas of* Da
>     Bei Zhou,
> *I have received love, forgiveness, compassion, light, and
> soul purification from you for my whole life. I am so
> grateful. I cannot honor you enough for your love,
> nourishment, training, and purification. I am mak-
> ing a vow to chant* Da Bei Zhou *to serve humanity
> and all souls as much as I can in this life and in all
> my future lifetimes.*

---

6. "Zhi Neng" means *intelligence and capabilities of the mind*. Zhi Neng Medicine was created by my most beloved spiritual father, Dr. and Master Zhi Chen Guo.

Guan Yin heard my vow and replied:

> *Dear my son, Zhi Gang,*
> *I am so pleased at your spiritual growth and by your*
> *love and compassion. I have taught, trained, and*
> *blessed you in this life and in many previous lives.*
> *You have passed my spiritual tests. So today I will*
> *transmit my spiritual compassion power to you. I*
> *will also transmit my thousand hands, thousand eyes*
> *spiritual power to your soul.*

I bowed to the floor continuously to Guan Yin and the eighty-seven buddhas of *Da Bei Zhou*. Their light shot through my whole body like lightning. That was one of the most powerful spiritual blessings I have ever received.

Since then I have chanted *Da Bei Zhou* much more than before to offer many, many blessings to humanity. I am honored to chant *Da Bei Zhou* to serve, heal, and transform people's lives.

I asked Guan Yin to transmit her spiritual thousand hands, thousand eyes abilities to two of my top teachers, Peter Hudoba and Michael Stevens, in November 2006 and to one spiritual leader, Dr. Barbara King, in June 2008. Guan Yin was delighted to offer them the same transmission.

From my early childhood to this day, the eighty-seven buddhas of *Da Bei Zhou* and the teachings and blessings from Ling Hui Sheng Shi have benefited my spiritual growth and my spiritual service tremendously. I cannot thank them enough.

HOW I RECEIVED THIS THIRD DIVINE SOUL SONG

On May 4, 2007, during my regular morning meditation, I chanted *Da Bei Zhou*. Guan Yin, or Ling Hui Sheng Shi, and the eighty-seven buddhas of *Da Bei Zhou* were present to bless me. The Divine was also there to observe my chanting. After I chanted *Da Bei Zhou* four times, the Divine said to me:

> *Zhi Gang,*
> *Today I am ready to give you my third major Soul*
> *Song, the Divine Soul Song of Compassion.*

The Divine gave me the words:

> *Lu La Li Lu     La Li Lu La     Li Lu La Li*
> *Lu La Li Lu     La Li Lu La     Li Lu La Li*
> *Lu La Li Lu     La Li Lu La     Li Lu La Li*
> *Lu La Li Lu     La Li Lu La     Li Lu La Li*

The English translation of this Soul Language is simply:

> *Compassion, compassion, compassion*
> *Compassion, compassion, compassion*
> *Compassion, compassion, compassion*
> *Compassion, compassion, compassion*

And here is the Chinese translation for reference:

> *Da ci da bei, da ci da bei, da ci da bei*
> *Da ci da bei, da ci da bei, da ci da bei*

*Da ci da bei, da ci da bei, da ci da bei*
*Da ci da bei, da ci da bei, da ci da bei*

After I received the words of this Divine Soul Song, I asked the Divine to give me the melody. The Divine told me: *Sing my Soul Song, the Divine Soul Song of Compassion. The melody will flow out from your mouth.* I followed the Divine's guidance. Instantly, the melody flowed out through my Soul Song.

You can listen to a sample of this Divine Soul Song on track 3 of the CD enclosed within this book. See figure 5 in the insert for the musical notation.

After I received this Divine Soul Song, I sang it a lot. Every time I sing this Divine Soul Song, I receive incredible blessings of divine compassion. I also continually receive blessings from Ling Hui Sheng Shi and the eighty-seven buddhas of *Da Bei Zhou.* I am extremely grateful to all of them.

APPLY THE DIVINE SOUL SONG OF COMPASSION TO HEAL, REJUVENATE, AND TRANSFORM YOU, HUMANITY, MOTHER EARTH, AND ALL UNIVERSES

Let us apply the Divine Soul Song of Compassion to boost energy. This is the way to do it:

*Dear soul, mind, and body of the Divine Soul Song of*
  *Compassion,*
*I love you, honor you, and appreciate you.*
*Please boost my energy.*
*I am very grateful.*
*Thank you.*

Then sing or chant the words to this Divine Soul Song:

> *Lu La Li Lu   La Li Lu La   Li Lu La Li*
> *Lu La Li Lu   La Li Lu La   Li Lu La Li*
> *Lu La Li Lu   La Li Lu La   Li Lu La Li*
> *Lu La Li Lu   La Li Lu La   Li Lu La Li*
>
> *Compassion, compassion, compassion*
> *Compassion, compassion, compassion*
> *Compassion, compassion, compassion*
> *Compassion, compassion, compassion . . .*

Generally speaking, sing for three to five minutes per time, three to five times per day, the more, the better. There are no time limits. Close the practice in the usual way:

> *Hao! Hao! Hao!*
> *Thank you. Thank you. Thank you.*

The second practice is to apply this Divine Soul Song to boost your stamina and vitality:

> *Dear soul, mind, and body of the Divine Soul Song of*
>   *Compassion,*
> *I love you, honor you, and appreciate you.*
> *Please boost my stamina and vitality.*
> *I am very grateful.*
> *Thank you.*

Then sing or chant the words to this Divine Soul Song:

*Lu La Li Lu    La Li Lu La    Li Lu La Li*
*Lu La Li Lu    La Li Lu La    Li Lu La Li*
*Lu La Li Lu    La Li Lu La    Li Lu La Li*
*Lu La Li Lu    La Li Lu La    Li Lu La Li*

*Compassion, compassion, compassion*
*Compassion, compassion, compassion*
*Compassion, compassion, compassion*
*Compassion, compassion, compassion . . .*

Generally speaking, sing for three to five minutes per time, three to five times per day, the more, the better. There are no time limits. Close in the usual way.

The third practice is to apply this Divine Soul Song to offer universal healing:

> *Dear soul, mind, and body of the Divine Soul Song of*
> *    Compassion,*
> *I love you, honor you, and appreciate you.*
> *Please offer a healing to Mother Earth, all planets, all*
> *    stars, all galaxies, and all universes.*
> *I am very grateful.*
> *Thank you.*

Then sing or chant the words to this Divine Soul Song:

*Lu La Li Lu    La Li Lu La    Li Lu La Li*
*Lu La Li Lu    La Li Lu La    Li Lu La Li*
*Lu La Li Lu    La Li Lu La    Li Lu La Li*
*Lu La Li Lu    La Li Lu La    Li Lu La Li*

*Compassion, compassion, compassion*
*Compassion, compassion, compassion*
*Compassion, compassion, compassion*
*Compassion, compassion, compassion . . .*

Generally speaking, sing for three to five minutes per time, three to five times per day, the more, the better. There are no time limits. Close in the usual way.

The fourth practice is to apply this Divine Soul Song to open and expand compassion within ourselves. Join me now:

*Dear soul, mind, and body of the Divine Soul Song of*
  *Compassion,*
*I love you, honor you, and appreciate you.*
*Please offer me a blessing to develop the greatest com-*
  *passion in my soul, heart, mind, and body so that I*
  *can be a better servant of humanity and all souls.*
*I am very grateful.*
*Thank you.*

Then sing or chant the words to this Divine Soul Song:

*Lu La Li Lu    La Li Lu La    Li Lu La Li*
*Lu La Li Lu    La Li Lu La    Li Lu La Li*
*Lu La Li Lu    La Li Lu La    Li Lu La Li*
*Lu La Li Lu    La Li Lu La    Li Lu La Li*

*Compassion, compassion, compassion*
*Compassion, compassion, compassion*
*Compassion, compassion, compassion*
*Compassion, compassion, compassion . . .*

Sing for at least three to five minutes per time, three to five times per day, the more, the better. There are no time limits.

*Hao! Hao! Hao!*
*Thank you. Thank you. Thank you.*

DIVINE SOUL DOWNLOAD OF THE DIVINE SOUL SONG
OF COMPASSION

Now I'm going to offer the first Divine Soul Download in this book as a divine gift to every reader. I will ask the Divine to offer a Divine Soul Transplant to every reader. This Divine Soul Transplant is named:

### Divine Soul Transplant of the
### Divine Soul Song of Compassion

This is a huge golden light soul that will be permanently downloaded to your soul. The Divine gave me the honor of transmitting the Divine's souls in July 2003 as the Divine's servant, vehicle, and channel. Every time I offer Divine Soul Transplants, I have to make a sincere request and totally honor the Divine. To transmit divine souls within a book, I have to preprogram the downloads with the Divine. Do not ask for anything different or more. It will not work.

Sit up straight. Put the tip of your tongue near the roof of your mouth. Relax. Open your heart and soul.

Prepare!

### Divine Soul Transplant of the
### Divine Soul Song of Compassion
### Silent download!

Close your eyes for thirty seconds to receive this major divine soul treasure.

> *Hao! Hao! Hao!*
> *Thank you. Thank you. Thank you.*

Thank you, Divine.

We are extremely honored that the Divine offers the Divine's soul treasures to every reader. Congratulations on receiving this treasure! If this is your first time to receive a Divine Soul Transplant, I will say three times *Congratulations!* to you.

The Divine Soul Transplant of the Divine Soul Song of Compassion carries the power of divine compassion to heal, rejuvenate, purify, and transform life. You can apply this divine soul for healing, rejuvenation, purification, and transformation of any aspect of life. You can invoke this priceless treasure anytime and anywhere. Here is how to practice. Do it with me now.

Let us invoke this divine soul to boost our immunity:

> *Dear soul, mind, and body of the divine soul of the*
>     *Divine Soul Song of Compassion downloaded to my*
>     *soul,*
> *I love you, honor you, and appreciate you.*
> *Please boost my immunity.*
> *I am very grateful.*
> *Thank you.*

Then chant for at least three minutes, silently or aloud:

> *Divine Permanent Soul Song Treasure of Divine*
>     *Compassion,*
> *Boost my immunity. Thank you, Divine.*

*Divine Permanent Soul Song Treasure of Divine*
  *Compassion,*
*Boost my immunity. Thank you, Divine.*
*Divine Permanent Soul Song Treasure of Divine*
  *Compassion,*
*Boost my immunity. Thank you, Divine.*
*Divine Permanent Soul Song Treasure of Divine*
  *Compassion,*
*Boost my immunity. Thank you, Divine.*

Generally speaking, chant for three to five minutes per time, three to five times per day, the more, the better. There are no time limits. Close the practice as usual.

According to the World Health Organization, nearly 12 percent of the world's population suffers from mental disorders. The WHO says that some four hundred fifty million people worldwide experience a mental illness that could benefit from professional diagnosis and treatment. Problems associated with mental illness and other mental disorders will continue to rise in Mother Earth's transition period. Mental disorders cause great suffering to those who have them. Mental disorders are also a burden to the loved ones and friends of those who have them. Those who suffer from mental disorders can benefit from our greatest compassion and from divine compassion.

*Dear soul, mind, and body of the divine soul of the*
  *Divine Soul Song of Compassion downloaded to my*
  *soul,*
*I love you, honor you, and appreciate you.*
*Please turn on to offer divine compassion to all who*
  *suffer from mental disorders.*

*Offer them a blessing of healing and peace.*
*I am very grateful.*
*Thank you. Thank you. Thank you.*

Then chant for at least three minutes, silently or aloud:

*Divine Permanent Soul Song Treasure of Divine*
   *Compassion,*
*Bless all of them. Thank you, Divine.*
*Divine Permanent Soul Song Treasure of Divine*
   *Compassion,*
*Bless all of them. Thank you, Divine.*
*Divine Permanent Soul Song Treasure of Divine*
   *Compassion,*
*Bless all of them. Thank you, Divine.*
*Divine Permanent Soul Song Treasure of Divine*
   *Compassion,*
*Bless all of them. Thank you, Divine.*

After chanting, close:

*Hao! Hao! Hao!*
*Thank you. Thank you. Thank you.*

You can apply this Divine Soul Download to transform every aspect of life. The power of Divine Compassion is beyond words. When you practice, you will experience life transformation through this power.

# Divine Soul Songs of Divine Universal Laws

THE UNIVERSE IS divided into the yang universe and the yin universe. The yang universe is the physical world. The yin universe is the spiritual world. Universal laws apply to both universes. There are four major universal laws. They are:

- Yin Yang
- Five Elements
- Message Energy Matter
- Universal Service

## The First Divine Universal Law:
## The Universal Law of Yin Yang

Yin Yang is the first Divine Universal Law. It is an ancient philosophy and theory that summarizes and describes everything in the universe, from the smallest to the largest, for both living and inanimate things.

## BASIC PHILOSOPHY AND CONCEPTS OF YIN YANG

Yin Yang theory was released in *The Yellow Emperor's Internal Classic,* the authoritative book of traditional Chinese medicine. It has also guided Taoist practice for thousands of years.

Yin Yang is a relative concept; it is not absolute. Everything can be divided into yin and yang. Also, any two things can be compared to determine which is yin and which is yang relative to the other.

Everything that has a fire characteristic belongs to yang. A fire characteristic is hot and bright, moves upward and outward, and is excited, fast, and vigorous.

Everything that has a water characteristic belongs to yin. A water characteristic is cool and dark, moves inward and downward, and is calm, slow, and peaceful.

Complements and opposites are yin-yang pairs. Some common pairs are listed below in Table 1:

Table 1. Common Yin Yang Pairs

| *Yin* | *Yang* |
|---|---|
| water | fire |
| slow | fast |
| woman | man |
| cold | hot |
| dark | light |
| passive | active |
| quiet | noisy |

| | |
|---|---|
| down | up |
| moon | sun |
| night | day |
| Earth | Heaven |
| winter | summer |
| soul | body |

The internal organs of the body can also be categorized as yin or yang as shown in Table 2. In traditional Chinese medicine the yin organs are the *zang* (pronounced *dzahng*) organs; the yang organs are the *fu* (pronounced *foo*) organs. Each major internal organ has a corresponding organ that is its yin-yang complement.

Table 2. Paired Yin and Yang Organs

| *Yin (zang)* | *Yang (fu)* |
|---|---|
| liver | gallbladder |
| heart | small intestine |
| spleen | stomach |
| lungs | large intestine |
| kidneys | urinary bladder |

Yin and yang are opposing but also interdependent and interchangeable. Each depends on the other for its existence. Night would not exist without day. Each transforms the other. Each transforms into the other. Each changes constantly. Night transforms into day and vice versa. Yin and yang are always in relative balance; yin wanes as yang waxes and vice versa.

Yin and yang are infinitely divisible. Let me use the kidney as an example. The kidney is yin relative to the urinary bladder, which is yang. The kidney itself can be subdivided into kidney yin and kidney yang. Each kidney cell can also be divided into yin and yang aspects. The membrane of a cell is yang; the nucleus is yin. The nucleus of a cell can in turn be divided into its yin and yang aspects. External parts of the nucleus are yang; internal parts are yin. Anything can be subdivided endlessly into yin and yang components.

In traditional Chinese medicine, yin-yang imbalance is the root cause of every sickness. Balancing yin and yang is the solution for healing in traditional Chinese medicine. In Soul Mind Body Medicine, balancing soul, mind, and body is the solution for healing. Soul, mind, and body all can be divided into yin and yang. Therefore, balancing yin and yang is the solution for healing in Soul Mind Body Medicine also.

## Divine Soul Song of Yin Yang

The Divine has a Soul Song for each universal law. Each one is a newly released divine practical soul treasure for healing; boosting energy, vitality, stamina, and immunity; preventing sickness; rejuvenation and prolonging life; balancing Heaven, Earth, and human beings; and healing humanity, Mother Earth, planets, stars, galaxies, and universes.

### HOW I RECEIVED THE DIVINE SOUL SONG OF YIN YANG

Five thousand years ago in traditional Chinese medicine, *The Yellow Emperor's Internal Classic* released Yin Yang theory. It has guided the practice of traditional Chinese medicine ever since. It has served millions of people worldwide throughout history. Five thousand years later, on May 8, 2008, in my regular early-morning meditation, the Divine told me:

> *Dear Zhi Gang,*
> *Today I am going to give you my fourth major Soul*
>   *Song, the Divine Soul Song of Yin Yang. This is my*
>   *healing treasure for humanity.*

I replied, "Thank you, Divine. I am extremely honored to receive your Divine Soul Song of Yin Yang. I understand how powerful this Divine Soul Song must be. To balance yin and yang is to heal all sicknesses."

The Divine said:

> *You are right. To balance yin and yang is the major heal-*
> *ing principle in history. My Divine Soul Song of Yin Yang*
> *could help everyone balance their yin and yang. This is my*
> *healing treasure to empower people to heal themselves. You*
> *have been teaching self-healing for more than twenty years*
> *as I guided you to do. This Divine Soul Song is another*
> *step. Everyone can receive further benefits from it.*

I replied, "Thank you so much. I am extremely honored to receive this priceless treasure."

The Divine continued:

> *Let me teach you about my Soul Song of Yin Yang. There*
> *are seven houses of the soul in a human being. They are in*
> *the core of the body. From lowest to highest, they are:*

- *First—just above the perineum, which is the region between the genitals and the anus*
- *Second—the area between the first soul house and the navel*
- *Third—the area of the navel*
- *Fourth—the Message Center, or heart chakra*
- *Fifth—the throat*
- *Sixth—the brain*
- *Seventh—above the crown chakra*

*There is also one area named the Wai Jiao, which is the space in front of the spinal column. It is the biggest space in the body* (see figure 6 in the insert). *From the first soul house, move up to the second soul house, then the third, fourth, fifth, sixth, and seventh soul houses. Then turn down through the Wai Jiao back to the first soul house.*

I replied, "Dear Divine, thank you so much for the teaching. I understand that you are showing me the key energy circle for the whole body. I am very grateful and honored. I do have one question. In traditional Chinese medicine, the Ren meridian flows through the front midline of the body to the top of the head. The Du meridian flows through the back midline within the spinal cord to the top of the head. The Ren and Du meridians connect to form a vertical energy circle, which is itself a yin yang circle. You are teaching me to go up the middle of the body through the seven soul houses and then to go down through the Wai Jiao in front of the spinal column. How is this yin yang energy circle different from the Ren-Du circle?"

The Divine replied:

*The circle of the Ren-Du meridians is the yin yang circle*
*in traditional Chinese medicine and in Taoist practice. It*
*is the Outer Yin Yang Circle. The circle I am showing you*
*now is the Inner Yin Yang Circle.* **The Inner Yin Yang**
**Circle directs the Outer Yin Yang Circle.** *This is the*
*greatest secret to balancing yin and yang in the body.*

I bowed down to the Divine 108 times to thank the Divine
for revealing this divine secret to me to share with humanity.
I was excited and speechless. Then the Divine started to show
me the sacred Soul Song of Yin Yang for every soul house. Listen
to it on track 6 of the enclosed audio CD. (See figure 7 in the
insert for the musical notation for this Divine Soul Song. On my
website, www.drsha.com, you can also watch a video of me teaching this Divine Soul Song and sing along with me.)

The first soul house is just above the Hui Yin (pronounced
*hway yeen*) acupuncture point, which is in the perineum, the area
between the genitals and the anus.

The Divine Soul Song of Yin Yang for the first soul house is:

*Hei Ya*
*Hei Ya Hei Ya You*
*Hei Ya Hei Ya You*
*Hei Ya Hei Ya Hei Ya You*
*Hei Ya Hei Ya Hei Ya Hei Ya You*

"Hei" (pronounced *hay*) is the key sound for the first soul
house.

"Ya" (pronounced *yah*) and "you" (pronounced *yoe*) are
sounds that are common to the Divine Soul Song of Yin Yang for
every soul house.

The second soul house is between the first soul house and the navel. This places the second soul house in the lower abdomen roughly at the level of the Lower Dan Tian (see page lviii for an explanation of the Lower Dan Tian).

The Divine Soul Song of Yin Yang for the second soul house is:

> *Heng Ya*
> *Heng Ya Heng Ya You*
> *Heng Ya Heng Ya You*
> *Heng Ya Heng Ya Heng Ya You*
> *Heng Ya Heng Ya Heng Ya Heng Ya You*

"Heng" (pronounced *hung*) is the key sound for the second soul house.

The third soul house is at the level of the navel.

The Divine Soul Song of Yin Yang for the third soul house is:

> *Hong Ya*
> *Hong Ya Hong Ya You*
> *Hong Ya Hong Ya You*
> *Hong Ya Hong Ya Hong Ya You*
> *Hong Ya Hong Ya Hong Ya Hong Ya You*

"Hong" (pronounced *hohng*) is the key sound for the third soul house.

The fourth soul house is the Message Center, which is also known as the heart chakra.

The Message Center is one of the most important energy centers in the body and is *the* most important spiritual center. It is the center for love, forgiveness, compassion, emotions, healing, karma, Soul Language, soul communication, life transformation, and soul enlightenment.

To locate the Message Center, start from the point at the middle of your sternum or breastbone (in traditional Chinese medicine, this is the Shan Zhong acupuncture point), then go 2.5 *cun* inside your body. (As I explained in the introduction, the *cun* is a unit of measurement used in traditional Chinese medicine. One *cun* is defined as the width of the top joint of the thumb at its widest part. Although this varies from person to person, it is roughly equivalent to one inch.) That is the center of your Message Center, which is a fist-sized energy center.

The Divine Soul Song of Yin Yang for the fourth soul house is:

> *Ah Ya*
> *Ah Ya Ah Ya You*
> *Ah Ya Ah Ya You*
> *Ah Ya Ah Ya Ah Ya You*
> *Ah Ya Ah Ya Ah Ya Ah Ya You*

"Ah" (pronounced *ah*) is the key sound for the fourth soul house.

The fifth soul house is in the throat.

The Divine Soul Song of Yin Yang for the fifth soul house is:

> *Xi Ya*
> *Xi Ya Xi Ya You*
> *Xi Ya Xi Ya You*
> *Xi Ya Xi Ya Xi Ya You*
> *Xi Ya Xi Ya Xi Ya Xi Ya You*

"Xi" (pronounced *shee*) is the key sound for the fifth soul house.

The sixth soul house is in the brain.

The Divine Soul Song of Yin Yang for the sixth soul house is:

> *Yi Ya*
> *Yi Ya Yi Ya You*
> *Yi Ya Yi Ya You*
> *Yi Ya Yi Ya Yi Ya You*
> *Yi Ya Yi Ya Yi Ya Yi Ya You*

"Yi" (pronounced *yee*) is the key sound for the sixth soul house.

The seventh soul house is above the center of the top of the head, above the crown chakra.

The Divine Soul Song of Yin Yang for the seventh soul house is:

> *Weng Ya*
> *Weng Ya Weng Ya You*
> *Weng Ya Weng Ya You*
> *Weng Ya Weng Ya Weng Ya You*
> *Weng Ya Weng Ya Weng Ya Weng Ya You*

"Weng" (pronounced *wung*) is the key sound for the seventh soul house.

After the seven soul houses we continue to the Wai Jiao, which is the space in front of the spinal column. The Wai Jiao is the biggest space within the body. It is a vital area for circulation of energy and matter.

The Divine Soul Song of Yin Yang for the Wai Jiao is:

*You Ya*
*You Ya You Ya You*
*You Ya You Ya You*
*You Ya You Ya You Ya You*
*You Ya You Ya You Ya You Ya You*

"You" (pronounced *yoe*) is the key sound for the Wai Jiao.

Then the Divine taught me to chant the entire Inner Yin Yang Circle four times:

*Hei Heng Hong Ah Xi Yi Weng You*
*Hei Heng Hong Ah Xi Yi Weng You*
*Hei Heng Hong Ah Xi Yi Weng You*
*Hei Heng Hong Ah Xi Yi Weng You*

You can listen to me singing this Inner Yin Yang Circle on track 4 of the enclosed audio CD.

The Divine continued:

Hei Heng Hong Ah Xi Yi Weng You *forms the most important energy circle in the body.* (See figure 8 in the insert.) *Every sickness is caused by blockages in soul, mind, and body. Soul blockages are karma. Mind blockages are energy blockages. Body blockages are matter blockages. Blockages in soul, mind, and body will appear as blockages in this circle. To promote free flow of energy in this circle is to remove all blockages in soul, mind, and body. This circle is the Inner Yin Yang Circle.*

*I am teaching you this so that you can share this teaching with humanity.*

I was profoundly moved and touched. I understood from the bottom of my heart that the Divine had just released the top healing treasure and tool to empower humanity to heal. I told the Divine, "Thank you so much for this sacred teaching. I am extremely honored to receive it. I am extremely privileged to be able to release it to humanity."

The Divine continued:

> *There is another sacred wisdom and practice I am*
> *    going to teach you now.*
> *This is the sacred and secret matter circle for rejuvena-*
> *    tion and long life.*
> *The Divine Soul Song for this circle is:*

> *You Weng Yi Xi Ah Hong Heng Hei*
> *You Weng Yi Xi Ah Hong Heng Hei*
> *You Weng Yi Xi Ah Hong Heng Hei*
> *You Weng Yi Xi Ah Hong Heng Hei*

> *When you sing this Soul Song or chant these words, the circle starts from the genital area, goes in front of and then inside the tailbone, then up through the spinal cord to the brain and the Bai Hui acupuncture point in the crown chakra.* (The Bai Hui acupuncture point, pronounced *bye hway,* is in the center of the top of the head.) *Then it goes down through the brain to the roof of the mouth, then down the middle of the body through the other houses of the soul to the first soul house just above the Hui Yin acupuncture point and perineum. This is the most important matter circle in the body.* (See figure 9 in the insert.)

You can listen to me singing this most important matter circle on track 5 of the enclosed audio CD.

When I heard this divine teaching, I remembered that my spiritual father, Dr. and Master Zhi Chen Guo, told me that energy in the roof of the mouth transforms to liquid (saliva). When this saliva drips down to the mouth, swallow it and visualize it traveling down to your Lower Dan Tian. When the saliva arrives at the Lower Dan Tian, this liquid will turn into a golden light ball to nourish your Lower Dan Tian and your whole body. I was profoundly appreciative of this teaching from Master Guo.

The Divine asked me to practice this new matter circle for a few minutes. I did it right away. My mouth produced a lot of saliva. I swallowed it. I felt relaxed, energized, nourished, and rejuvenated.

This is how I received this major divine sacred teaching of the Divine Soul Song of Yin Yang and the Divine Yin Yang Energy Circle and Divine Yin Yang Matter Circle that are vital parts of this Divine Soul Song. The first circle, *Hei Heng Hong Ah Xi Yi Weng You,* is the most important energy circle in the body for healing all sicknesses of the physical, emotional, mental, and spiritual bodies. The second circle, *You Weng Yi Xi Ah Hong Heng Hei,* is the most important matter circle in the body for rejuvenation and long life. The music for the entire Divine Soul Song of Yin Yang is provided in figure 7 in the insert.

I bowed to the Divine 108 times to show my greatest appreciation. My conversation with the Divine ended.


PRACTICE THE DIVINE SOUL SONG OF YIN YANG

The Divine also showed me how to practice the Divine Soul Song of Yin Yang using the Four Power Techniques I introduced in my book *Power Healing.*[7] The Four Power Techniques are Soul Power, Body Power, Mind Power, and Sound Power.

- Soul Power is *soul over matter,* which means using the power of soul to heal, bless, and transform every aspect of life. All you have to do is say *hello* and ask.
- Body Power is the use of specific body and hand positions for healing and energy development.
- Mind Power is *mind over matter,* which means using the power of mind—including intention and creative visualization—to heal, bless, and transform.
- Sound Power is the use of vibrational healing sounds, healing mantras, and Divine Soul Songs.

A focus and benefit of this practice is to develop the power of the seven houses of the soul. Let's review these seven important locations in the body and the Divine Soul Song sound associated with each of them:

- Hei     First Soul House (Hui Yin area)
- Heng    Second Soul House (between the Hui Yin area and the navel)
- Hong    Third Soul House (navel area)
- Ah      Fourth Soul House (Message Center)
- Xi      Fifth Soul House (throat)
- Yi      Sixth Soul House (brain)
- Weng    Seventh Soul House (just above the crown chakra)

---

7. See also *Soul Mind Body Medicine,* pp. 118–119.

There is a general principle to follow for Body Power in this practice: sit with one palm under the Hui Yin area (males sit on left palm; females sit on right palm). This palm will remain anchored throughout the practice of the Divine Soul Song of Yin Yang. I will call this the *fixed palm*. The other palm moves to the area of each soul house as indicated in each step that follows. I will call this the *moving palm*.

## 1. First Soul House

| | |
|---|---|
| Soul Power | Say *hello: Dear soul, mind, and body of my first soul house, I love you. You have the power to develop and purify yourself. Do a good job. Thank you.* |
| Body Power | Sit on the fixed palm under the Hui Yin area. Place the moving palm over the fixed hand. See figure 10. |
| Mind Power | Visualize golden light in the first soul house. |
| Sound Power | Sing or chant the words to the Divine Soul Song of Yin Yang for the first soul house: |

*Hei Ya*
*Hei Ya Hei Ya You*
*Hei Ya Hei Ya You*
*Hei Ya Hei Ya Hei Ya You*
*Hei Ya Hei Ya Hei Ya Hei Ya You*

## 2. Second Soul House

| | |
|---|---|
| Soul Power | Say *hello: Dear soul, mind, and body of my second soul house, I love you. You have the power to develop and purify yourself. Do a good job. Thank you.* |

| Body Power | Sit on the fixed palm under the Hui Yin area. Place the moving palm over your lower abdomen (Lower Dan Tian). See figure 11. |
| Mind Power | Visualize golden light in the second soul house. |
| Sound Power | Sing or chant the words to the Divine Soul Song of Yin Yang for the second soul house: |

*Heng Ya*
*Heng Ya Heng Ya You*
*Heng Ya Heng Ya You*
*Heng Ya Heng Ya Heng Ya You*
*Heng Ya Heng Ya Heng Ya Heng Ya You*

## 3. Third Soul House

| Soul Power | Say *hello: Dear soul, mind, and body of my third soul house, I love you. You have the power to develop and purify yourself. Do a good job. Thank you.* |
| Body Power | Sit on the fixed palm under the Hui Yin area. Place the moving palm over your navel. See figure 12. |
| Mind Power | Visualize golden light in the third soul house. |
| Sound Power | Sing or chant the words to the Divine Soul Song of Yin Yang for the third soul house: |

*Hong Ya*
*Hong Ya Hong Ya You*
*Hong Ya Hong Ya You*
*Hong Ya Hong Ya Hong Ya You*
*Hong Ya Hong Ya Hong Ya Hong Ya You*

## 4. Fourth Soul House

| | |
|---|---|
| Soul Power | Say *hello: Dear soul, mind, and body of my fourth soul house, I love you. You have the power to develop and purify yourself. Do a good job. Thank you.* |
| Body Power | Sit on the fixed palm under the Hui Yin area. Place the moving palm over your Message Center. See figure 13. |
| Mind Power | Visualize golden light in the fourth soul house. |
| Sound Power | Sing or chant the words to the Divine Soul Song of Yin Yang for the fourth soul house: |

*Ah Ya*
*Ah Ya Ah Ya You*
*Ah Ya Ah Ya You*
*Ah Ya Ah Ya Ah Ya You*
*Ah Ya Ah Ya Ah Ya Ah Ya You*

## 5. Fifth Soul House

| | |
|---|---|
| Soul Power | Say *hello: Dear soul, mind, and body of my fifth soul house, I love you. You have the power to develop and purify yourself. Do a good job. Thank you.* |
| Body Power | Sit on the fixed palm under the Hui Yin area. Place the moving palm over your throat. See figure 14. |
| Mind Power | Visualize golden light in the fifth soul house. |
| Sound Power | Sing or chant the words to the Divine Soul Song of Yin Yang for the fifth soul house: |

*Xi Ya*
*Xi Ya Xi Ya You*
*Xi Ya Xi Ya You*
*Xi Ya Xi Ya Xi Ya You*
*Xi Ya Xi Ya Xi Ya Xi Ya You*

## 6. Sixth Soul House

| | |
|---|---|
| Soul Power | Say *hello: Dear soul, mind, and body of my sixth soul house, I love you. You have the power to develop and purify yourself. Do a good job. Thank you.* |
| Body Power | Sit on the fixed palm under the Hui Yin area. Place the moving palm over your forehead. See figure 15. |
| Mind Power | Visualize golden light in the sixth soul house. |
| Sound Power | Sing or chant the words to the Divine Soul Song of Yin Yang for the sixth soul house:<br>*Yi Ya*<br>*Yi Ya Yi Ya You*<br>*Yi Ya Yi Ya You*<br>*Yi Ya Yi Ya Yi Ya You*<br>*Yi Ya Yi Ya Yi Ya Yi Ya You* |

## 7. Seventh Soul House

| | |
|---|---|
| Soul Power | Say *hello: Dear soul, mind, and body of my seventh soul house, I love you. You have the power to develop and purify yourself. Do a good job. Thank you.* |
| Body Power | Sit on the fixed palm under the Hui Yin area. Place the moving palm over your crown chakra. See figure 16. |

| Mind Power | Visualize golden light in the seventh soul house. |
|---|---|
| Sound Power | Sing or chant the words to the Divine Soul Song of Yin Yang for the seventh soul house: |

*Weng Ya*
*Weng Ya Weng Ya You*
*Weng Ya Weng Ya You*
*Weng Ya Weng Ya Weng Ya You*
*Weng Ya Weng Ya Weng Ya Weng Ya You*

## 8. Wai Jiao

| Soul Power | Say *hello: Dear soul, mind, and body of my Wai Jiao, I love you. You have the power to develop and purify yourself. Do a good job. Thank you.* |
|---|---|
| Body Power | Sit on the fixed palm under the Hui Yin area. Place the moving palm over the back of the neck. See figure 17 for front and back views. |
| Mind Power | Visualize golden light in the Wai Jiao. |
| Sound Power | Sing or chant the words to the Divine Soul Song of Yin Yang for the Wai Jiao: |

*You Ya*
*You Ya You Ya You*
*You Ya You Ya You*
*You Ya You Ya You Ya You*
*You Ya You Ya You Ya You Ya You*

## 9. Yin Yang Energy Circle

| Soul Power | Say *hello: Dear soul, mind, and body of my Inner Yin Yang Energy Circle, I love you. You have the* |
|---|---|

*power to develop and purify yourself. Do a good job. Thank you.*

| | |
|---|---|
| Body Power | Sit on the fixed palm under the Hui Yin area; place the moving palm over the crown chakra. See figure 18. |
| Mind Power | Visualize golden light in each soul house moving from the first soul house in the Hui Yin area, up the center of the body to the seventh soul house above the Bai Hui acupuncture point at the top of the head, then down the back of the body in front of the spinal column to the first soul house. |
| Sound Power | Sing or chant the words for the energy circle four times: |

*Hei Heng Hong Ah Xi Yi Weng You*
*Hei Heng Hong Ah Xi Yi Weng You*
*Hei Heng Hong Ah Xi Yi Weng You*
*Hei Heng Hong Ah Xi Yi Weng You*

## 10. Yin Yang Matter Circle

| | |
|---|---|
| Soul Power | Say *hello: Dear soul, mind, and body of my Yin Yang Matter Circle, I love you. You have the power to develop and purify yourself. Do a good job. Thank you.* |
| Body Power | Sit on the fixed palm under the Hui Yin area; place the moving palm over the crown chakra. See figure 18. |
| Mind Power | Visualize golden light in each soul house moving from the first soul house in the Hui Yin area, up the spinal cord to the seventh soul house |

above the Bai Hui acupuncture point at the top of the head, then down the center of the body through the sixth, fifth, fourth, third, and second soul houses back to the first soul house.

Sound Power     Sing or chant the words for the matter circle four times:
*You Weng Yi Xi Ah Hong Heng Hei*
*You Weng Yi Xi Ah Hong Heng Hei*
*You Weng Yi Xi Ah Hong Heng Hei*
*You Weng Yi Xi Ah Hong Heng Hei*

Now let's do the entire practice of the Divine Sacred Soul Song of Yin Yang straight through from beginning to end:

*Dear soul, mind, and body of my seven soul houses,*
   *Wai Jiao, Inner Yin Yang Energy Circle, and Yin*
   *Yang Matter Circle,*
*I love you.*
*You have the power to develop and purify yourselves.*
*Do a good job.*
*Thank you.*

*Hei Ya*
*Hei Ya Hei Ya You*
*Hei Ya Hei Ya You*
*Hei Ya Hei Ya Hei Ya You*
*Hei Ya Hei Ya Hei Ya Hei Ya You*

*Heng Ya*
*Heng Ya Heng Ya You*
*Heng Ya Heng Ya You*

*Heng Ya Heng Ya Heng Ya You*
*Heng Ya Heng Ya Heng Ya Heng Ya You*

*Hong Ya*
*Hong Ya Hong Ya You*
*Hong Ya Hong Ya You*
*Hong Ya Hong Ya Hong Ya You*
*Hong Ya Hong Ya Hong Ya Hong Ya You*

*Ah Ya*
*Ah Ya Ah Ya You*
*Ah Ya Ah Ya You*
*Ah Ya Ah Ya Ah Ya You*
*Ah Ya Ah Ya Ah Ya Ah Ya You*

*Xi Ya*
*Xi Ya Xi Ya You*
*Xi Ya Xi Ya You*
*Xi Ya Xi Ya Xi Ya You*
*Xi Ya Xi Ya Xi Ya Xi Ya You*

*Yi Ya*
*Yi Ya Yi Ya You*
*Yi Ya Yi Ya You*
*Yi Ya Yi Ya Yi Ya You*
*Yi Ya Yi Ya Yi Ya Yi Ya You*

*Weng Ya*
*Weng Ya Weng Ya You*
*Weng Ya Weng Ya You*
*Weng Ya Weng Ya Weng Ya You*
*Weng Ya Weng Ya Weng Ya Weng Ya You*

*You Ya*
*You Ya You Ya You*
*You Ya You Ya You*
*You Ya You Ya You Ya You*
*You Ya You Ya You Ya You Ya You*

*Hei Heng Hong Ah Xi Yi Weng You*
*Hei Heng Hong Ah Xi Yi Weng You*
*Hei Heng Hong Ah Xi Yi Weng You*
*Hei Heng Hong Ah Xi Yi Weng You*

*You Weng Yi Xi Ah Hong Heng Hei*
*You Weng Yi Xi Ah Hong Heng Hei*
*You Weng Yi Xi Ah Hong Heng Hei*
*You Weng Yi Xi Ah Hong Heng Hei*

*Hao! Hao! Hao!*
*Thank you. Thank you. Thank you.*

## THE POWER AND SIGNIFICANCE OF THE SEVEN SOUL HOUSES

I have just led you in the practice of the Divine Soul Song of Yin Yang. This practice goes through the seven soul houses, the Wai Jiao, the Inner Yin Yang Energy Circle, and the Yin Yang Matter Circle. Now let me explain the power and significance of the seven soul houses.

Each soul house is important and significant. Each soul house has a different significance for the soul journey. Each one is directly related to your spiritual standing. The higher the soul house your soul resides in, the higher your spiritual standing in Heaven. The soul's journey is to climb Heaven's stairs step by step, to be uplifted to higher and higher soul houses and spiritual standing.

The first soul house, which is the area above the Hui Yin acupuncture point, or perineum, is the beginning, the base, or the root. It is the generating source of energy and light. On the physical level, this area is also the generator of life and energy. It is the engine that produces the driving force to generate and propel energy through the remaining six soul houses and through the entire body.

The first soul house is exactly that; it is the first house in which a soul resides on its journey. It is the beginning of the soul journey. A human being's soul has been on its journey for many, many lifetimes. If the soul sits in the first soul house, the soul is still at the beginning stages of the journey. The first soul house is very important, but in your soul journey you do not want to stay in this position.

The second soul house is in the lower abdomen, which is the area of the Lower Dan Tian, between the first soul house and the level of the navel. The second soul house is important in the soul journey because when a soul reaches this position it has gained great virtue. It has made significant progress, but it still has a very long journey ahead.

The second soul house is connected with the well-being and balance of the foundational energy of the Lower Dan Tian. It is connected with the well-being and balance of all creation. *As in the big universe* (nature), *so, too, in the small universe* (human being). As I revealed in *The Power of Soul,* the authoritative book of my entire Soul Power Series, the lower abdomen is also a secret soul center of soul intelligence, wisdom, and knowledge. In this area there is much circulation of message, energy, and matter, influencing every aspect of one's being. This second soul house connects with all of these aspects of all creation, including the Soul World and the Divine.

The third soul house is important because it is the last one for a soul to pass through on its journey to enlightenment. When a soul reaches this level it has made real progress. Souls are quite happy to have moved to this level. They are very eager to advance further because they know the next step is their enlightenment.

The fourth soul house is very special. When a soul sits in the Message Center, it has reached the level of enlightenment. Its soul standing has changed significantly. Reaching this level usually requires many hundreds and thousands of lifetimes, although it can also be accomplished in an instant through a Divine Order. Being enlightened transforms the quality of service you can offer. It becomes higher and more powerful. At the same time, your book in the Akashic Records is transferred to a special hall for those who are enlightened. Your ability to communicate with the Soul World increases significantly. The teachings, wisdom, and practices you receive from the Divine and the entire Soul World will be on an entirely different level. It is a major milestone on the soul journey, but it is only the beginning of the enlightenment journey.

The fourth soul house is the center for healing, karma, love, forgiveness, compassion, soul communication, transformation, enlightenment, and much more. All of these qualities also affect your physical journey. When your soul sits in the fourth soul house, many blockages are removed. Your well-being, including your physical, emotional, and mental health, can improve in a powerful way.

The fifth soul house is in the throat. The souls of very few people reach this level through their own efforts. It is possible to achieve this soul standing by receiving more Divine Orders and divine gifts. This soul house is a bridge between the heart and the mind. It helps to integrate the wisdom of the heart and the mind. When this happens, the service you can give increases significantly again. Your ability to understand your own soul journey and that of others increases greatly. On the physical level, the blessings bring about not only greater healing in every aspect of life but also substantial rejuvenation and prolongation of life. For many people, this soul house is connected with soul memories. Healing of these memories can take place on a very deep level. As this happens, reversal of physical issues often occurs at an accelerated rate.

The sixth soul house is in the brain. As the soul reaches this level, consciousness is transformed. The connection and alignment with divine consciousness are much stronger. The ability to communicate with the Soul World grows further. On the physical level, when a soul resides in the brain, it heals and rejuvenates every aspect of the physical body in a special way. The brain determines, directs, or influences every function of the body. When the soul resides in the brain, the brain's influence has reached a level of divine presence and light.

The seventh and last soul house is just above the crown chakra. This is the highest position. It is the beginning, in a very special way, of your soul's journey to enter Tian Wai Tian (see the introduction for a brief explanation of Tian Wai Tian). When a soul reaches Tian Wai Tian, reincarnation is no longer necessary. This is a blessing beyond words. This is the heart's desire and ultimate goal of your soul. On the physical level, a soul that resides in the seventh soul house has reached a position where it truly can be in charge. It is able to direct every aspect of your life in a powerful way, including the physical, mental, emotional, relationship, and financial aspects. It is a great honor and privilege to reach this soul house. Very few have accomplished it through their own efforts.

All seven soul houses connect with aspects of creation, with the balancing of yin and yang, and with the practice of the Divine. As you practice with the Divine Soul Song of Yin Yang, you are connecting with the soul journeys of the Divine and of all universes. You are connecting with all humanity and Mother Earth. As your soul moves from one soul house to the next, this connection of humanity, Mother Earth, and the Divine becomes concrete, practical, and real in your daily life. Words cannot fully express the benefits you receive. Your practice benefits humanity, Mother Earth, and all universes. The practice of the Divine Soul Song of Yin Yang is a very special blessing and gift.

## SECRET WISDOM OF YIN YANG

To balance yin and yang is to heal. To balance yin and yang is to transform life. Everything in the universe can be divided into yin and yang. For example, tai chi is a major practice of Yin Yang. Tai chi uses visualization and movement to promote and balance the flow of chi (vital energy or life force) in the yin organs and yang organs, and in the yin meridians and yang meridians.

Consider the Yin Yang symbol (see figure 19). A white fish and a black fish join as one. The white fish represents yang. The black fish represents yin. Everything can be divided into yin and yang: every human being, every system, every organ, every cell, every cell unit, every DNA and RNA, every smallest bit of matter inside the body, every planet, every star, every galaxy, and every universe. Yin Yang is a Universal Law because it can summarize and describe everything.

Yin and yang are independent but united. Day and night are different. Light and dark are different. Man and woman are different. But they are all united and connected. Male is yang, but it can be subdivided into yin and yang again. For example, the front side of the body is yin, while the back side of the body is yang. The heart is a yin organ, while the small intestine is its paired yang organ.

Another important wisdom of Yin Yang is that yin is never absolute yin; yang is always within yin. In the same way, yang is never absolute yang; yin is always within yang. The Yin Yang symbol presents exactly this wisdom. Inside the white fish there is a black eye. This means yin within yang. Inside the black fish there is a white eye. This means yang within yin.

How does this wisdom apply to the human body? This is a *qian gu zhi mi* (pronounced *chyen goo jee mee*)—a "thousand-year ancient mystery." At this moment, the Divine told me that the Divine is going to reveal for the first time the secret of this *qian gu zhi mi*. The Divine will explain how to understand the white and black eyes inside our bodies. Remember, I am not *writing* this book. I receive divine teaching in the moment and "flow" it out. I offer teaching on how to gain these abilities in my second book of the Soul Power Series, *Soul Communication*. I welcome you to study this teaching and open your four main spiritual communication channels to learn wisdom directly from the Divine anytime, anywhere. If you gain advanced soul communication abilities, you will be able to "write" books in the same way.

Five thousand years ago the Yellow Emperor explained the important and fundamental concept of yin and yang within the body—namely, the entire front half of the body belongs to yin; the entire back half of the body belongs to yang. But nowhere has anyone written an explanation of where the white eye and the black eye are. Here is the mystery revealed: the Message Center is the white eye in the black fish (the front half of the body); the Snow Mountain Area is the black eye in the white fish (the back half of the body).

The Snow Mountain Area is one of two key foundational energy centers in the body. (The other is the Lower Dan Tian, which I described on page lviii.) To locate it, imagine a line going from your navel straight back through your body. This line connects your navel to the Ming Men acupuncture point on your back. Along this line, go one-third of the way in from your back toward your navel. From this point, go straight down about 2.5 *cun* (see page lviii). That is the center of this fist-sized energy center.

The Snow Mountain Area is:

- the prenatal energy center; it connects with the energy of your parents and other ancestors and holds the essence of their energy
- the key to quality of life and long life
- the energy source for the kidneys
- energy food for the brain and Third Eye
- the starting point of the four major meridians (Ren, Du, Dai, Chong) of traditional Chinese medicine

"Snow Mountain Area" is a Buddhist term. Taoists call this area the Golden Urn. Traditional Chinese medicine calls it the Ming Men area, which means the *gate of life*. In yoga this area is known as kundalini. Developing the power of the Snow Mountain Area is vital for every aspect of life.

The black fish that represents the front side of the body also represents the spiritual world. Therefore, the white eye—the

Message Center—in the black fish represents the physical world within the spiritual world. The spiritual world communicates with the physical being through the white eye. The secret wisdom here is that the Divine and the spiritual world communicate with and guide us through our Message Centers. If your Message Center is not fully open and of the highest purity, you will not receive complete teachings and guidance from the Divine and the spiritual world.

To fully open and completely purify your Message Center is to receive complete teachings and blessing from the Divine and the spiritual world. This is the importance and significance of opening your spiritual communication channels.

The white fish that represents the back side of the body also represents the physical world. Therefore, the black eye—the Snow Mountain Area—in the white fish represents the spiritual world within the physical world. The physical being connects with the spiritual world through the black eye. The secret wisdom here is that to open your Third Eye and other soul communication abilities, focus on your Snow Mountain Area. If your Snow Mountain Area is not fully developed and of the highest purity, the Divine and the spiritual world cannot communicate with you completely.

To fully develop and completely purify your Snow Mountain Area is to send your complete and purest messages to the Divine and the spiritual world.

## A TOP DIVINE PRACTICE OF THE DIVINE SOUL SONG OF YIN YANG REVEALED AS I WROTE THIS BOOK

It is now 12:30 PM Eastern Daylight Time on September 9, 2008. I am flowing this book with a student. We just took a break for a few minutes. During the break we practiced the Inner Yin Yang Energy Circle and the Yin Yang Matter Circle by chanting the Energy and Matter Circles of the Divine Soul Song of Yin Yang: *Hei Heng Hong Ah Xi Yi Weng You* and *You Weng Yi Xi Ah Hong Heng Hei,* respectively. Suddenly the Divine showed me a most profound and sacred divine wisdom and practice for this Soul Song. Now I am honored to reveal this divine treasure to humanity on the spot. I am asking my student to type this new divine secret wisdom and practice, which is named:

## Divine Sacred *Tian Di Ren* Soul Practice to Reach the Tao

"Tian," as I have explained, means *Heaven*. "Di" (pronounced *dee*) means Earth. "Ren" means *human being*. So the name of this practice translates as the "Divine Sacred Heaven, Earth, Human Being Soul Practice to Reach the Tao." Tao is *the Way*. It is the fundamental laws, principles, and nature of the universe. It is unlimited and cannot be defined or named. To reach the Tao is to reach the ultimate condition. It is the divine condition.

Let me explain the practice and lead you to do it with me. Then I will explain its power and significance. You will understand why it is named "Divine Sacred *Tian Di Ren* Soul Practice to Reach the Tao."

Apply the Four Power Techniques with this new secret practice:

Soul Power: Say *hello* with me like this:

> *Dear soul, mind, and body of my Inner Yin Yang*
> *Energy Circle and my Yin Yang Matter Circle,*
> *I love you.*
> *You have the power to clear and purify yourselves.*

*You have the power to heal, rejuvenate, bless, and*
  *transform my soul, mind, and body.*
*You have the power to help me reach the Tao.*
*Do a good job.*
*I am very grateful.*
*Thank you.*

Body Power: If you are a male, put your right palm over your
Message Center and your left palm over your Ming Men acupuncture point, which can be located by imagining a line from
your navel straight back through your body. The Ming Men acupuncture point is the point where this line reaches your back. If
you are a female, put your left palm over your Message Center
and your right palm over your Ming Men acupuncture point.

Sound Power: Sing or chant the words of the Divine Soul
Songs of the Yin Yang Energy Circle and Yin Yang Matter Circle
in the following order (see figure 20 for the music):

*Hei Heng Hong Ah Xi Yi Weng You*
*You Weng Yi Xi Ah Hong Heng Hei*
*You Weng Yi Xi Ah Hong Heng Hei*
*Hei Heng Hong Ah Xi Yi Weng You*

Mind Power: As you sing or chant the words to the **first line,**
*Hei Heng Hong Ah Xi Yi Weng You,* you will focus in turn on two
points on your body. First, as you sing or chant *Hei Heng Hong
Ah Xi Yi Weng,* focus gently on the Bai Hui acupuncture point at
the top of your head. If your Third Eye is open, you will see a
light beam going from the Hui Yin acupuncture point in your
perineum up the center of your body through the seven soul

houses beam to the Bai Hui point at the top of your head. Then as you start to sing *You,* shift your focus immediately to the Hui Yin point. The light beam will form an arc from the Bai Hui point down through the Wai Jiao back to the Hui Yin point. Therefore, when you practice this first line, there is a light circle that follows the path of the Inner Yin Yang Energy Circle. Figure 21 will make this clear for you.

As you sing or chant the words to the **second line,** *You Weng Yi Xi Ah Hong Heng Hei,* you will again focus in turn on two points on your body. First, as you sing or chant *You,* focus gently on the Bai Hui point. The light beam will go back up from the Hui Yin into your tailbone and then up through your spinal column and brain to the Bai Hui point. Then as you start to sing *Weng Yi Xi Ah Hong Heng Hei,* shift your focus to the Hui Yin point again. The light beam will go down from the Bai Hui point straight through the seven houses of the soul and back to the Hui Yin point. Therefore, when you practice this second line, there is a light circle that follows the path of the Yin Yang Matter Circle. See figure 22.

As you sing or chant the words to the **third line,** *You Weng Yi Xi Ah Hong Heng Hei,* your mind will focus in a different way. First, as you chant *You,* focus gently on the center of Heaven *and* the center of Mother Earth at the same time. Two arcs of light will flow from your body to the universe. The first light arc comes out from your Message Center, goes up to the top of your head, exits through the Bai Hui point, and extends to the center of Heaven. The second light arc comes out from your Snow Mountain Area, goes down to the Hui Yin point, goes further down through the middle of both legs to the Yong Quan (Kidney 1) acupuncture points (located on the sole of each foot between the second and third metatarsal bones, about one-third the distance from the webs of the toes to the heel),[8] and then extends to the center of Mother Earth. Next, as you start to sing *Weng Yi Xi Ah Hong Heng Hei,* shift your focus to your Message Center and Snow Mountain Area at the same time. The light arcs will return from the center of Heaven and the center of Mother Earth outside your body directly to your Message Center and Snow Mountain Area, respectively, so that each one completes a circle. Therefore, when you practice this third line, there are two light circles. One connects you with Heaven through your Message Center. The other connects you with Mother Earth through your Snow Mountain Area. See figure 23.

Finally, we come to the **fourth line** and circle, *Hei Heng Hong Ah Xi Yi Weng You.* As you sing or chant the words *Hei Heng Hong Ah Xi Yi Weng,* again focus gently on both the center of Heaven and the center of Mother Earth. Two light arcs will flow out from your Message Center and Snow Mountain Area. The light arc from your Message Center goes out through your Bai Hui point to the center of Heaven. The light arc from your Snow Mountain Area goes down the center of your legs and out through your Yong Quan points to the center of Mother Earth. Then, as you chant *You,* shift your focus to your Message Center and Snow Mountain Area. Light returns from the center of Heaven outside your body directly to your Message Center. At the same time, light returns from the center of Mother Earth outside your body directly to your Snow Mountain Area. See figure 24.

---

8. An alternative description of the location of the Yong Quan point is: on the sole, in the depression when the foot is in plantar flexion, approximately at the junction of the anterior one-third and posterior two-thirds of the line connecting the base of the second and third toes and the heel.

Practice with me now. Place your hands in the Body Power position described above. Invoke Soul Power by saying *hello* as indicated above. Let's go through the practice four times. You may need to practice more to learn the Mind Power visualizations so that they become natural and you do not have to think about them. Then you will be able to fully experience the power of this sacred practice. Start!

*Hei Heng Hong Ah Xi Yi Weng You*
*You Weng Yi Xi Ah Hong Heng Hei*
*You Weng Yi Xi Ah Hong Heng Hei*
*Hei Heng Hong Ah Xi Yi Weng You*

*Hei Heng Hong Ah Xi Yi Weng You*
*You Weng Yi Xi Ah Hong Heng Hei*
*You Weng Yi Xi Ah Hong Heng Hei*
*Hei Heng Hong Ah Xi Yi Weng You*

*Hei Heng Hong Ah Xi Yi Weng You*
*You Weng Yi Xi Ah Hong Heng Hei*
*You Weng Yi Xi Ah Hong Heng Hei*
*Hei Heng Hong Ah Xi Yi Weng You*

*Hei Heng Hong Ah Xi Yi Weng You*
*You Weng Yi Xi Ah Hong Heng Hei*
*You Weng Yi Xi Ah Hong Heng Hei*
*Hei Heng Hong Ah Xi Yi Weng You*

*Hao! Hao! Hao!*
*Thank you. Thank you. Thank you.*

This is *Tian Di Ren He Yi* practice. Heaven, Earth, and human being join as one. ("He yi," pronounced *huh yee,* means *join as one.*)


## THE POWER AND SIGNIFICANCE OF THE DIVINE SACRED *TIAN DI REN* SOUL PRACTICE TO REACH THE TAO

The Divine Sacred *Tian Di Ren* Soul Practice to Reach the Tao has power and significance beyond what I can explain in words.

Singing or chanting the words to the **first line**, *Hei Heng Hong Ah Xi Yi Weng You,* promotes the most important energy circle in the body. All of the energies of all of your systems, organs, cells, and meridians will gather together to join this most important energy circle. If this circle flows, all energy circles will follow. This is the Inner Yin Yang Energy Circle.

The pathway of the Inner Yin Yang Energy Circle is:

- Energy starts from the Hui Yin acupuncture point in the perineum.
- It flows up through the center of the body and the seven soul houses to the Bai Hui acupuncture point at the top of the head.
- From there it flows down through the Wai Jiao and returns to the Hui Yin.

Five thousand years ago, *The Yellow Emperor's Internal Classic* and Taoist teaching revealed the first yin yang circle. The pathway of that original yin yang circle is:

- Energy starts from the Hui Yin.
- It flows up the Ren meridian, which is in the front

midline of the body close to the surface, to the Bai
Hui point.

- From there it flows down the Du meridian, which is
in the back midline of the body within the spinal
cord, and returns to the Hui Yin.

This Ren-Du meridian circle is also a yin yang circle. This
yin yang circle has been practiced for thousands of years. It has
guided traditional Chinese medicine and Taoist practitioners.
Now that the Divine has given me the Inner Yin Yang Energy
Circle, the Divine told me that this ancient original yin yang
circle will be called the Outer Yin Yang Energy Circle. The Outer
Yin Yang Energy Circle was released five thousand years ago. The
Inner Yin Yang Energy Circle was revealed in September 2008.
Both yin yang circles are important. The Outer Yin Yang Energy
Circle and the Inner Yin Yang Energy Circle have a yin yang re-
lationship themselves. The Outer Yin Yang Energy Circle is the
yang circle of the pair; the Inner Yin Yang Energy Circle is the
yin circle.

The vital wisdom and knowledge is:

**The Inner Yin Yang Energy Circle directs
the Outer Yin Yang Energy Circle.**

According to traditional Chinese medicine and Taoist practice, if the Outer Yin Yang Energy Circle flows, all the other energy circles in the body will flow. This is important wisdom. But
after revealing the Inner Yin Yang Energy Circle, the Divine told
me to share with you and humanity that:

**If the Inner Yin Yang Energy Circle flows,
the Outer Yin Yang Energy Circle will follow.**

Then all the other energy circles in the body will follow, including the energy circles of all systems, organs, cells, cell units, DNA and RNA, spaces between cells, and the smallest matter within cells.

I cannot honor the Divine enough for releasing this sacred wisdom and practice to humanity. Millions of people have searched for secret energy practices throughout history. Many serious practitioners have meditated in mountains, temples, and caves for thirty or fifty years—and even for their entire lives—trying to discover secret practices. Why is the Divine releasing this divine secret at this time? It is because we live in a special time. In the Soul Light Era, beginning with this historic period of Mother Earth's transition and Heaven's reconstruction, Heaven is coming to Earth. There are no words and no thoughts that are enough to appreciate and honor the Divine for this divine sacred teaching, wisdom, and practice. It will serve millions and billions of spiritual seekers and practitioners in all nations. I am extremely honored.

Let me continue to explain the practice.

Singing the **second line**, *You Weng Yi Xi Ah Hong Heng Hei*, promotes the most important matter circle in the body. This is a divine sacred matter circle, the Divine Yin Yang Matter Circle.

Energy is "tiny" or refined matter. When energy flows, matter will flow also. At the highest level and frequency, energy *is* matter and matter *is* energy. The pathway of this Divine Yin Yang Matter Circle is:

- Matter starts in the Hui Yin area.
- It moves back to the tailbone and then flows up through the spinal cord to the brain and the Bai Hui point at the top of the head.

- From the Bai Hui point, it drops down to the palate.
- It continues down the center of the body through the remaining soul houses and returns to the Hui Yin area.

This is a matter circle because the spinal cord and brain are made of matter. However, although this is a matter circle, in fact, matter and energy both flow through the spinal cord and brain. When energy reaches the palate, the energy will transform to liquid (saliva). This liquid will drop from the palate into the mouth. This liquid is produced by Heaven. In ancient spiritual practice there is a renowned statement:

### Tian yi sheng shui

"Tian" means *Heaven*. "Yi" means *one*. "Sheng" (pronounced *shung*) means *produces*. "Shui" (pronounced *shway*) means *water*. So this statement means *Heaven produces water*.

This is an ancient theoretical teaching and goal of Xiu Lian practice (see page xliv for a definition of Xiu Lian), but *where* and *how* does Heaven produce water in the body? Xiu Lian practitioners know that this is one of the most profound secrets for energy and spiritual practice. There have been some ancient practices, but they cannot go far enough. They do not make Heaven-produced water a complete reality. How and where to do it has been a mystery. With this divine sacred matter circle, the Divine has released the secret to this mystery. Again, I have no words to express my honor and gratitude to the Divine.

Let me explain further.

When energy in the matter circle reaches the palate, the energy will transform to liquid and then drop down into the mouth. Energy is yang. Liquid is yin. So this transformation of energy to liquid is yang-to-yin transformation. After the liquid descends down the center of the body through the fifth (throat), fourth (Message Center), and third (navel area) soul houses, it will arrive at the Lower Dan Tian area (second soul house). There, the liquid will transform into a golden light ball. This is yin-to-yang transformation.

The saliva produced in the palate area is a high-level inner nutrient to nourish the whole body. This liquid will transform into a golden light ball in the Lower Dan Tian, one of your two key foundational energy centers. This liquid also nourishes and provides the matter foundation for the golden light ball and Lower Dan Tian.

In summary, in the flow of this matter circle you can experience transformation from energy to matter in the palate area and transformation from matter to energy in the Lower Dan Tian area. This is the most profound secret for rejuvenation and long life.

I have studied Taoism my whole life. I am one of the major Taoist lineage holders. I have practiced Taoist secrets my whole life. In Taoist teaching, every practitioner knows the renowned statement: *Lian jing hua qi. Lian qi hua shen. Lian shen hua xu. Lian xu hua tao.* This means: Transform *jing* to *qi*. Transform *qi* to *shen*. Transform *shen* to *xu*. Transform *xu* to *tao*.

*Jing qi shen xu tao* is pronounced *jing chee shun shü dow. Jing, qi, shen, xu,* and *tao* are five different layers of matter, energy, and message. "Jing" literally means *the essence of matter.* "Qi" is *vital energy.* "Shen" is *refined energy* that is related with the soul. "Xu" means *emptiness* and *nothingness.* "Tao" is *the Way,* the laws and principles of the universe (the equivalent of the divine condition in Taoist teaching).

*Jing qi shen xu tao* are different layers of matter. They become more and more refined.

*Jing qi shen xu tao* are different layers of energy. They become more and more refined.

*Jing qi shen xu tao* are different layers of message. Message is soul. They also become more and more refined.

In fact, at the highest and most refined level, matter, energy, and message are one.

Taoist practitioners have understood *jing qi shen xu tao* for thousands of years. But they are not given a single practice to actually transform *jing* to *qi* to *shen* to *xu* to *tao*.

This **second line** of the Divine Sacred *Tian Di Ren* Soul Practice to Reach the Tao, *You Weng Yi Xi Ah Hong Heng Hei,* is the secret and sacred practice to transform *jing* to *qi, qi* to *shen, shen* to *xu,* and *xu* to *tao*.

In this circle there are three major matter-energy, or yin-yang, transformations. The first is the transformation of energy to matter in the palate area. The second is the transformation from matter to energy in the Lower Dan Tian Area. The third is another transformation from energy to matter in the tailbone area.

Every time energy transforms to matter, it refines the matter.

Every time matter transforms to energy, it refines the energy.

Therefore, this practice is to refine matter, energy, and message. Further and further refinement is exactly the process of *jing qi shen xu tao. Jing* refines to *qi. Qi* refines to *shen. Shen* refines to *xu. Xu* refines to *tao*. When you do this practice, *jing qi shen xu tao* in your whole body will be refined further and further. The matter, energy, and message in your whole body will be refined further and further. The matter, energy, and message in every system, every organ, every cell, every cell unit, every DNA and RNA, every space, and every smallest bit of matter will be refined further and further. Therefore, this divine sacred matter circle practice is one of the greatest secrets the Divine has given to humanity so far.

If one's matter, energy, and message refine further and further, true rejuvenation will happen. Complete health in soul, mind, and body will happen. This Divine Yin Yang Matter Circle practice is to move in the direction of immortality. It is far, far beyond what humanity can imagine and comprehend.

One must practice this circle countless times to rejuvenate further and further, to prolong life further and further, and to move in the direction of immortality. Of course, to reach immortality there will be many more requirements in every aspect of life, but this sacred matter circle practice is vital for anyone who strives to move to that realm.

The first chapter of *The Yellow Emperor's Internal Classic* includes the following profound and relevant sentences:

> *Shang gu zhen ren*
> *Ti xie tian di*
> *Ba wo yin yang*
> *Hu xi jing qi*
> *Jing shen nei shou*
> *Ji rou ruo yi*
> *Shou bi tian di*
> *Wu you zhong shi*

"Shang gu zhen ren" means *the real saint in ancient times*.

"Ti xie tian di" means *mastered and followed the universal principles and laws of Heaven and Earth*. This means to follow the Tao, the Way of Heaven, Earth, and the universe.

"Ba wo yin yang" means *mastered and followed yin and yang*.

"Hu xi jing qi" means *breathed the essence of energy and matter from the universe*.

"Jing shen nei shou" means *focused inside the body*. The principle of visualizing and concentrating inside the body is the top guidance for meditation and for energy and spiritual practice. Keep the mind inside the body to boost energy, stamina, vitality, and immunity and to purify matter, energy, and message for the systems, organs, and cells.

"Ji rou ruo yi" means *to balance, purify, and refine matter, energy, and message as one*. This is the final destiny for all layers of matter, energy, and message.

"Shou bi tian di" means *life is as long as Heaven's and Earth's*.

"Wu you zhong shi" means *immortality will happen*. Physical life has no end.

In these sentences, the Yellow Emperor explained five thousand years ago how the highest saints in ancient times moved toward immortality. These sentences summarize the vital philosophy, wisdom, principles, and practices of that time for reaching immortality. Now the Divine has guided me that the Divine Sacred *Tian Di Ren* Soul Practice to Reach the Tao is *the* vital philosophy, principle, purification, refinement, and practice to move to immortality. I am honored to receive this divine secret practice and to share it with millions of people who are searching for the true secrets of rejuvenation, prolonging life, purification, enlightenment, and immortality. I am speechless. To say *thank you* to the Divine is far from enough. I am deeply honored and profoundly touched and humbled.

I am honored to continue to try to explain the significance of this profound wisdom and knowledge and the power of this practice. No matter how much I understand it and no matter how deeply I appreciate it, words cannot explain enough the significance and the power of what the Divine has just taught me. I just received this teaching. I shared it with you right away. Let us practice more and more. We will understand and realize the power and significance of this practice further and further.

As you sing or chant the words to the **third line**, *You Weng Yi Xi Ah Hong Heng Hei,* start with *You* and focus on the center of Heaven above you and the center of Earth below you (figure 23). Energy and light[9] from your Message Center move to the center of Heaven. Energy and light from your Snow Mountain Area move to the center of Mother Earth. Your mind is focused on *tian xin*[10] (Heaven's center) and *di xin* (Earth's center) together. Light from your Message Center moves straight up to your brain and out through your Bai Hui point. Light from your Snow Mountain Area goes down to your Hui Yin, where it divides in two and goes down your legs and out through your Yong Quan points at the bottom of your feet to the center of Mother Earth.

A very important principle is to be sure your mind's focus on Heaven's center and Earth's center is *gentle*. You do not need to visualize them too strongly. Neither do you need to visualize light from your Message Center to Heaven's center and light from your Snow Mountain Area to Earth's center too strongly. Be natural. Do not force. I want to repeat this for emphasis. Where you

---

9. Energy is qi. Light is the essence of qi. Light is refined energy.

10. "Xin," pronounced *sheen,* means *heart* or *center.*

concentrate is where energy and light will move. But *if you concentrate too strongly, it is not right.* Think *gently* of Heaven's center and of Earth's center. Strong visualization is not proper. In ancient meditation and qi gong wisdom, *yi zhong qi huo*—thinking heavily produces fire. You must remember this point.

The profound secret is that when you concentrate on Heaven's and Earth's centers, your energy and light connect right away with their energy and light. The moment you sing *You* and your mind is on the centers, right away beams of light from Heaven's center and Earth's center will shoot to you. They will arrive instantaneously at your Message Center from Heaven and at your Snow Mountain Area from Earth.

As you continue to sing the **rest of the third line**, *Weng Yi Xi Ah Hong Heng Hei,* you shift your gentle focus to your Message Center and Snow Mountain Area. Heaven's energy and light and Earth's energy and light will continue to pour into your Message Center and Snow Mountain Area. This third-line practice literally connects your energy and light to Heaven's and Earth's energy and light. This is the core *Tian Di Ren* practice. Heaven's center and Earth's center will give you their essence to nourish, boost, purify, transform, enlighten, and refine your energy and light to higher and higher frequencies.

Heaven and Earth are pure servants of the Divine. They carry the essence of universal yang and the essence of universal yin. A spiritual being who knows this secret, and especially one who knows how to practice in this way, will receive divine yin-yang essence beyond comprehension. Words and thoughts are not enough to express the benefits.

In fact, practicing the third line connects your energy, light, and matter with Heaven's energy, light, and matter and Earth's energy, light, and matter through your Message Center, Snow

Mountain Area, and Divine Yin Yang Matter Circle, which is the most important matter circle or yin circle (matter is yin, energy is yang). Singing the **fourth line**, *Hei Heng Hong Ah Xi Yi Weng You*, continues this connection through your Message Center, Snow Mountain Area, and Inner Yin Yang Circle, which is the most important energy circle or yang circle (energy is yang, matter is yin).

I am honored to explain the benefits of this practice.

Earlier in this chapter I shared a major yin-yang secret that the Divine released as I was flowing this book. The front half of a human being is the yin side, or black fish. The Message Center is the white eye in the black fish. The back half of the body is the yang side, or white fish. The Snow Mountain Area is the black eye in the white fish. The black fish represents the spiritual world. The white eye represents the physical world. The spiritual world connects with the physical world through the white eye. The white fish represents the physical world. The physical world connects with the spiritual world through the black eye. The Message Center and Snow Mountain Area are the white eye and black eye, respectively. They are most important energy and spiritual centers because they are the vital centers for communicating with Heaven and Earth.

Heaven's center carries the essence of universal yang. It carries the most nourishing nutrients and the most refined, profound, and pure energy and light from Heaven. Even Heaven has different frequencies of energy and light. A practitioner needs to practice, practice, and practice. Heaven will deliver energy and light to you step by step. One's spiritual standing is very important. Heaven's light has five layers: golden, rainbow, purple, crystal, and beyond crystal (the highest). To reach a high spiritual standing is first to reach soul enlightenment and then to reach more and more advanced levels of enlightenment. The higher the level of soul enlightenment you achieve, which is to say the higher the spiritual standing your soul reaches, the higher the frequency and layer of light Heaven's center will release to you.

If millions of people do this practice, each person could receive different layers of frequency and light. But the more you practice, the more purification you could receive. The more purification you receive, the more refined the energy and light Heaven will give to you. The more refined the energy and light Heaven gives to you, the more rejuvenation and long life you could achieve. Immortality is to move much further in this direction.

The same wisdom applies to your Snow Mountain Area when it connects with Earth's center. The higher your spiritual standing, the higher the frequencies of energy and light you will receive from Earth's center and the greater the benefits for rejuvenation and long life you will receive.

The Divine Sacred *Tian Di Ren* Soul Practice to Reach the Tao is one of the highest spiritual practices because Heaven's and Earth's centers carry divine love, forgiveness, compassion, and light. The more you practice, the more you receive divine healing, blessing, purification, transformation, and enlightenment. This practice is also an energy practice. The more you practice, the more refined the energy Heaven and Earth will give to you. This practice is also a matter practice. The more you practice, the more refined the matter you will receive from Heaven and Earth.

This is a universal matter, energy, and message practice. This is a spiritual energy and matter practice. This is a universal soul, mind, and body practice. This is a Divine Oneness practice. The benefits and significance of this practice are beyond explanation and comprehension.

Practice more. Purify your soul, heart, mind, and body more. Transform them more. Enlighten them further. This is a Divine Universal Oneness practice. Feel honor and total appreciation to do this practice. The benefits are boundless.

I wish every reader, every spiritual being, and every human being will receive the maximum benefits from this divine sacred practice. The wisdom is profound. The power is unlimited.

Practice. Practice. Practice.

Benefit. Benefit. Benefit.

Hao! Hao! Hao!

Thank you. Thank you. Thank you.

## APPLY THE DIVINE SOUL SONG OF YIN YANG TO HEAL AND TRANSFORM YOU, HUMANITY, MOTHER EARTH, AND ALL UNIVERSES

As with any Divine Soul Song, the Divine Soul Song of Yin Yang can be applied directly for healing and transformation. Do it with me now:

> *Dear Divine Soul Song of Yin Yang,*
> *I love you, honor you, and appreciate you.*
> *Please give me a healing* (you may request specific
>     healing for the physical, emotional, mental, or
>     spiritual bodies).
> *Please give a healing to my loved ones* (you may make
>     specific requests).

*Please give a healing to humanity* (you may make
specific requests).
*Please give a healing to Mother Earth* (you may make
specific requests).
*Please give a healing to all universes* (you may make
specific requests).
*I am very grateful.*
*Thank you.*

Then sing the Divine Soul Song of Yin Yang or chant its
words. At the same time, use the Body Power hand positions and
Mind Power visualizations of golden light that we used in the
basic practice described on pages 119–129. Start!

*Hei Ya*
*Hei Ya Hei Ya You*
*Hei Ya Hei Ya You*
*Hei Ya Hei Ya Hei Ya You*
*Hei Ya Hei Ya Hei Ya Hei Ya You*

*Heng Ya*
*Heng Ya Heng Ya You*
*Heng Ya Heng Ya You*
*Heng Ya Heng Ya Heng Ya You*
*Heng Ya Heng Ya Heng Ya Heng Ya You*

*Hong Ya*
*Hong Ya Hong Ya You*
*Hong Ya Hong Ya You*
*Hong Ya Hong Ya Hong Ya You*
*Hong Ya Hong Ya Hong Ya Hong Ya You*

*Ah Ya*
*Ah Ya Ah Ya You*
*Ah Ya Ah Ya You*
*Ah Ya Ah Ya Ah Ya You*
*Ah Ya Ah Ya Ah Ya Ah Ya You*

*Xi Ya*
*Xi Ya Xi Ya You*
*Xi Ya Xi Ya You*
*Xi Ya Xi Ya Xi Ya You*
*Xi Ya Xi Ya Xi Ya Xi Ya You*

*Yi Ya*
*Yi Ya Yi Ya You*
*Yi Ya Yi Ya You*
*Yi Ya Yi Ya Yi Ya You*
*Yi Ya Yi Ya Yi Ya Yi Ya You*

*Weng Ya*
*Weng Ya Weng Ya You*
*Weng Ya Weng Ya You*
*Weng Ya Weng Ya Weng Ya You*
*Weng Ya Weng Ya Weng Ya Weng Ya You*

*You Ya*
*You Ya You Ya You*
*You Ya You Ya You*
*You Ya You Ya You Ya You*
*You Ya You Ya You Ya You Ya You*

*Hei Heng Hong Ah Xi Yi Weng You*
*Hei Heng Hong Ah Xi Yi Weng You*
*Hei Heng Hong Ah Xi Yi Weng You*
*Hei Heng Hong Ah Xi Yi Weng You*

*You Weng Yi Xi Ah Hong Heng Hei*
*You Weng Yi Xi Ah Hong Heng Hei*
*You Weng Yi Xi Ah Hong Heng Hei*
*You Weng Yi Xi Ah Hong Heng Hei*

*Hao! Hao! Hao!*
*Thank you. Thank you. Thank you.*

Remember, every time you sing or chant the words of a Divine Soul Song, you are serving the Divine Mission. The Divine Mission is:

**To gather all souls and hearts together to create
divine consciousness and divine love, peace, and harmony
for you, humanity, Mother Earth, and all universes.**

## DIVINE SOUL DOWNLOADS OF THE DIVINE
## SOUL SONG OF YIN YANG

Now I am delighted to share with you that I have asked the Divine to preprogram ten Divine Soul Downloads of the Divine Soul Song of Yin Yang for you and every reader of this book. You can receive these downloads as you continue to read this section. I have committed to offering Divine Soul Downloads in every book of the Soul Power Series. In chapter 2 you have already received the first Divine Soul Download offered as a divine gift in this book: a Divine Soul Transplant of the Divine Soul Song of Compassion.

The first Divine Soul Download of the Divine Soul Song of Yin Yang (and the second Divine Soul Download offered in this book) is:

### Divine Soul Transplant of the Divine Soul Song *Hei*

Prepare! Sit up straight. Put the tip of your tongue near the roof of your mouth. Totally relax. Open your heart and soul to receive this divine treasure. Tell the Divine: *Dear Divine, I am very grateful and honored to receive this permanent divine soul. I am ready to receive it. Thank you.* (If you are not ready to receive this and the other divine gifts, simply tell the Divine: *Dear Divine, I am not ready to receive these gifts yet. Thank you.* The Divine will download his new divine souls only to ready ones.)

If you are ready, prepare. Say one more time: *Dear Divine, I am ready to receive. Thank you.* In the next thirty seconds the Divine will download it to your soul.

### Divine Soul Transplant of the Divine Soul Song *Hei*
### Silent download!

Now close your eyes for thirty seconds to receive this major divine soul treasure.

*Hao! Hao! Hao!*
*Thank you. Thank you. Thank you.*

Thank you, Divine.

Congratulations! You have received a Divine Soul Transplant of the Divine Soul Song *Hei* for the first soul house.

Now prepare for the second Divine Soul Download of the Divine Soul Song of Yin Yang (and the third Divine Soul Download offered in this book):

## Divine Soul Transplant of the Divine Soul Song *Heng*

Prepare! Sit up straight. Put the tip of your tongue near the roof of your mouth. Totally relax. Open your heart and soul to receive this divine treasure. Tell the Divine: *Dear Divine, I am very grateful and honored to receive this permanent divine soul. I am ready to receive it. Thank you.* In the next thirty seconds the Divine will download it to your soul.

## Divine Soul Transplant of the Divine Soul Song *Heng*
## Silent download!

Now close your eyes for thirty seconds to receive this major divine soul treasure.

> *Hao! Hao! Hao!*
> *Thank you. Thank you. Thank you.*

Thank you, Divine.

Congratulations! You have received a Divine Soul Transplant of the Divine Soul Song *Heng* for the second soul house.

Now prepare for the third Divine Soul Download of the Divine Soul Song of Yin Yang (and the fourth Divine Soul Download offered in this book):

## Divine Soul Transplant of the Divine Soul Song *Hong*

Prepare! Sit up straight. Put the tip of your tongue near the roof of your mouth. Totally relax. Open your heart and soul to receive this divine treasure. Tell the Divine: *Dear Divine, I am very grateful and honored to receive this permanent divine soul. I am ready to receive it. Thank you.* In the next thirty seconds the Divine will download it to your soul.

## Divine Soul Transplant of the Divine Soul Song *Hong* Silent download!

Now close your eyes for thirty seconds to receive this major divine soul treasure.

> *Hao! Hao! Hao!*
> *Thank you. Thank you. Thank you.*

Thank you, Divine.

Congratulations! You have received a Divine Soul Transplant of the Divine Soul Song *Hong* for the third soul house.

Now prepare for the fourth Divine Soul Download of the Divine Soul Song of Yin Yang (and the fifth Divine Soul Download offered in this book):

## Divine Soul Transplant of the Divine Soul Song *Ah*

Prepare! Sit up straight. Put the tip of your tongue near the roof of your mouth. Totally relax. Open your heart and soul to receive this divine treasure. Tell the Divine: *Dear Divine, I am very grateful and honored to receive this permanent divine soul. I am ready to receive it. Thank you.* In the next thirty seconds the Divine will download it to your soul.

### Divine Soul Transplant of the Divine Soul Song *Ah*
### Silent download!

Now close your eyes for thirty seconds to receive this major divine soul treasure.

> *Hao! Hao! Hao!*
> *Thank you. Thank you. Thank you.*

Thank you, Divine.

Congratulations! You have received a Divine Soul Transplant of the Divine Soul Song *Ah* for the fourth soul house.

Now prepare for the fifth Divine Soul Download of the Divine Soul Song of Yin Yang (and the sixth Divine Soul Download offered in this book):

### Divine Soul Transplant of the Divine Soul Song *Xi*

Prepare! Sit up straight. Put the tip of your tongue near the roof of your mouth. Totally relax. Open your heart and soul to receive this divine treasure. Tell the Divine: *Dear Divine, I am very grateful and honored to receive this permanent divine soul. I am ready to receive it. Thank you.* In the next thirty seconds the Divine will download it to your soul.

### Divine Soul Transplant of the Divine Soul Song *Xi*
### Silent download!

Now close your eyes for thirty seconds to receive this major divine soul treasure.

> *Hao! Hao! Hao!*
> *Thank you. Thank you. Thank you.*

Thank you, Divine.

Congratulations! You have received a Divine Soul Transplant of the Divine Soul Song *Xi* for the fifth soul house.

Now prepare for the sixth Divine Soul Download of the Divine Soul Song of Yin Yang (and the seventh Divine Soul Download offered in this book):

## Divine Soul Transplant of the Divine Soul Song *Yi*

Prepare! Sit up straight. Put the tip of your tongue near the roof of your mouth. Totally relax. Open your heart and soul to receive this divine treasure. Tell the Divine: *Dear Divine, I am very grateful and honored to receive this permanent divine soul. I am ready to receive it. Thank you.* In the next thirty seconds the Divine will download it to your soul.

## Divine Soul Transplant of the Divine Soul Song *Yi*
## Silent download!

Now close your eyes for thirty seconds to receive this major divine soul treasure.

> *Hao! Hao! Hao!*
> *Thank you. Thank you. Thank you.*

Thank you, Divine.

Congratulations! You have received a Divine Soul Transplant of the Divine Soul Song *Yi* for the sixth soul house.

Now prepare for the seventh Divine Soul Download of the Divine Soul Song of Yin Yang (and the eighth Divine Soul Download offered in this book):

## Divine Soul Transplant of the Divine Soul Song *Weng*

Prepare! Sit up straight. Put the tip of your tongue near the roof of your mouth. Totally relax. Open your heart and soul to receive this divine treasure. Tell the Divine: *Dear Divine, I am very grateful and honored to receive this permanent divine soul. I am ready to receive it. Thank you.* In the next thirty seconds the Divine will download it to your soul.

## Divine Soul Transplant of the Divine Soul Song *Weng* Silent download!

Now close your eyes for thirty seconds to receive this major divine soul treasure.

> *Hao! Hao! Hao!*
> *Thank you. Thank you. Thank you.*

Thank you, Divine.

Congratulations! You have received a Divine Soul Transplant of the Divine Soul Song *Weng* for the seventh soul house.

Now prepare for the eighth Divine Soul Download of the Divine Soul Song of Yin Yang (and the ninth Divine Soul Download offered in this book):

## Divine Soul Transplant of the Divine Soul Song *You*

Prepare! Sit up straight. Put the tip of your tongue near the roof of your mouth. Totally relax. Open your heart and soul to receive this divine treasure. Tell the Divine: *Dear Divine, I am very grateful and honored to receive this permanent divine soul. I am ready to receive it. Thank you.* In the next thirty seconds the Divine will download it to your soul.

## Divine Soul Transplant of the Divine Soul Song *You* Silent download!

Now close your eyes for thirty seconds to receive this major divine soul treasure.

> *Hao! Hao! Hao!*
> *Thank you. Thank you. Thank you.*

Thank you, Divine.

Congratulations! You have received a Divine Soul Transplant of the Divine Soul Song *You* for the Wai Jiao.

Now prepare for the ninth Divine Soul Download of the Divine Soul Song of Yin Yang (and the tenth Divine Soul Download offered in this book):

## Divine Soul Transplant of the Divine Soul Song *Hei Heng Hong Ah Xi Yi Weng You*

Prepare! Sit up straight. Put the tip of your tongue near the roof of your mouth. Totally relax. Open your heart and soul to receive this divine treasure. Tell the Divine: *Dear Divine, I am*

*very grateful and honored to receive this permanent divine soul. I am*
*ready to receive it. Thank you.* In the next thirty seconds the Divine will download it to your soul.

## Divine Soul Transplant of the Divine Soul Song
### *Hei Heng Hong Ah Xi Yi Weng You*
### Silent download!

Now close your eyes for thirty seconds to receive this major divine soul treasure.

> *Hao! Hao! Hao!*
> *Thank you. Thank you. Thank you.*

Thank you, Divine.

Congratulations! You have received a Divine Soul Transplant of the Divine Soul Song *Hei Heng Hong Ah Xi Yi Weng You* for the Divine Yin Yang Energy Circle.

Finally, prepare for the tenth Divine Soul Download of the Divine Soul Song of Yin Yang (and the eleventh Divine Soul Download offered in this book):

## Divine Soul Transplant of the Divine Soul Song
### *You Weng Yi Xi Ah Hong Heng Hei*

Prepare! Sit up straight. Put the tip of your tongue near the roof of your mouth. Totally relax. Open your heart and soul to receive this divine treasure. Tell the Divine: *Dear Divine, I am very grateful and honored to receive this permanent divine soul. I am ready to receive it. Thank you.* In the next thirty seconds the Divine will download it to your soul.

## Divine Soul Transplant of the Divine Soul Song
### *You Weng Yi Xi Ah Hong Heng Hei*
### Silent download!

Now close your eyes for thirty seconds to receive this major divine soul treasure.

*Hao! Hao! Hao!*
*Thank you. Thank you. Thank you.*

Thank you, Divine.

Congratulations! You have received a Divine Soul Transplant of the Divine Soul Song *You Weng Yi Xi Ah Hong Heng Hei* for the Divine Yin Yang Matter Circle.

You have just received ten priceless divine souls that are permanent and practical divine soul treasures. Divine souls carry divine love, forgiveness, compassion, and light. Divine love melts all blockages and transforms all life. Divine forgiveness brings inner peace and inner joy. Divine compassion boosts energy, stamina, vitality, and immunity. Divine light heals, prevents sickness, rejuvenates, prolongs life, and transforms consciousness and every aspect of life. Divine souls also carry divine creation, manifestation, and transformation abilities. The ten divine souls you have received in this section are so powerful that you can apply them instantly for healing, rejuvenation, and life transformation. Invoke them. Apply them. Benefit from them. In the next section I will show you how.

APPLY DIVINE SOUL DOWNLOADS OF THE DIVINE SOUL
SONG OF YIN YANG TO HEAL YOU, OTHERS, HUMANITY,
MOTHER EARTH, AND ALL UNIVERSES

Let me teach you the sacred and secret wisdom for applying the
ten Divine Soul Downloads of the Divine Soul Song of Yin Yang
that you have just received.

### *First Practice: Self-healing the genital area and boosting energy*

If you want to heal a sickness in the genitals, such as genital her-
pes, you can apply the Divine Soul Transplant of the Divine Soul
Song *Hei* and the Divine Soul Transplant of the Divine Soul
Song *Hei Heng Hong Ah Xi Yi Weng You* because the sexual organs are at or near the first soul house in the Hui Yin area. If you
want to boost energy, apply the same two Divine Soul Transplants because the Hui Yin area is the source of energy. We include the Divine Soul Transplant of the Divine Soul Song *Hei
Heng Hong Ah Xi Yi Weng You* for the Divine Inner Yin Yang
Energy Circle because healing for the Inner Yin Yang Energy
Circle benefits healing for anything else.

    Here's how to do it:

> *Dear divine souls of the Divine Soul Song* Hei *and the
> Divine Soul Song* Hei Heng Hong Ah Xi Yi Weng
> You *downloaded to my soul,*
> *I love you, honor you, and appreciate you.*
> *Please turn on to heal my genital area* (you may make
> specific requests) *and to boost my energy.*
> *I am very grateful.*
> *Thank you.*

Then sing or chant the words:

> *Hei Ya*
> *Hei Ya Hei Ya You*
> *Hei Ya Hei Ya You*
> *Hei Ya Hei Ya Hei Ya You*
> *Hei Ya Hei Ya Hei Ya Hei Ya You*
>
> *Hei Heng Hong Ah Xi Yi Weng You*
> *Hei Heng Hong Ah Xi Yi Weng You*
> *Hei Heng Hong Ah Xi Yi Weng You*
> *Hei Heng Hong Ah Xi Yi Weng You*

Sing or chant this nine-line practice at least four times. There is no time limit. The longer you sing or chant, the better.

> *Hao! Hao! Hao!*
> *Thank you. Thank you. Thank you.*

Let me explain how this practice works. The Divine Soul Transplant of the Divine Soul Song *Hei* carries divine frequency with divine love, forgiveness, compassion, and light. When you invoke this divine soul, this treasure vibrates the Hui Yin area to remove soul, mind, and body blockages there. It also boosts energy because that area is the source of energy in the body.

The Divine guides us to sing or chant the nine lines above four times. The first five lines shake the genital area (above the Hui Yin point). The last four lines move energy through the whole Inner Yin Yang Circle. When energy flows freely in this circle, yin and yang will be balanced. Blockages of soul, mind, and body will be removed. You could receive remarkable healing from these divine soul treasures and this practice.

*Second Practice: Self-healing the lower abdomen area below the navel, including the small intestine, large intestine, uterus, ovaries, prostate gland, and urinary bladder*

If you have any unhealthy conditions in these organs or in this area, here is how to apply the Divine Soul Transplant of the Divine Soul Song *Heng* and the Divine Soul Transplant of the Divine Soul Song *Hei Heng Hong Ah Xi Yi Weng You* to self-heal. Join me to do it now:

> *Dear divine souls of the Divine Soul Song* Heng *and the Divine Soul Song* Hei Heng Hong Ah Xi Yi Weng You *downloaded to my soul,*
> *I love you, honor you, and appreciate you.*
> *Please turn on to heal and rejuvenate the organs in my lower abdomen.* (You may make specific healing requests.)
> *I am very grateful.*
> *Thank you.*

Then sing or chant the words:

> *Heng Ya*
> *Heng Ya Heng Ya You*
> *Heng Ya Heng Ya You*
> *Heng Ya Heng Ya Heng Ya You*
> *Heng Ya Heng Ya Heng Ya Heng Ya You*
>
> *Hei Heng Hong Ah Xi Yi Weng You*
> *Hei Heng Hong Ah Xi Yi Weng You*
> *Hei Heng Hong Ah Xi Yi Weng You*
> *Hei Heng Hong Ah Xi Yi Weng You*

Sing or chant this nine-line practice at least four times. There is no time limit. The longer you sing or chant, the better.

> *Hao! Hao! Hao!*
> *Thank you. Thank you. Thank you.*

Let me explain how this practice works. When you invoke the divine soul of the Divine Soul Song *Heng,* this treasure vibrates the lower abdomen to remove soul, mind, and body blockages there. It also boosts energy, because the two major foundational energy centers, the Lower Dan Tian and the Snow Mountain Area, lie between the genitals and the navel.

The Divine guides us to sing or chant the above four times. The first five lines shake the entire lower abdomen area, including all the organs there, the Lower Dan Tian, and the Snow Mountain Area. The last four lines move energy through the whole Inner Yin Yang Circle. When energy flows freely in this circle, yin ang yang will be balanced. Blockages of soul, mind, and body will be removed. You could receive remarkable healing from these divine soul treasures and this practice.

*Third Practice: Self-healing the upper abdomen area from the level of the navel to the diaphragm, including the spleen, stomach, pancreas, liver, gallbladder, kidneys, and adrenal glands.*

If you have any unhealthy conditions in these organs or in this area, here is how to apply the Divine Soul Transplant of the Divine Soul Song *Hong* and the Divine Soul Transplant of the Divine Soul Song *Hei Heng Hong Ah Xi Yi Weng You* to self-heal.

Let's do it now:

*Dear divine souls of the Divine Soul Song* Hong *and*
  *the Divine Soul Song* Hei Heng Hong Ah Xi Yi
  Weng You *downloaded to my soul,*
*I love you, honor you, and appreciate you.*
*Please turn on to heal the organs in my upper abdo-*
  *men.* (You may make specific healing requests for
  this area, but it is not necessary.)
*I am very grateful.*
*Thank you.*

Then sing or chant the words:

*Hong Ya*
*Hong Ya Hong Ya You*
*Hong Ya Hong Ya You*
*Hong Ya Hong Ya Hong Ya You*
*Hong Ya Hong Ya Hong Ya Hong Ya You*

*Hei Heng Hong Ah Xi Yi Weng You*
*Hei Heng Hong Ah Xi Yi Weng You*
*Hei Heng Hong Ah Xi Yi Weng You*
*Hei Heng Hong Ah Xi Yi Weng You*

Sing or chant this nine-line practice at least four times. There
is no time limit. The longer you sing or chant, the better.

*Hao! Hao! Hao!*
*Thank you. Thank you. Thank you.*

This practice works because the divine soul of the Divine
Soul Song *Hong* and the Divine Soul Song itself shake the entire

area of the upper abdomen. Blockages of soul, mind, and body in that area could be removed. The divine soul of the Divine Soul Song *Hei Heng Hong Ah Xi Yi Weng You* and the Divine Soul Song itself will balance the energy in the Inner Yin Yang Circle for healing and recovery of all.

*Fourth Practice: Self-healing the heart and chest area, including the heart, lungs, bronchial tubes, and esophagus; self-healing all emotional imbalances; and opening your Message Center to develop your spiritual channels*

If you have any unhealthy physical conditions in these organs or in this area, or any emotional imbalances, including depression, anxiety, worry, grief, fear, guilt, and more, here is how to apply the Divine Soul Transplant of the Divine Soul Song *Ah* and the Divine Soul Transplant of the Divine Soul Song *Hei Heng Hong Ah Xi Yi Weng You* to self-heal. You can also use this practice to open your Message Center and your spiritual communication channels.

Do it with me now:

> *Dear divine souls of the Divine Soul Song* Ah *and the Divine Soul Song* Hei Heng Hong Ah Xi Yi Weng You *downloaded to my soul,*
> *I love you, honor you, and appreciate you.*
> *Please turn on to heal my heart, lungs, bronchial tubes, and esophagus.* (You may make specific healing requests.)
> *Please balance my emotions.* (You may make specific requests for emotional imbalances.)

> *Please fully open and fully develop my Message Center*
> *and spiritual communication channels.*
> *I am very grateful.*
> *Thank you.*

Then sing or chant the words:

*Ah Ya*
*Ah Ya Ah Ya You*
*Ah Ya Ah Ya You*
*Ah Ya Ah Ya Ah Ya You*
*Ah Ya Ah Ya Ah Ya Ah Ya You*

*Hei Heng Hong Ah Xi Yi Weng You*
*Hei Heng Hong Ah Xi Yi Weng You*
*Hei Heng Hong Ah Xi Yi Weng You*
*Hei Heng Hong Ah Xi Yi Weng You*

Sing or chant this nine-line practice at least four times. There is no time limit. The longer you sing or chant, the better.

> *Hao! Hao! Hao!*
> *Thank you. Thank you. Thank you.*

This practice works because this divine soul of the Divine Soul Song *Ah* and the Divine Soul Song itself shake the entire area of the heart and chest, which includes the Message Center. The Message Center is the emotional center. All kinds of emotional imbalances are due to blockages in the Message Center. To clear blockages in the Message Center is to balance all emotions. Blockages of soul, mind, and body in that area could be removed.

The divine soul of the Divine Soul Song *Hei Heng Hong Ah Xi Yi Weng You* will balance the energy in the Inner Yin Yang Circle for healing and recovery.

In addition, there are four major spiritual channels: Soul Language, Direct Soul Communication, Third Eye, and Direct Knowing. The Message Center is the foundation for all of them. You must open your Message Center in order to develop your spiritual channels. The Divine Soul Song of Yin Yang is a pure divine singing and chanting treasure. The Divine Soul Transplant of the Divine Soul Song *Ah* is another priceless divine treasure to open your Message Center in order to develop all four main spiritual channels.

*Fifth Practice: Self-healing the throat area, including the thyroid and parathyroid glands, larynx, and vocal cords*

If you have any unhealthy conditions in these organs or in this area, here is how to apply the Divine Soul Transplant of the Divine Soul Song *Xi* and the Divine Soul Transplant of the Divine Soul Song *Hei Heng Hong Ah Xi Yi Weng You* to self-heal.

Join me to do it now:

> *Dear divine souls of the Divine Soul Song* Xi *and the Divine Soul Song* Hei Heng Hong Ah Xi Yi Weng You *downloaded to my soul,*
> *I love you, honor you, and appreciate you.*
> *Please turn on to heal the organs in my throat.* (You may make specific healing requests for this area, but it is not necessary.)
> *I am very grateful.*
> *Thank you.*

Then sing or chant the words:

*Xi Ya*
*Xi Ya Xi Ya You*
*Xi Ya Xi Ya You*
*Xi Ya Xi Ya Xi Ya You*
*Xi Ya Xi Ya Xi Ya Xi Ya You*

*Hei Heng Hong Ah Xi Yi Weng You*
*Hei Heng Hong Ah Xi Yi Weng You*
*Hei Heng Hong Ah Xi Yi Weng You*
*Hei Heng Hong Ah Xi Yi Weng You*

Sing or chant this nine-line practice at least four times. There is no time limit. The longer you sing or chant, the better.

*Hao! Hao! Hao!*
*Thank you. Thank you. Thank you.*

This practice works because this divine soul of the Divine Soul Song *Xi* and the Divine Soul Song itself shake the entire area of the throat. Blockages of soul, mind, and body in that area could be removed. *Hei Heng Hong Ah Xi Yi Weng You* will balance the energy in the Inner Yin Yang Circle for healing and recovery.

*Sixth Practice: Self-healing the head area, including the brain, eyes, tongue, mouth and gums, nose, sinuses, ears, face, hair, and pharynx; boosting mind power; and opening the Third Eye*

If you have any unhealthy conditions in these organs or in this area, here is how to apply the Divine Soul Transplant of the

Divine Soul Song *Yi* and the Divine Soul Transplant of the Divine Soul Song *Hei Heng Hong Ah Xi Yi Weng You* to self-heal. You can also use this practice to increase your mind power and open your Third Eye.

Say *hello* with me first:

> *Dear divine souls of the Divine Soul Song* Yi *and the Divine Soul Song* Hei Heng Hong Ah Xi Yi Weng You *downloaded to my soul,*
> *I love you, honor you, and appreciate you.*
> *Please turn on to heal the organs in my head.* (You may make specific healing requests for this area, but it is not necessary.)
> *Please boost my Mind Power and open* (or *further open) my Third Eye.*
> *I am very grateful.*
> *Thank you.*

Then sing or chant the words:

> *Yi Ya*
> *Yi Ya Yi Ya You*
> *Yi Ya Yi Ya You*
> *Yi Ya Yi Ya Yi Ya You*
> *Yi Ya Yi Ya Yi Ya Yi Ya You*
>
> *Hei Heng Hong Ah Xi Yi Weng You*
> *Hei Heng Hong Ah Xi Yi Weng You*
> *Hei Heng Hong Ah Xi Yi Weng You*
> *Hei Heng Hong Ah Xi Yi Weng You*

Sing or chant this nine-line practice at least four times. There is no time limit. The longer you sing or chant, the better.

> *Hao! Hao! Hao!*
> *Thank you. Thank you. Thank you.*

This practice works because this divine soul of the Divine Soul Song *Yi* and the Divine Soul Song itself shake the entire head. Blockages of soul, mind, and body in the head could be removed. *Hei Heng Hong Ah Xi Yi Weng You* will balance the energy in the Inner Yin Yang Circle for healing and recovery.

This practice will also develop your Zu Qiao (pronounced *zoo chow*). The Zu Qiao is the key energy center for mind power. It is a cherry-sized energy center located in the bone cavity between the eyebrows. This practice also stimulates and develops the Third Eye, which, like the Zu Qiao, is also in the head.

*Seventh Practice: Self-healing the whole body through the seventh soul house*

Here is how to apply the Divine Soul Transplant of the Divine Soul Song *Weng* and the Divine Soul Transplant of the Divine Soul Song *Hei Heng Hong Ah Xi Yi Weng You* for total self-healing.

Invoke these two divine souls with me:

> *Dear divine souls of the Divine Soul Song* Weng *and the Divine Soul Song* Hei Heng Hong Ah Xi Yi Weng You *downloaded to my soul,*

*I love you, honor you, and appreciate you.*
*Please turn on to heal my whole body.*
*I am very grateful.*
*Thank you.*

Then sing or chant the words:

*Weng Ya*
*Weng Ya Weng Ya You*
*Weng Ya Weng Ya You*
*Weng Ya Weng Ya Weng Ya You*
*Weng Ya Weng Ya Weng Ya Weng Ya You*

*Hei Heng Hong Ah Xi Yi Weng You*
*Hei Heng Hong Ah Xi Yi Weng You*
*Hei Heng Hong Ah Xi Yi Weng You*
*Hei Heng Hong Ah Xi Yi Weng You*

Sing or chant this nine-line practice at least four times. There is no time limit. The longer you sing or chant, the better.

*Hao! Hao! Hao!*
*Thank you. Thank you. Thank you.*

Why does this practice offer you healing for the whole body? Because your seventh soul house is around the Bai Hui acupuncture point, which is located on the crown of your head. The Bai Hui point gathers the energies of hundreds of other acupuncture points. Two major vertical meridians, the Ren (front midline) and Du (back midline), connect and end at the Bai Hui point. To vibrate the seventh soul house and the Bai Hui area is to directly stimulate the Ren and Du meridians. This can balance the Ren and Du meridians for total healing.

After practicing

> *Weng Ya*
> *Weng Ya Weng Ya You*
> *Weng Ya Weng Ya You*
> *Weng Ya Weng Ya Weng Ya You*
> *Weng Ya Weng Ya Weng Ya Weng Ya You*

to stimulate the Bai Hui, another secret is to follow that by practicing

> *Hei Ya*
> *Hei Ya Hei Ya You*
> *Hei Ya Hei Ya You*
> *Hei Ya Hei Ya Hei Ya You*
> *Hei Ya Hei Ya Hei Ya Hei Ya You*

to stimulate the Hui Yin. The Hui Yin is the acupuncture point where the Ren and Du meridians connect and begin. Stimulating the Hui Yin and Bai Hui together further balances yin and yang for total healing. You are stimulating and promoting free flow in the Outer Yin Yang Circle.

*Eighth Practice: Self-healing the whole body through the Wai Jiao*

If you have any unhealthy conditions anywhere in your body, you can invoke the Divine Soul Transplant of the Divine Soul Song *You* and the Divine Soul Transplant of the Divine Soul Song *Hei Heng Hong Ah Xi Yi Weng You* for self-healing because

*You* stimulates the Wai Jiao. Every sickness will also manifest as a blockage in the Wai Jiao. To clear the Wai Jiao is to heal the whole body.

Do it with me now:

> *Dear divine souls of the Divine Soul Song* You *and the Divine Soul Song* Hei Heng Hong Ah Xi Yi Weng You *downloaded to my soul,*
> *I love you, honor you, and appreciate you.*
> *Please turn on to heal and rejuvenate my whole body.*
>     (You may also make specific healing requests, but it is not necessary.)
> *I am very grateful.*
> *Thank you.*

Then sing or chant the words:

> *You Ya*
> *You Ya You Ya You*
> *You Ya You Ya You*
> *You Ya You Ya You Ya You*
> *You Ya You Ya You Ya You Ya You*
>
> *Hei Heng Hong Ah Xi Yi Weng You*
> *Hei Heng Hong Ah Xi Yi Weng You*
> *Hei Heng Hong Ah Xi Yi Weng You*
> *Hei Heng Hong Ah Xi Yi Weng You*

Sing or chant this nine-line practice at least four times. There is no time limit. The longer you sing or chant, the better.

*Hao! Hao! Hao!*
*Thank you. Thank you. Thank you.*

This practice works because this divine soul of the Divine Soul Song *You* and the Divine Soul Song itself vibrate the entire Wai Jiao. Blockages of soul, mind, and body in the Wai Jiao could be removed. *Hei Heng Hong Ah Xi Yi Weng You* will balance the energy in the Inner Yin Yang Circle, which goes through the Wai Jiao, for further healing and recovery.

*Ninth Practice: Total self-healing for the physical, emotional, mental, and spiritual bodies*

If you have any blockages or imbalances of the physical, emotional, mental, and spiritual bodies, invoke the Divine Soul Transplant of the Divine Soul Song *Hei Heng Hong Ah Xi Yi Weng You* for self-healing. To clear blockages in the Inner Yin Yang Circle is to clear blockages in all four bodies.

Here is how to do it:

*Dear divine soul of the Divine Soul Song* Hei Heng Hong Ah Xi Yi Weng You *downloaded to my soul,*
*I love you, honor you, and appreciate you.*
*Please turn on to clear all blockages in my Inner Yin Yang Circle to give me total healing for my soul, heart, mind, and body.* (You may make specific healing requests.)
*I am very grateful.*
*Thank you.*

Then sing or chant the words of the Divine Soul Song of the Divine Yin Yang Energy Circle:

*Hei Heng Hong Ah Xi Yi Weng You*
*Hei Heng Hong Ah Xi Yi Weng You*
*Hei Heng Hong Ah Xi Yi Weng You*
*Hei Heng Hong Ah Xi Yi Weng You*

Sing these four lines at least four times, the longer, the better.

This practice works because the divine soul of the Divine Soul Song *Hei Heng Hong Ah Xi Yi Weng You* and the Divine Soul Song itself balance the energy in the Inner Yin Yang Circle for healing and recovery.

*Tenth Practice: Rejuvenation and long life*

Invoke the Divine Soul Transplant of the Divine Soul Song *You Weng Yi Xi Ah Hong Heng Hei* for rejuvenation and long life.
Practice with me:

> *Dear divine soul of the Divine Soul Song* You Weng
>     Yi Xi Ah Hong Heng Hei *downloaded to my soul,*
> *I love you, honor you, and appreciate you.*
> *Please turn on to clear all blockages in my Yin Yang*
>     *Matter Circle in order to rejuvenate my systems, or-*
>     *gans, cells, cell units, DNA, RNA, spaces between*
>     *my organs and cells, and the smallest matter in*
>     *my cells.*
> *I am very grateful.*
> *Thank you.*

FIGURE 1: Body Power Technique to Calm a Strong Energy Reaction
in the Body

# Love, Peace and Harmony

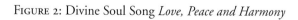

FIGURE 2: Divine Soul Song *Love, Peace and Harmony*

# Divine Soul Song for World Soul Healing, Peace and Enlightenment

Figure 3: Divine Soul Song for World Soul Healing, Peace and Enlightenment

# God Gives His Heart to Me

FIGURE 4: Divine Soul Song *God Gives His Heart to Me*

# Divine Soul Song of Compassion

FIGURE 5: Divine Soul Song of Compassion

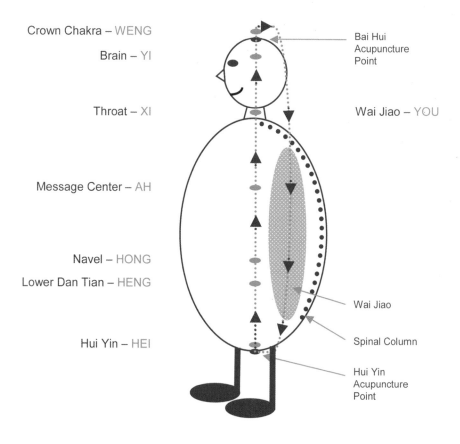

Crown Chakra – WENG
Brain – YI

Bai Hui
Acupuncture
Point

Throat – XI

Wai Jiao – YOU

Message Center – AH

Navel – HONG
Lower Dan Tian – HENG

Wai Jiao

Hui Yin – HEI

Spinal Column

Hui Yin
Acupuncture
Point

FIGURE 6: Seven Houses of the Soul and Wai Jiao

# Divine Soul Song of Yin Yang

* Hei, Heng, Hong, Ah, Xi, Yi, Weng, You

FIGURE 7: Divine Soul Song of Yin Yang

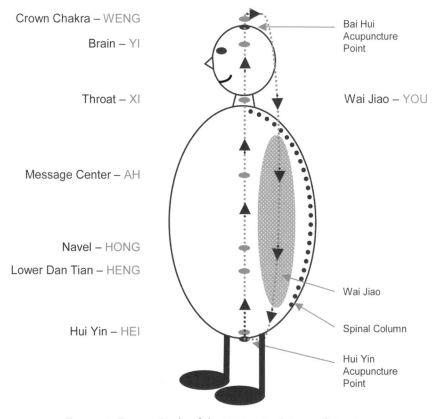

Crown Chakra – WENG

Brain – YI

Throat – XI

Message Center – AH

Navel – HONG

Lower Dan Tian – HENG

Hui Yin – HEI

Bai Hui
Acupuncture
Point

Wai Jiao – YOU

Wai Jiao

Spinal Column

Hui Yin
Acupuncture
Point

FIGURE 8: Energy Circle of the Divine Soul Song of Yin Yang

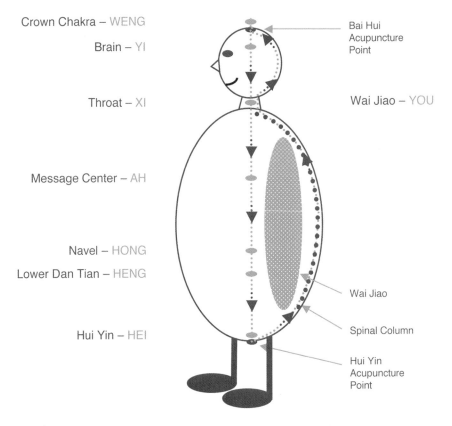

Crown Chakra – WENG

Brain – YI

Throat – XI

Message Center – AH

Navel – HONG

Lower Dan Tian – HENG

Hui Yin – HEI

Bai Hui
Acupuncture
Point

Wai Jiao – YOU

Wai Jiao

Spinal Column

Hui Yin
Acupuncture
Point

FIGURE 9: Matter Circle of the Divine Soul Song of Yin Yang

FIGURE 10: Divine Soul Song of
Yin Yang—Body Power for First
Soul House

FIGURE 11: Divine Soul Song of
Yin Yang—Body Power for Second
Soul House

FIGURE 12: Divine Soul Song of
Yin Yang—Body Power for Third
Soul House

FIGURE 13: Divine Soul Song of
Yin Yang—Body Power for Fourth
Soul House

FIGURE 14: Divine Soul Song of Yin Yang—Body Power for Fifth Soul House

FIGURE 15: Divine Soul Song of Yin Yang—Body Power for Sixth Soul House

FIGURE 16: Divine Soul Song of Yin Yang—Body Power for Seventh Soul House

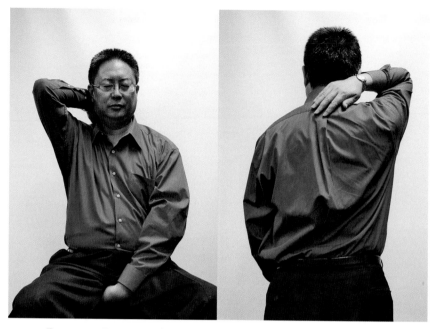

FIGURE 17: Divine Soul Song of Yin Yang—Body Power forWai Jiao

FIGURE 19: Yin Yang Symbol

FIGURE 18: Divine Soul Song of
Yin Yang—Body Power for Energy
and Matter Circles

FIGURE 20: Divine Sacred *Tian Di Ren* Soul Practice to Reach the Tao

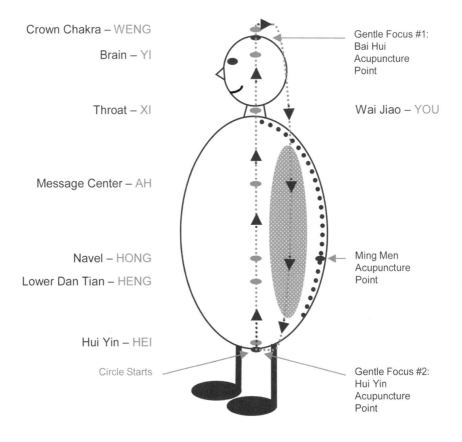

Crown Chakra – WENG

Brain – YI

Gentle Focus #1:
Bai Hui
Acupuncture
Point

Throat – XI

Wai Jiao – YOU

Message Center – AH

Navel – HONG

Lower Dan Tian – HENG

Ming Men
Acupuncture
Point

Hui Yin – HEI

Circle Starts

Gentle Focus #2:
Hui Yin
Acupuncture
Point

FIGURE 21: Divine Sacred *Tian Di Ren* Soul Practice to Reach the Tao:
Circle 1 Mind Power

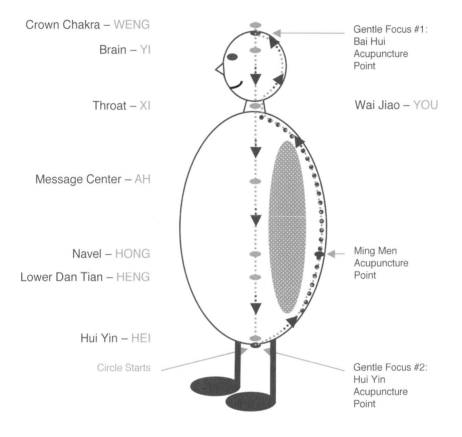

Crown Chakra – WENG

Brain – YI

Gentle Focus #1:
Bai Hui
Acupuncture
Point

Throat – XI

Wai Jiao – YOU

Message Center – AH

Navel – HONG

Ming Men
Acupuncture
Point

Lower Dan Tian – HENG

Hui Yin – HEI

Circle Starts

Gentle Focus #2:
Hui Yin
Acupuncture
Point

FIGURE 22: Divine Sacred *Tian Di Ren* Soul Practice to Reach the Tao:
Circle 2 Mind Power

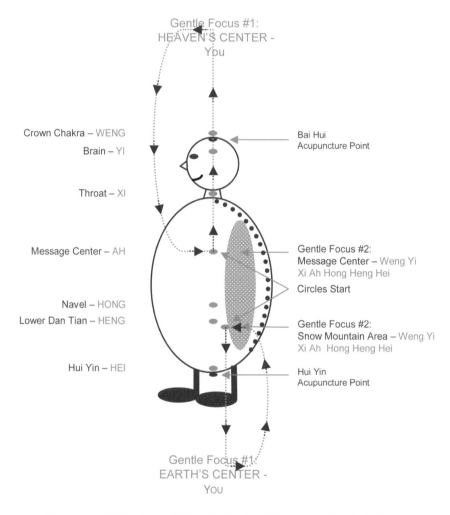

**Figure 23:** Divine Sacred *Tian Di Ren* Soul Practice to Reach the Tao:
Circle 3 Mind Power

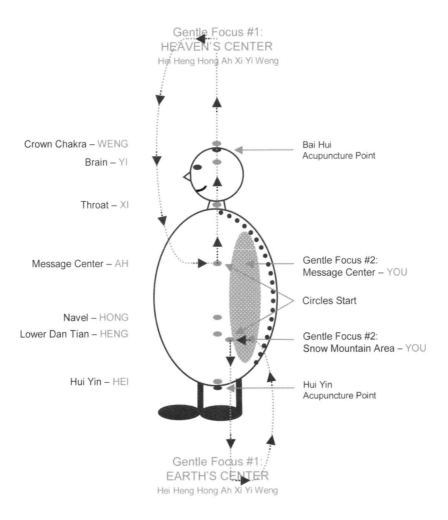

FIGURE 24: Divine Sacred *Tian Di Ren* Soul Practice to Reach the Tao:
Circle 4 Mind Power

FIGURE 25: Universal Connection Hand Position

FIGURE 26: Universal Connection
for the First Soul House

FIGURE 27: Universal Connection
for the Second Soul House

FIGURE 28: Universal Connection for the Third Soul House

FIGURE 29: Universal Connection for the Fourth Soul House

FIGURE 30: Universal Connection for the Fifth Soul House

FIGURE 31: Universal Connection
for the Sixth Soul House

FIGURE 32: Universal Connection
for the Seventh Soul House

FIGURE 33: Universal Connection
for the Wai Jiao

FIGURE 34: Divine Soul Song of Five Elements

FIGURE 35: Divine Soul Song of Wood Element—Body Power for *Jiao*

FIGURE 36: Divine Soul Song of Fire Element—Body Power for *Zhi*

FIGURE 37: Divine Soul Song of Earth Element—Body Power for *Gong*

FIGURE 38: Divine Soul Song of Metal Element—Body Power for *Shang*

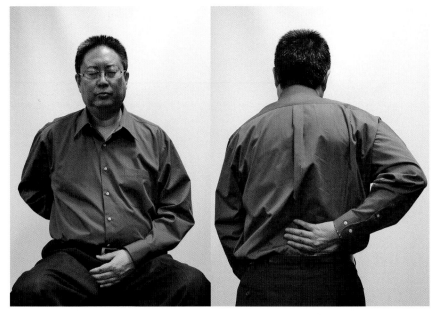

FIGURE 39: Divine Soul Song of Water Element—Body Power for *Yu*

FIGURE 40: Divine Soul Song *Ai* for All
Five Elements—Body Power for *Ai*

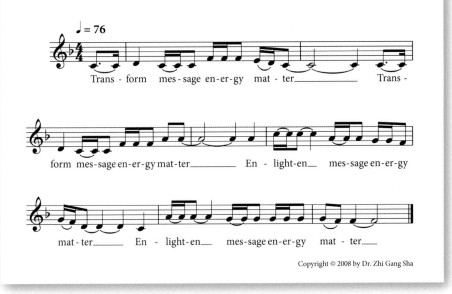

FIGURE 41: Divine Soul Song of Message Energy Matter

# Divine Soul Song of Universal Service

FIGURE 42: Divine Soul Song of Universal Service

Then sing or chant the words of the Divine Soul Song of the
Divine Yin Yang Matter Circle:

*You Weng Yi Xi Ah Hong Heng Hei*
*You Weng Yi Xi Ah Hong Heng Hei*
*You Weng Yi Xi Ah Hong Heng Hei*
*You Weng Yi Xi Ah Hong Heng Hei*

Sing these four lines at least four times, the longer, the
better.

This practice works because the divine soul of the Divine
Soul Song *You Weng Yi Xi Ah Hong Heng Hei* and the Divine
Soul Song itself transform energy to matter in a sacred and
secret way.

Energy is created in the Hui Yin area. It then moves in front
of the tailbone, passes through three secret energy holes, and en-
ters the spinal cord to become matter. This is the first vital transformation in the body from energy to matter.

Energy also flows up the spinal cord to the brain and the Bai
Hui point. From there, it flows back down to the palate, where
the energy transforms to matter as liquid (saliva) that drips down
into the mouth. This is the second vital transformation in the
body from energy to matter.

The Divine Yin Yang Matter Circle of *You Weng Yi Xi Ah
Hong Heng Hei* continues to flow in this way. The more you
chant, the more these two vital transformations from energy to
matter happen.

Every time these two vital transformations from energy to
matter happen, the energy and matter in the body become more
and more refined. To highly refine energy and matter in the body
is the key secret of rejuvenation and long life.

ANOTHER SACRED PRACTICE TO HEAL, REJUVENATE, AND
TRANSFORM YOUR SOUL, MIND, AND BODY JUST REVEALED

In September 2008 I was in Honolulu as part of my 2008 World
Healing and Teaching Tour. I started to travel in April and continued to do so into December. Every week I am healing and
teaching wherever in the world the Divine guides me to go. It is
a very heavy travel and teaching schedule. On September 26 I
was awakened by the Divine at 4:00 AM. The Divine told me:

> *Zhi Gang,*
> *Let me further teach you the secrets, wisdom,*
> *knowledge, and practices of the Divine Soul Song of*
> *Yin Yang. I especially want to teach you more about*
> *the sacred practice of* Tian Di Ren He Yi *(Heaven*
> *Earth Human Being Join as One).*

I was so excited. Whenever the Divine teaches me something
new, I never feel it's too much. It doesn't matter whether it's in
the middle of a workshop or retreat, while I'm writing a book, on
an airplane, in my regular morning meditation, or in the middle
of the night. I feel extremely honored to learn new divine secrets.

Then the Divine told me to sit up. I sat up right away. The
Divine was giving me a private workshop. The teachings in the
next few pages are exactly the Divine's direct teaching to me
about the Divine's sacred practice. I'm honored to share this
teaching with you in this book. I'm delighted to have the opportunity because this book is still in the preparation stages. It is the
perfect time to put more secrets, wisdom, knowledge, and practices in this book.

As soon as I receive some teaching or wisdom, I love to give it out. Why should I keep it? This teaching, wisdom, and practice are for you and all humanity, to benefit the entire world. There is also an important spiritual law: *The only way to receive new secrets and wisdom is to share the old secrets and wisdom.* I am honored to share. I am honored to be your servant. I am honored to be a servant of humanity and the Divine.

I sat in a half lotus. You can sit in any position when you do this practice, such as a full lotus if you are flexible enough or with naturally crossed legs. You can sit on a chair. You can also do this practice standing up or lying down. The Divine told me that no specific position is required. The Divine told me that you can even do this practice while you are walking.

Then the Divine told me: *Use the Four Power Techniques to do this sacred practice, but first call your soul to sit in your **first soul house**.* I said *hello* to my soul: "Dear my beloved soul, I love you. Please sit just above the Hui Yin area in the first soul house. Thank you." My soul immediately sat there with crossed legs, just as I do when I meditate.

Body Power: The Divine said to use the Universal Connection hand position. You do this by forming an "O" with your hands and fingers, with the tips of your thumbs almost touching and with the fingers of your right hand resting on the fingers of your left hand. This special hand position can be held as shown in figure 25, with the thumbs above the fingers. It can also be turned upside down so that the thumbs are below the fingers. The Divine guided me in each step of this practice, as I will explain step by step.

The Divine then told me: *Put your hands in this position, close to your body in front of the genital area.* (See figure 26.)

Sound Power: The Divine said, *Now sing or chant the words*

*Hei Ya*
*Hei Ya Hei Ya You*
*Hei Ya Hei Ya You*
*Hei Ya Hei Ya Hei Ya You*
*Hei Ya Hei Ya Hei Ya Hei Ya You*

You will recognize this as the Divine Soul Song of Yin Yang for the first soul house.

Mind Power: The Divine's direction was to watch the golden light ball and golden liquid spring rotating in your first soul house. They will vibrate and further purify and cleanse your first soul house and your soul together. This is Mind Power. The Divine said that a person whose Third Eye is not open should visualize the golden light ball and golden liquid spring rotating counterclockwise in the first soul house to purify and cleanse this soul house and the soul together. If your Third Eye is open, you can directly see this movement.

Soul Power: The Divine guided me to ask my soul to shine in my first soul house to purify; to boost energy, stamina, vitality, and immunity; and to transform my soul frequency to divine soul frequency. I followed exactly what the Divine asked me to do for Soul Power. I said *hello* like this: "Dear my soul, I love you. Please receive the golden light and golden liquid in my first soul house to purify; boost energy, stamina, vitality, and immunity; and transform your soul frequency to divine soul frequency. Do a good job. Thank you."

The Divine told me to continue with Soul Power in this way:

*Dear Divine,*
  *"I love you. I am extremely honored that you taught me your Divine Soul Song of Yin Yang and Divine Soul*

*Song of Five Elements a few months ago and that now you are continuing to show me further secrets and practices of your Divine Soul Song of Yin Yang. Please continue to bless my first soul house and my soul to purify my soul further as a servant of humanity and of you. Thank you."*

The moment I made this request, the Divine started shooting light to me. The Divine poured a huge amount of golden light, rainbow light, purple light, and crystal light to my soul and my first soul house. My first soul house exploded with intense light. It was blindingly bright. Then the Divine confirmed: *This is the Soul Power for this practice.* I replied, "Dear Divine, I cannot bow down to you enough."

Immediately, the Divine continued to teach me, saying: *Sing once more:*

> *Hei Ya*
> *Hei Ya Hei Ya You*
> *Hei Ya Hei Ya You*
> *Hei Ya Hei Ya Hei Ya You*
> *Hei Ya Hei Ya Hei Ya Hei Ya You*

I did.
Then the Divine said: *Now sing:*

> *Hei Heng Hong Ah Xi Yi Weng You*

I did.
The Divine continued:

*Look at your soul. Your soul has a Hui Yin area. Your soul has a Ren meridian, a Du meridian, and a Wai Jiao. Whatever your physical body has, your soul has. Follow the teaching I gave you before for the Divine Soul Song of Yin Yang practice. When you sing* Hei Heng Hong Ah Xi Yi Weng, *light from your soul's Hui Yin area will flow up the soul's seven soul houses to the soul's Bai Hui point. When you sing* You, *light will flow down in front of your soul's spinal column through the soul's Wai Jiao to the soul's Hui Yin area.*

I was excited and very appreciative because I learned clearly at that moment a new wisdom:

**Whatever the physical body has,
the soul has also.**

It makes great sense. We have physical acupuncture; the Divine has soul acupuncture. We have physical herbs; the Divine and Heaven's herb garden have soul herbs. We have physical surgery; the Divine has Soul Operations. We have physical organ transplants; the Divine has Divine Soul Transplants. Therefore, a soul has its own systems, organs, cells, cell units, DNA, RNA, spaces between cells, and smallest matter in the cells. A soul has its own soul acupuncture points and soul meridians. This is a major new soul wisdom that I clearly understood and appreciated at that moment.

Then the Divine said to sing:

*You Weng Yi Xi Ah Hong Heng Hei*

The Divine guided me to again follow the earlier *Tian Di Ren* practice:

> *When you sing* You *this time, visualize light from your soul's Hui Yin point going to the soul's tailbone area, and then into your soul's spinal column, where it moves up to your soul's Bai Hui point.*
>
> *When you sing* Weng Yi Xi Ah Hong Heng Hei, *visualize light going down through the seven soul houses from top to bottom.*
>
> *Then sing one more time:*

You Weng Yi Xi Ah Hong Heng Hei

> *When you sing* You *this time, connect your mind with* tian xin (Heaven's center) *and* di xin (Earth's center).

The instant I focused my mind gently on *tian xin* and *di xin*, multicolored beams of light shot from Heaven and Earth to my soul and my first soul house.

The Divine continued:

> *After singing* You, *as you start to sing* Weng Yi Xi Ah Hong Heng Hei, *focus your mind right away on your soul's Message Center and your soul's Snow Mountain Area.*

*Tian xin* and *di xin* continued to shoot light and liquid to my soul and my first soul house.

Finally, I sang *Hei Heng Hong Ah Xi Yi Weng You* again. As I sang *Hei Heng Hong Ah Xi Yi Weng,* I again focused gently on both the center of Heaven and the center of Mother Earth. As I sang *You,* I shifted my focus to my soul's Message Center and Snow Mountain Area. Beautiful light and liquid continued to pour from Heaven's center and Earth's center to nourish and purify my soul and my first soul house.

The Divine continued:

> *Now ask your soul to sit in your* **second soul house** *and move your hands up in front of your second soul house.*

I said *hello* to my soul again: "Dear my beloved soul, please sit between my Hui Yin area and navel in the second soul house. Thank you." My soul instantly moved up from my first soul house. I moved my hands up in front of my lower abdomen, still in the basic Universal Connection hand position with my thumbs above my fingers. (See figure 27.)

Soul Power is to ask my soul to shine and to ask for Heaven's and Earth's blessings:

> *Dear my soul, I love you. Please receive golden light*
> *and golden liquid in my second soul house to purify;*
> *boost energy, stamina, vitality, and immunity; and*
> *transform your soul frequency to divine soul fre-*
> *quency. Do a good job. Thank you.*
> *Dear Divine, dear Heaven, and dear Mother Earth,*
> *I love you, honor you, and appreciate you. Please*
> *continue to bless my second soul house and my*
> *soul to purify my soul further. I am very grateful.*
> *Thank you.*

Then the Divine said: *Sing my Soul Song for the second soul house.*

I sang:

*Heng Ya*
*Heng Ya Heng Ya You*
*Heng Ya Heng Ya You*
*Heng Ya Heng Ya Heng Ya You*
*Heng Ya Heng Ya Heng Ya Heng Ya You*

Exactly as with the first soul house, the Mind Power is to visualize a golden light ball and a golden liquid spring rotating and vibrating in my second soul house and on my soul.

Then I sang *Hei Heng Hong Ah Xi Yi Weng.* I saw light flow up from my soul's Hui Yin point through my soul's seven soul houses to my soul's Bai Hui point.

Next I sang *You.* Light flowed down through my soul's Wai Jiao.

Then I sang *You Weng Yi Xi Ah Hong Heng Hei.* As I sang *You,* light flowed up from my soul's Hui Yin to my soul's tailbone, and then up through my soul's spinal cord to my soul's brain and my soul's Bai Hui point. As I then sang *Weng Yi Xi Ah Hong Heng Hei,* light flowed down through the soul's seven soul houses.

I sang *You Weng Yi Xi Ah Hong Heng Hei* again, focusing, as in the practice for the first soul house, on *tian xin* and *di xin.* Light flowed down from Heaven and Earth through the seven soul houses within my soul.

Last, I sang *Hei Heng Hong Ah Xi Yi Weng You* again.

As I sang *Hei Heng Hong Ah Xi Yi Weng,* my mind again focused on *tian xin* and *di xin.* Then when I sang *You,* my mind shifted to my soul's Message Center and my soul's Snow Mountain Area. Beautiful multicolored light shot back from Heaven and Earth to my soul and my second soul house.

Then the Divine told me that the next step was to move my soul up to the **third soul house.** I said *hello* to my soul again: "Dear my beloved soul, please sit behind my navel in the third soul house. Thank you." Then I followed exactly the same techniques that I shared for the first two soul houses, starting with moving my hands up over my navel, maintaining the basic Universal Connection hand position. (See figure 28.) I applied Soul Power as before by asking my soul to receive golden light and golden liquid and asking for Heaven's and Earth's blessings.

I sang the Divine Soul Song of Yin Yang for the third soul house:

> *Hong Ya*
> *Hong Ya Hong Ya You*
> *Hong Ya Hong Ya You*
> *Hong Ya Hong Ya Hong Ya You*
> *Hong Ya Hong Ya Hong Ya Hong Ya You*

Then, as before, I sang the *Tian Di Ren* circles:

> *Hei Heng Hong Ah Xi Yi Weng You*
> *You Weng Yi Xi Ah Hong Heng Hei*
> *You Weng Yi Xi Ah Hong Heng Hei*
> *Hei Heng Hong Ah Xi Yi Weng You*

I followed exactly the same Mind Power and Soul Power techniques.

Then the Divine told me to ask my soul to sit in the **fourth**

**soul house.** I said *hello*: "Dear my beloved soul, please sit in my heart chakra, or Message Center, the fourth soul house. Thank you." It did immediately. I moved my hands up in front of my Message Center, turning the Universal Connection hand position upside down so that my thumbs were below my fingers (see figure 29), and started to sing the Divine Soul Song of Yin Yang for the fourth soul house:

*Ah Ya*
*Ah Ya Ah Ya You*
*Ah Ya Ah Ya You*
*Ah Ya Ah Ya Ah Ya You*
*Ah Ya Ah Ya Ah Ya Ah Ya You*

I saw a golden light ball and a golden liquid spring purifying, nourishing, and brightening my soul and my fourth soul house. Then I did the four-line Tian Di Ren practice:

*Hei Heng Hong Ah Xi Yi Weng You*
*You Weng Yi Xi Ah Hong Heng Hei*
*You Weng Yi Xi Ah Hong Heng Hei*
*Hei Heng Hong Ah Xi Yi Weng You*

As I sang the first two lines, the light circle rotated inside my soul.

As I sang the last two lines, the light circle connected with *tian xin* and *di xin* together exactly as I explained for the first soul house.

Then the Divine told me to ask my soul to sit in the **fifth soul house.** I moved my hands in front of my throat, thumbs still below my fingers (figure 30). I said *hello* to my soul again:

*Dear my beloved soul, I love you. Please sit in my
throat. Please receive golden light and golden liquid
in my fifth soul house to purify; boost energy, stamina, vitality, and immunity; and transform your
soul frequency to divine soul frequency. Do a good
job. Thank you.*

I said *hello* to Heaven and Earth again:

*Dear Divine, dear Heaven, and dear Mother Earth, I
love you, honor you, and appreciate you. Please continue to bless my fifth soul house and my soul to purify my soul further. I am very grateful. Thank you.*

I sang the Divine Soul Song of Yin Yang for the fifth soul
house:

*Xi Ya
Xi Ya Xi Ya You
Xi Ya Xi Ya You
Xi Ya Xi Ya Xi Ya You
Xi Ya Xi Ya Xi Ya Xi Ya You*

Then I sang the four Yin Yang Energy and Matter Circles,
following the same principles of the *Tian Di Ren* practice:

*Hei Heng Hong Ah Xi Yi Weng You
You Weng Yi Xi Ah Hong Heng Hei
You Weng Yi Xi Ah Hong Heng Hei
Hei Heng Hong Ah Xi Yi Weng You*

The Divine then told me to put my soul inside my brain. I did: "Dear my beloved soul, please sit in my brain in the **sixth soul house.** Thank you." I moved my hands in front of my forehead, thumbs below the fingers (see figure 31), and sang the Divine Soul Song of Yin Yang for the sixth soul house:

> *Yi Ya*
> *Yi Ya Yi Ya You*
> *Yi Ya Yi Ya You*
> *Yi Ya Yi Ya Yi Ya You*
> *Yi Ya Yi Ya Yi Ya Yi Ya You*

Then I did the *Tian Di Ren* practice, following the same principles as for the previous soul houses. I sang:

> *Hei Heng Hong Ah Xi Yi Weng You*
> *You Weng Yi Xi Ah Hong Heng Hei*
> *You Weng Yi Xi Ah Hong Heng Hei*
> *Hei Heng Hong Ah Xi Yi Weng You*

Then the Divine told me to ask my soul to sit above my head. I said *hello*: "Dear my beloved soul, please sit above my crown chakra and Bai Hui point in the **seventh soul house.** Thank you." As at every step in this practice, I also asked my soul to receive golden light and golden liquid to purify and transform its soul frequency. I asked for Heaven's and Earth's blessings again as well. Then I moved my hands above my head in the Universal Connection position with my thumbs below my fingers (see figure 32) and sang the Divine Soul Song of Yin Yang for the seventh soul house:

*Weng Ya*
*Weng Ya Weng Ya You*
*Weng Ya Weng Ya You*
*Weng Ya Weng Ya Weng Ya You*
*Weng Ya Weng Ya Weng Ya Weng Ya You*

Then I did *Tian Di Ren* practice for my soul as it sat above my head.

Then the Divine told me to ask my soul to sit in my back upper chest in front of my spinal column in the Wai Jiao. I said *hello* to my soul again:

> *Dear my beloved soul, I love you. Please sit in the upper part of my Wai Jiao. Please receive golden light and golden liquid in my Wai Jiao to purify; boost energy, stamina, vitality, and immunity; and transform your soul frequency to divine soul frequency. Do a good job. Thank you.*

I said *hello* to Heaven and Earth again:

> *Dear Divine, dear Heaven, and dear Mother Earth, I love you, honor you, and appreciate you. Please continue to bless my Wai Jiao and my soul to purify my soul further. I am very grateful. Thank you.*

I moved my hands behind my neck in the Universal Connection position, thumbs still below my fingers (figure 33), and sang the Divine Soul Song of Yin Yang for the Wai Jiao:

> *You Ya*
> *You Ya You Ya You*

*You Ya You Ya You*
*You Ya You Ya You Ya You*
*You Ya You Ya You Ya You Ya You*

Then the Divine asked me to do the *Tian Di Ren* practice again:

> *Hei Heng Hong Ah Xi Yi Weng You*
> *You Weng Yi Xi Ah Hong Heng Hei*
> *You Weng Yi Xi Ah Hong Heng Hei*
> *Hei Heng Hong Ah Xi Yi Weng You*

Finally, the Divine told me to ask my soul to sit in my Ling Gong. The Ling Gong, or "Soul Temple," lies between the Message Center and heart. ("Ling" means *soul*. "Gong" means *temple*.) I moved my hands in the inverted Universal Connection position, with my thumbs below my fingers, in front of my Ling Gong. For this part of the practice, the Divine taught me to sing the Divine Soul Song for All Five Divine Elements in the Whole Body. I will discuss this Divine Soul Song in the next section.

> *Ai Ya* ("Ai" is pronounced *eye*.)
> *Ai Ya Ai Ya You*
> *Ai Ya Ai Ya You*
> *Ai Ya Ai Ya Ai Ya You*
> *Ai Ya Ai Ya Ai Ya Ai Ya You*

Then I concluded with the *Tian Di Ren* practice:

> *Hei Heng Hong Ah Xi Yi Weng You*
> *You Weng Yi Xi Ah Hong Heng Hei*

*You Weng Yi Xi Ah Hong Heng Hei*
*Hei Heng Hong Ah Xi Yi Weng You*

When I was done, the Divine told me: *This is the further teaching for you today.* I instantly bowed down to the floor one thousand times in appreciation. I felt that even if I had bowed down from that moment to the end of my life I could not honor the Divine enough for releasing these divine sacred soul secrets, wisdom, knowledge, and practices to help humanity. I cannot bow down to the Divine enough for the countless Divine Soul Transplants the Divine has given to humanity through my service for the last six years. I cannot honor the Divine enough. I am forever grateful.

I realized how deep and profound are the secrets the Divine has given through this practice. To summarize:

- The seven soul houses are the keys for healing, rejuvenation, and prolonging life.
- This practice is a breakthrough divine soul method for divine healing, prevention of sickness, rejuvenation, and prolonging life.
- You must also purify and transform the frequency of your soul and your soul houses further and further.
- This practice brings the *Tian Di Ren* (Heaven Earth Human Being) practice directly to your soul and your soul houses for purification and transformation.

*Hao! Hao! Hao!*
*Thank you. Thank you. Thank you.*

## The Second Divine Universal Law:
## The Universal Law of Five Elements

Five thousand years ago *The Yellow Emperor's Internal Classic*, the authoritative book of traditional Chinese medicine, revealed the philosophy and theory of Five Elements. This theory is the second Divine Universal Law.

BASIC CONCEPTS OF FIVE ELEMENTS

The Five Elements are Wood, Fire, Earth, Metal, and Water. They represent the five natures found throughout all universes. There are Wood, Fire, Earth, Metal, and Water elements on Mother Earth. The five natures are also in stars. Entire galaxies and universes can also be divided into the five natures of the Five Elements.

*Everything* can be classified into the Five Elements. Table 3 below shows how many common things are represented by the Five Elements, including weather, the seasons, and direction. Traditional Chinese medicine has applied the theory of Five Elements for five thousand years. Table 3 also shows how Five Elements theory applies to organs, tissues, and other aspects of the human body.

The table illustrates how the Five Elements connect with nature and with the body. To balance the Five Elements is to balance everything. To balance the Five Elements in the body is to heal and maintain optimum health.

The Five Elements are related and interact in four main ways:

- Generating
- Controlling

Table 3. Five Elements

| Element | Yin Organ | Yang Organ | Body Tissue | Body Fluid | Sense | Unbalanced Emotion | Balanced Emotion |
|---------|-----------|------------|-------------|------------|-------|--------------------|--------------------|
| Wood | Liver | Gallbladder | Tendons Nails | Tears | Eyes Sight | Anger | Patience |
| Fire | Heart | Small Intestine | Blood Vessels | Sweat | Tongue Taste | Depression Anxiety Excitability | Joy |
| Earth | Spleen | Stomach | Muscles | Saliva | Mouth Lips Speech | Worry | Love Compassion |
| Metal | Lung | Large Intestine | Skin | Mucus | Nose Smell | Grief Sadness | Courage |
| Water | Kidney | Urinary Bladder | Bones Joints | Urine | Ear Hearing | Fear | Calmness |

- Overcontrolling
- Reverse Controlling

The *generating* relationship can be understood as a mother-son relationship. The mother gives birth to the son. The mother generates and nourishes the son. The Five Elements are related via the following mother-son pairs:

- Wood produces (is the mother of) Fire.
- Fire produces Earth.
- Earth produces Metal.
- Metal produces Water.
- Water produces Wood.

These relationships can be seen in the natural world, where wood ignites to start a fire, a fire produces ash, earth can be mined for metal, metal carries water (as in a bucket or a pipe), and plants grow from spring rain.

Applying this to the organs of the body, a healthy mother

Table 3. Five Elements (contd.)

| Element | Finger | Taste | Color | Weather | Season | Direction | Phase | Energy |
|---------|--------|-------|-------|---------|--------|-----------|-------|--------|
| Wood | Index | Sour | Green | Windy | Spring | East | New Yang | Generative |
| Fire | Middle | Bitter | Red | Hot | Summer | South | Full Yang | Expansive |
| Earth | Thumb | Sweet | Yellow | Damp | Change of seasons | Central | Yin/Yang Balance | Stabilizing |
| Metal | Ring | Pungent | White | Dry | Autumn | West | New Yin | Contracting |
| Water | Little | Salty | Blue | Cold | Winter | North | Full Yin | Conserving |

organ nourishes the son organ. Therefore, a liver with balanced soul, energy, and matter without blockages will fully nourish the soul, energy, and matter of the heart. In the same way, a healthy heart will nourish the spleen, a healthy spleen will nourish the lungs, healthy lungs will nourish the kidneys, and healthy kidneys will nourish the liver.

The *controlling* relationship shows the order of dominance or control among the Five Elements:

- Wood controls Earth.
- Earth controls Water.
- Water controls Fire.
- Fire controls Metal.
- Metal controls Wood.

In the natural world, wood draws nutrients from earth, earth dams water, water puts out fire, fire melts metal, and metal chops wood.

The *overcontrolling* and *reverse controlling* relationships are unbalanced relationships that can be used to describe and explain pathological conditions in the organs of the body. These relationships and conditions are caused by soul, energy, and matter blockages.

Five Elements theory can be used to guide how to balance the physical body, emotional body, mental body, and spiritual body. It can be applied to balance nature. It can be used to balance planets, stars, galaxies, and universes.

## Divine Soul Song of Five Elements

The Divine Soul Song of Five Elements is another newly released divine practical soul treasure for healing; boosting energy, vitality, stamina, and immunity; preventing sickness; rejuvenation and prolonging life; for balancing Heaven, Earth, and human beings; and for healing humanity, Mother Earth, planets, stars, galaxies, and universes.

HOW I RECEIVED THE DIVINE SOUL SONG
OF FIVE ELEMENTS

During my daily morning conversation with the Divine on June 4, 2008, the Divine gave me the Divine Soul Song of Five Elements. Here is what the Divine told me:

> *Zhi Gang,*
> *I released my Soul Song of Yin Yang to you a short*
> *while ago. You understand the significance and the*
> *power of Yin Yang. You also understand the signifi-*
> *cance and power of Five Elements. Yin Yang and*

*Five Elements are the number-one and number-two*
*universal laws. I release these two Soul Songs to you*
*to ask you to share them with humanity. They are*
*my soul treasures to heal and transform humanity,*
*Mother Earth, and all universes.*

*Zhi Gang,*
*You know* jiao, zhi, gong, shang, *and* yu, *five basic*
*sounds in ancient music* [pronounced *jee-yow* (as
one syllable), *jee, gawng, shang,* and *yü,* respec-
tively]. *Expand them to be my Soul Song of Five*
*Elements.*

Then the Divine gave me more details.
The Divine Soul Song of Wood Element is:

*Jiao Ya*
*Jiao Ya Jiao Ya You*
*Jiao Ya Jiao Ya You*
*Jiao Ya Jiao Ya Jiao Ya You*
*Jiao Ya Jiao Ya Jiao Ya Jiao Ya You*

The Divine Soul Song of Fire Element is:

*Zhi Ya*
*Zhi Ya Zhi Ya You*
*Zhi Ya Zhi Ya You*
*Zhi Ya Zhi Ya Zhi Ya You*
*Zhi Ya Zhi Ya Zhi Ya Zhi Ya You*

The Divine Soul Song of Earth Element is:

*Gong Ya*
*Gong Ya Gong Ya You*
*Gong Ya Gong Ya You*
*Gong Ya Gong Ya Gong Ya You*
*Gong Ya Gong Ya Gong Ya Gong Ya You*

The Divine Soul Song of Metal Element is:

*Shang Ya*
*Shang Ya Shang Ya You*
*Shang Ya Shang Ya You*
*Shang Ya Shang Ya Shang Ya You*
*Shang Ya Shang Ya Shang Ya Shang Ya You*

The Divine Soul Song of Water Element is:

*Yu Ya*
*Yu Ya Yu Ya You*
*Yu Ya Yu Ya You*
*Yu Ya Yu Ya Yu Ya You*
*Yu Ya Yu Ya Yu Ya Yu Ya You*

Finally, the Divine gave me the Divine Soul Song *Ai* for All Five Elements:

*Ai Ya*
*Ai Ya Ai Ya You*
*Ai Ya Ai Ya You*
*Ai Ya Ai Ya Ai Ya You*
*Ai Ya Ai Ya Ai Ya Ai Ya You*

Listen to the Divine Soul Song of Five Elements on track 7 of the enclosed audio CD. See figure 34 in the insert for the music. The melody is identical to that of the Divine Soul Songs of the Seven Soul Houses in the Divine Soul Song of Yin Yang.

The Divine continued to guide me: *The Divine Soul Song of Five Elements can offer healing to humanity, pets, nature, planets, stars, galaxies, and universes.*

Divine Soul Songs carry divine frequency and vibration with divine love, forgiveness, compassion, and light. Their power is beyond words and imagination.

PRACTICE THE DIVINE SOUL SONG OF FIVE ELEMENTS

The Divine also showed me how to practice the Divine Soul Song of Five Elements using the Four Power Techniques for healing, rejuvenation, and prolonging life.

There is a general principle to follow for Body Power in this practice: place one palm over the Lower Dan Tian or lower abdomen (males use the left palm; females use the right palm). This palm will remain anchored throughout the practice of the Divine Soul Song of Five Elements. I will call this the *fixed palm*. The other palm moves over the appropriate yin organ or the Message Center as indicated in the summary in table 4 below, as well as in each step of the practice that follows. I will call this the *moving palm*.

Now I will describe the practice step by step.

## 1. Divine Soul Song of Wood Element

Soul Power     Say *hello: Dear soul, mind, and body of my liver, I love you. You have the power to heal and rejuvenate yourself. Do a good job. Thank you.*

Table 4. Practice of the Divine Soul Song of Five Elements

| Element | Yin Organ | Yang Organ | Color | Sacred Sound |
|---------|-----------|------------|-------|--------------|
| Wood | Liver | Gallbladder | **Green** | Jiao |
| Fire | Heart | Small Intestine | **Red** | Zhi |
| Earth | Spleen | Stomach | **Yellow** | Gong |
| Metal | Lungs | Large Intestine | **White** | Shang |
| Water | Kidneys | Urinary Bladder | **Blue** | Yu |
| All | (Message Center for Whole Body) | | **Rainbow** | Ai |

Body Power    Place the fixed palm over the Lower Dan Tian. Place the moving palm over the liver, which is the major Wood organ. See figure 35 in the insert.

Mind Power    Visualize **green light** radiating in your liver.

Sound Power    Sing or chant the words to the Divine Soul Song of Wood Element:

*Jiao Ya*
*Jiao Ya Jiao Ya You*
*Jiao Ya Jiao Ya You*
*Jiao Ya Jiao Ya Jiao Ya You*
*Jiao Ya Jiao Ya Jiao Ya Jiao Ya You*

## 2. Divine Soul Song of Fire Element

Soul Power    Say *hello: Dear soul, mind, and body of my heart, I love you. You have the power to heal and rejuvenate yourself. Do a good job. Thank you.*

| Body Power | Place the fixed palm over the Lower Dan Tian. Place the moving palm over the heart, which is the major Fire organ. See figure 36. |
| Mind Power | Visualize **red light** radiating in your heart. |
| Sound Power | Sing or chant the words to the Divine Soul Song of Fire Element: |

*Zhi Ya*
*Zhi Ya Zhi Ya You*
*Zhi Ya Zhi Ya You*
*Zhi Ya Zhi Ya Zhi Ya You*
*Zhi Ya Zhi Ya Zhi Ya Zhi Ya You*

## 3. Divine Soul Song of Earth Element

| Soul Power | Say *hello: Dear soul, mind, and body of my spleen, I love you. You have the power to heal and rejuvenate yourself. Do a good job. Thank you.* |
| Body Power | Place the fixed palm over the Lower Dan Tian. Place the moving palm over the spleen, which is the major Earth organ. See figure 37. |
| Mind Power | Visualize **golden light** radiating in your spleen. |
| Sound Power | Sing or chant the words to the Divine Soul Song of Earth Element: |

*Gong Ya*
*Gong Ya Gong Ya You*
*Gong Ya Gong Ya You*
*Gong Ya Gong Ya Gong Ya You*
*Gong Ya Gong Ya Gong Ya Gong Ya You*

## 4. Divine Soul Song of Metal Element

| Soul Power | Say *hello: Dear soul, mind, and body of my lungs, I love you. You have the power to heal* |

*and rejuvenate yourselves. Do a good job. Thank you.*

| | |
|---|---|
| Body Power | Place the fixed palm over the Lower Dan Tian. Place the moving palm over a lung, which is the major Metal organ. See figure 38. |
| Mind Power | Visualize **white light** radiating in your lungs. |
| Sound Power | Sing or chant the words to the Divine Soul Song of Metal Element: |

*Shang Ya*
*Shang Ya Shang Ya You*
*Shang Ya Shang Ya You*
*Shang Ya Shang Ya Shang Ya You*
*Shang Ya Shang Ya Shang Ya Shang Ya You*

## 5. Divine Soul Song of Water Element

| | |
|---|---|
| Soul Power | Say *hello: Dear soul, mind, and body of my kidneys, I love you. You have the power to heal and rejuvenate yourselves. Do a good job. Thank you.* |
| Body Power | Place the fixed palm over the Lower Dan Tian. Place the moving palm over a kidney, which is the major Water organ. See figure 39. |
| Mind Power | Visualize **blue light** radiating in your kidneys. |
| Sound Power | Sing or chant the words to the Divine Soul Song of Water Element: |

*Yu Ya*
*Yu Ya Yu Ya You*
*Yu Ya Yu Ya You*
*Yu Ya Yu Ya Yu Ya You*
*Yu Ya Yu Ya Yu Ya Yu Ya You*

## 6. Divine Soul Song *Ai* for All Five Elements

Soul Power       Say *hello: Dear soul, mind, and body of my whole body, I love you. You have the power to heal and rejuvenate yourselves. Do a good job. Thank you.*

Body Power       Place the fixed palm over the Lower Dan Tian. Place the moving palm over the Message Center. See figure 40.

Mind Power       Visualize **rainbow light** vibrating in your whole body.

Sound Power       Sing or chant the words to the Divine Soul Song *Ai* for All Five Elements:
*Ai Ya*
*Ai Ya Ai Ya You*
*Ai Ya Ai Ya You*
*Ai Ya Ai Ya Ai Ya You*
*Ai Ya Ai Ya Ai Ya Ai Ya You*

"Ai" means *love* in Chinese. Love melts all blockages and transforms all life. The Divine Soul Song *Ai* for All Five Elements carries the power of divine love. All Divine Soul Songs carry the power of divine love.

Now let's do the practice of the Divine Sacred Soul Songs of Five Elements together straight through from beginning to end. I will also add the Divine Yin Yang Energy Circle and the Divine Yin Yang Matter Circle at the end of the practice:

> *Dear soul, mind, and body of my major organs and*
> *my whole body,*
> *I love you.*
> *You have the power to heal and rejuvenate yourselves.*

*Do a good job.*
*Thank you.*


*Dear soul, mind, and body of the Divine Soul Song of*
   *Five Elements,*
*I love you, honor you, and appreciate you.*
*Please offer me a blessing for healing and rejuvenation.*
*I am very grateful.*
*Thank you.*


*Jiao Ya*
*Jiao Ya Jiao Ya You*
*Jiao Ya Jiao Ya You*
*Jiao Ya Jiao Ya Jiao Ya You*
*Jiao Ya Jiao Ya Jiao Ya Jiao Ya You*


*Zhi Ya*
*Zhi Ya Zhi Ya You*
*Zhi Ya Zhi Ya You*
*Zhi Ya Zhi Ya Zhi Ya You*
*Zhi Ya Zhi Ya Zhi Ya Zhi Ya You*


*Gong Ya*
*Gong Ya Gong Ya You*
*Gong Ya Gong Ya You*
*Gong Ya Gong Ya Gong Ya You*
*Gong Ya Gong Ya Gong Ya Gong Ya You*


*Shang Ya*
*Shang Ya Shang Ya You*
*Shang Ya Shang Ya You*

*Shang Ya Shang Ya Shang Ya You*
*Shang Ya Shang Ya Shang Ya Shang Ya You*

*Yu Ya*
*Yu Ya Yu Ya You*
*Yu Ya Yu Ya You*
*Yu Ya Yu Ya Yu Ya You*
*Yu Ya Yu Ya Yu Ya Yu Ya You*

*Ai Ya*
*Ai Ya Ai Ya You*
*Ai Ya Ai Ya You*
*Ai Ya Ai Ya Ai Ya You*
*Ai Ya Ai Ya Ai Ya Ai Ya You*

*Hei Heng Hong Ah Xi Yi Weng You*
*Hei Heng Hong Ah Xi Yi Weng You*
*Hei Heng Hong Ah Xi Yi Weng You*
*Hei Heng Hong Ah Xi Yi Weng You*

*You Weng Yi Xi Ah Hong Heng Hei*
*You Weng Yi Xi Ah Hong Heng Hei*
*You Weng Yi Xi Ah Hong Heng Hei*
*You Weng Yi Xi Ah Hong Heng Hei*

*Hao! Hao! Hao!*
*Thank you. Thank you. Thank you.*

APPLY THE DIVINE SOUL SONG OF FIVE ELEMENTS TO HEAL, REJUVENATE, AND TRANSFORM YOU, HUMANITY, MOTHER EARTH, AND ALL UNIVERSES

To apply the Divine Soul Song of Five Elements to heal the Wood element, including the liver, gallbladder, tendons, eyes, and anger, do this practice with me now:

> *Dear Divine Soul Song of Wood Element,*
> *I love you, honor you, and appreciate you.*
> *Please heal my Wood organs and emotions.* (You may make specific requests.)
> *I am very grateful.*
> *Thank you.*

Use the Body Power and Mind Power techniques shared in the previous section.

Then sing or chant the words; as always, you may chant silently or aloud:

> *Jiao Ya*
> *Jiao Ya Jiao Ya You*
> *Jiao Ya Jiao Ya You*
> *Jiao Ya Jiao Ya Jiao Ya You*
> *Jiao Ya Jiao Ya Jiao Ya Jiao Ya You*

Sing for three to five minutes per time, three to five times per day—the more, the better.

Close the practice in the usual way:

> *Hao! Hao! Hao!*
> *Thank you. Thank you. Thank you.*

To apply the Divine Soul Song of Five Elements to heal the Fire element, including the heart, small intestine, blood vessels, tongue, and depression, anxiety, or excitability, do this practice with me now. Start by saying *hello:*

> *Dear Divine Soul Song of Fire Element,*
> *I love you, honor you, and appreciate you.*
> *Please heal my Fire organs and emotions* (you may
>     make specific requests).
> *I am very grateful.*
> *Thank you.*

Use the Body Power and Mind Power techniques shared in the previous section.

Then sing or chant the words:

> *Zhi Ya*
> *Zhi Ya Zhi Ya You*
> *Zhi Ya Zhi Ya You*
> *Zhi Ya Zhi Ya Zhi Ya You*
> *Zhi Ya Zhi Ya Zhi Ya Zhi Ya You*

Sing for three to five minutes per time, three to five times per day—the more, the better.

Close the practice in the usual way.

To apply the Divine Soul Song of Five Elements to heal the Earth element, including the spleen, stomach, muscles, mouth and lips, and worry, do this practice with me now:

> *Dear Divine Soul Song of Earth Element,*
> *I love you, honor you, and appreciate you.*

*Please heal my Earth organs and emotions* (you may
   make specific requests).
*I am very grateful.*
*Thank you.*

Use the Body Power and Mind Power techniques shared in
the previous section.

Then sing or chant the words:

*Gong Ya*
*Gong Ya Gong Ya You*
*Gong Ya Gong Ya You*
*Gong Ya Gong Ya Gong Ya You*
*Gong Ya Gong Ya Gong Ya Gong Ya You*

Sing for three to five minutes per time, three to five times per
day—the more, the better.

Close the practice in the usual way.

To apply the Divine Soul Song of Five Elements to heal the
Metal element, including the lungs, large intestine, skin, nose,
and grief or sadness, do this practice with me now:

*Dear Divine Soul Song of Metal Element,*
*I love you, honor you, and appreciate you.*
*Please heal my Metal organs and emotions* (you may
   make specific requests).
*I am very grateful.*
*Thank you.*

Use the Body Power and Mind Power techniques shared in
the previous section.

Then sing or chant the words:

> *Shang Ya*
> *Shang Ya Shang Ya You*
> *Shang Ya Shang Ya You*
> *Shang Ya Shang Ya Shang Ya You*
> *Shang Ya Shang Ya Shang Ya Shang Ya You*

Sing for three to five minutes per time, three to five times per day—the more, the better.

Close the practice in the usual way.

To apply the Divine Soul Song of Five Elements to heal the Water element, including the kidneys, urinary bladder, bones and joints, ears, and fear, do this practice with me now:

> *Dear Divine Soul Song of Water Element,*
> *I love you, honor you, and appreciate you.*
> *Please heal my Water organs and emotions* (you may
>     make specific requests).
> *I am very grateful.*
> *Thank you.*

Use the Body Power and Mind Power techniques shared in the previous section.

Then sing or chant the words:

> *Yu Ya*
> *Yu Ya Yu Ya You*
> *Yu Ya Yu Ya You*
> *Yu Ya Yu Ya Yu Ya You*
> *Yu Ya Yu Ya Yu Ya Yu Ya You*

Sing for three to five minutes per time, three to five times per day—the more, the better.

Close the practice in the usual way:

> *Hao! Hao! Hao!*
> *Thank you. Thank you. Thank you.*

DIVINE SOUL DOWNLOADS OF THE DIVINE SOUL SONG
OF FIVE ELEMENTS

Now I am delighted to share with you that I have asked the Divine to preprogram six Divine Soul Downloads of the Divine Soul Song of Five Elements.

I am offering the following permanent Divine Soul Downloads:

- Divine Soul Transplant of the Divine Soul Song *Jiao* for Wood Element
- Divine Soul Transplant of the Divine Soul Song *Zhi* for Fire Element
- Divine Soul Transplant of the Divine Soul Song *Gong* for Earth Element
- Divine Soul Transplant of the Divine Soul Song *Shang* for Metal Element
- Divine Soul Transplant of the Divine Soul Song *Yu* for Water Element
- Divine Soul Transplant of the Divine Soul Song *Ai* for All Five Elements

These are the twelfth through seventeenth Divine Soul Downloads offered to readers of this book. I will offer these six treasures in a different way: by registration on my website. If you would like to receive these priceless divine treasures, visit www .drsha.com. On the home page you will find a link to "Soul Power Series Divine Downloads." After you complete your registration there as instructed, I will offer these Divine Soul Downloads in my Sunday Divine Blessings teleconference from 5:00 to 7:00 PM Pacific Time to those who have registered in the preceding week.

You are not required to be in the teleconference to receive these treasures, but you must register. You will then receive the Divine Soul Downloads the following Sunday whether you are in the teleconference or not. You are required to have a copy of this book, whether you purchased it or received it as a gift. Then register. Then the permanent treasures will be downloaded to your soul. Otherwise you cannot receive them.

The Divine told me that after my physical life ends, people can still receive the treasures by registering. The Divine will preprogram the downloads for people who register properly.

I welcome you and your loved ones to join my Divine Blessings teleconference every Sunday.

APPLY DIVINE SOUL DOWNLOADS OF THE DIVINE SOUL SONG OF FIVE ELEMENTS TO HEAL, REJUVENATE, AND TRANSFORM YOU, HUMANITY, MOTHER EARTH, AND ALL UNIVERSES

After you have registered and received the Divine Soul Downloads of the Divine Soul Song of Five Elements as I explained in the preceding section, you can immediately invoke and practice with the treasures. I would like to encourage you and lead you to invoke these divine treasures to offer universal service. The Five

Elements are the fundamental elements for everyone and everything in the universe. You can invoke these divine souls not only
to receive and offer blessings for human beings. You can invoke
these treasures to offer healing, blessing, rejuvenation, prolongation of life, and life transformation for animals, organizations,
cities, countries, Mother Earth, countless planets, stars, galaxies,
and universes. The applications of these Divine Soul Downloads
are unlimited.

For example, there are countless trees, flowers, and grasses on
Mother Earth and in the universes. They all belong to the Wood
element. There are also entire planets, stars, galaxies, and universes that belong to the Wood element. For example, the planet
Jupiter belongs to the Wood element.

Join me now to offer universal service to the Wood element.
Here is how to practice:

> *Dear divine soul of the Divine Soul Song Jiao for*
> *Wood Element downloaded to my soul,*[11]
> *I love you, honor you, and appreciate you.*
> *Please turn on to give divine healing, blessing, and*
> *transformation to my Wood organs, including the*
> *liver and gallbladder, and other related organs.*
> *Please also give divine healing, blessing, and transfor-*
> *mation to all trees, flowers, cities, countries, planets,*
> *stars, galaxies, and universes related to the Wood*
> *element.*
> *I am very grateful.*
> *Thank you.*

---

11. If you have not yet received this Divine Soul Transplant, replace this first line with: *Dear
Divine Soul Song of Divine Wood Element Jiao, I love you* . . . and make similar adjustments to
the following practices in this section.

Then sing or chant the words of this Divine Soul Song:

*Jiao Ya*
*Jiao Ya Jiao Ya You*
*Jiao Ya Jiao Ya You*
*Jiao Ya Jiao Ya Jiao Ya You*
*Jiao Ya Jiao Ya Jiao Ya Jiao Ya You*

Sing or chant three to five minutes per time, three to five times per day. The more you sing or chant, the better.

Close this and the following practices in the usual way.

Now let me show you how to do a group soul healing by applying Divine Soul Transplants of the Divine Soul Song of Five Elements. Whether you have a group of two people or thousands of people, this is the way to practice:

> *Dear Divine Soul Transplant of the Divine Soul Song*
>     Jiao *for Wood Element downloaded to my soul,*
> *I love you, honor you, and appreciate you.*
> *Please turn on to heal and rejuvenate our Wood element organs, including the liver, gallbladder, tendons, and eyes, and remove anger.* (You may also make relevant specific requests in this and in the following practices.)
> *We are very grateful.*
> *Thank you.*

Then sing or chant the words to this Divine Soul Song together.

*Jiao Ya*
*Jiao Ya Jiao Ya You*

*Jiao Ya Jiao Ya You*
*Jiao Ya Jiao Ya Jiao Ya You*
*Jiao Ya Jiao Ya Jiao Ya Jiao Ya You*

Sing this Divine Soul Song at least four times. There is no time limit to this practice—the longer, the better.

The next practice for group soul healing with these Divine Soul Downloads is:

> *Dear Divine Soul Transplant of the Divine Soul Song*
>    Zhi *for Fire Element downloaded to my soul,*
> *I love you, honor you, and appreciate you.*
> *Please turn on to heal and rejuvenate our Fire element*
>    *organs, including the heart, small intestine, blood*
>    *vessels, and tongue, and remove depression and*
>    *anxiety.*
> *We are very grateful.*
> *Thank you.*

Then sing or chant the words to this Divine Soul Song together:

*Zhi Ya*
*Zhi Ya Zhi Ya You*
*Zhi Ya Zhi Ya You*
*Zhi Ya Zhi Ya Zhi Ya You*
*Zhi Ya Zhi Ya Zhi Ya Zhi Ya You*

Sing this Divine Soul Song at least four times. There is no time limit to this practice—the longer, the better.

The third practice for group soul healing is:

*Dear Divine Soul Transplant of the Divine Soul Song*
   *Gong for Earth Element downloaded to my soul,*
*I love you, honor you, and appreciate you.*
*Please turn on to heal and rejuvenate our Earth ele-*
   *ment organs, including the spleen, stomach, muscles,*
   *and mouth and gums, and remove worry.*
*We are very grateful.*
*Thank you.*

Then sing or chant the words to this Divine Soul Song together:

*Gong Ya*
*Gong Ya Gong Ya You*
*Gong Ya Gong Ya You*
*Gong Ya Gong Ya Gong Ya You*
*Gong Ya Gong Ya Gong Ya Gong Ya You*

Sing this Divine Soul Song at least four times. There is no time limit to this practice—the longer, the better.

The fourth practice for group soul healing is:

*Dear Divine Soul Transplant of the Divine Soul Song*
   *Shang for Metal Element downloaded to my soul,*
*I love you, honor you, and appreciate you.*
*Please turn on to heal and rejuvenate our Metal ele-*
   *ment organs, including the lungs, large intestine,*
   *skin, and nose, and remove sadness and grief.*
*We are very grateful.*
*Thank you.*

Then sing or chant the words to this Divine Soul Song together:

*Shang Ya*
*Shang Ya Shang Ya You*
*Shang Ya Shang Ya You*
*Shang Ya Shang Ya Shang Ya You*
*Shang Ya Shang Ya Shang Ya Shang Ya You*

Sing this Divine Soul Song at least four times. There is no time limit to this practice—the longer, the better.

The fifth practice for group soul healing is:

*Dear Divine Soul Transplant of the Divine Soul Song*
   *Yu for Water Element downloaded to my soul,*
*I love you, honor you, and appreciate you.*
*Please turn on to heal and rejuvenate our Water ele-*
   *ment organs, including the kidneys, urinary blad-*
   *der, bones, and ears, and remove fear.*
*We are very grateful.*
*Thank you.*

Then sing or chant the words to this Divine Soul Song together:

*Yu Ya*
*Yu Ya Yu Ya You*
*Yu Ya Yu Ya You*
*Yu Ya Yu Ya Yu Ya You*
*Yu Ya Yu Ya Yu Ya Yu Ya You*

Sing this Divine Soul Song at least four times. There is no time limit to this practice—the longer, the better.

The sixth practice for group soul healing is for all sicknesses of the physical, emotional, mental, and spiritual bodies:

> *Dear Divine Soul Transplant of the Divine Soul Song*
> *Ai for All Five Elements downloaded to my soul,*
> *I love you, honor you, and appreciate you.*
> *Please turn on to heal and rejuvenate our physical,*
> *emotional, mental, and spiritual bodies. (You may*
> *also make specific requests.)*
> *We are very grateful.*
> *Thank you.*

Then sing or chant the words to this Divine Soul Song:

> *Ai Ya*
> *Ai Ya Ai Ya You*
> *Ai Ya Ai Ya You*
> *Ai Ya Ai Ya Ai Ya You*
> *Ai Ya Ai Ya Ai Ya Ai Ya You*

Sing this Divine Soul Song at least four times. There is no time limit to this practice—the longer, the better.

> *Hao! Hao! Hao!*
> *Thank you. Thank you. Thank you.*

Now let me show you how to serve all of Mother Earth by applying Divine Soul Transplants of the Divine Soul Song of Five Elements to offer a soul healing.

It is well known that Mother Earth has major environmental imbalances. Many trees and entire forests are being destroyed. Land is mined until it is lifeless. Many bodies of water and much of the air are polluted. Polar ice is shrinking. Weather is becoming more extreme. The Divine Soul Transplants of the Divine Soul Song of Five Elements can serve Mother Earth with great healing. These divine souls can help balance the environment. They can help purify the water. They can help cleanse the air.

In 2001 the Divine told me:

*The divine solution to purify pollution is the soul solution. When millions of people sing or chant together, the frequency and the vibration of divine love, forgiveness, compassion, and light can purify pollution.*

I responded to the Divine: "I am delighted to wait for the day when millions of people will sing and chant together to purify pollution in the air and in the water." Dr. Masaru Emoto has done research on the effects of chanting, prayer, and message on purifying water. I wish the day that millions of people chant to purify pollution will come as soon as possible.

You can be an early bird! This is the way to do it. As always, we start by saying *hello.* Join me now:

*Dear Divine Soul Transplants of the Divine Soul Song
    of Five Elements downloaded to my soul,
I love you, honor you, and appreciate you.
Please turn on to heal and balance all Five Elements
    on Mother Earth.
Dear soul, mind, and body of Mother Earth,*

*Dear all Wood elements, including all trees, grasses,*
*and flowers on Mother Earth,*
*Dear all Fire elements, including heat, fire, and elec-*
*tricity on Mother Earth,*
*Dear all Earth elements, including soil and land on*
*Mother Earth,*
*Dear all Metal elements, including iron, steel, and all*
*kinds of metal instruments on Mother Earth,*
*Dear all Water elements, including oceans, rivers, and*
*other liquids on Mother Earth,*
*I love you, honor you, and appreciate you.*
*Please join us in singing or chanting to offer and re-*
*ceive blessings from the Divine Soul Transplants of*
*the Divine Soul Song of Five Elements and from the*
*Divine Soul Song of Five Elements itself.*
*We are very grateful.*
*Thank you. Thank you. Thank you.*

Everything has a soul. We are calling every soul of everything on Mother Earth to sing and chant together with us to receive a healing and blessing from Divine Soul Transplants of the Divine Soul Song of Five Elements.

The Divine taught me soul chanting in July 2003. Since then I have constantly called the souls of humanity, Mother Earth, planets, stars, galaxies, and universes to do soul singing or soul chanting of Soul Songs together to serve humanity, Mother Earth, and all universes. This book brings this soul singing and soul chanting soul service to humanity.

Let us receive the healing and blessing of Divine Soul Transplants of the Divine Soul Song of Five Elements and sing the

Divine Soul Song of Five Elements together. This is your service to Mother Earth. To serve is to transform. This service could benefit and transform every aspect of your life.

Sing or chant with me now, silently or aloud:

*Jiao Ya*
*Jiao Ya Jiao Ya You*
*Jiao Ya Jiao Ya You*
*Jiao Ya Jiao Ya Jiao Ya You*
*Jiao Ya Jiao Ya Jiao Ya Jiao Ya You*

*Zhi Ya*
*Zhi Ya Zhi Ya You*
*Zhi Ya Zhi Ya You*
*Zhi Ya Zhi Ya Zhi Ya You*
*Zhi Ya Zhi Ya Zhi Ya Zhi Ya You*

*Gong Ya*
*Gong Ya Gong Ya You*
*Gong Ya Gong Ya You*
*Gong Ya Gong Ya Gong Ya You*
*Gong Ya Gong Ya Gong Ya Gong Ya You*

*Shang Ya*
*Shang Ya Shang Ya You*
*Shang Ya Shang Ya You*
*Shang Ya Shang Ya Shang Ya You*
*Shang Ya Shang Ya Shang Ya Shang Ya You*

*Yu Ya*
*Yu Ya Yu Ya You*

*Yu Ya Yu Ya You*
*Yu Ya Yu Ya Yu Ya You*
*Yu Ya Yu Ya Yu Ya Yu Ya You*

*Ai Ya*
*Ai Ya Ai Ya You*
*Ai Ya Ai Ya You*
*Ai Ya Ai Ya Ai Ya You*
*Ai Ya Ai Ya Ai Ya Ai Ya You*

*Hei Heng Hong Ah Xi Yi Weng You*
*Hei Heng Hong Ah Xi Yi Weng You*
*Hei Heng Hong Ah Xi Yi Weng You*
*Hei Heng Hong Ah Xi Yi Weng You*

*You Weng Yi Xi Ah Hong Heng Hei*
*You Weng Yi Xi Ah Hong Heng Hei*
*You Weng Yi Xi Ah Hong Heng Hei*
*You Weng Yi Xi Ah Hong Heng Hei*

*Hao! Hao! Hao!*
*Thank you. Thank you. Thank you.*

In the same way, you can offer healing, blessings, and service to all planets, all stars, all galaxies, and all universes. Five Elements is a universal law. Sing the Divine Soul Song of Five Elements and ask the permanent Divine Soul Song Transplants of the Divine Soul Song of Five Elements to offer healing and transformation for humanity, Mother Earth, and all universes. The more you serve, the more blessings you will receive.

I wish you will serve more.

I wish you will serve well.

Thank you. Thank you. Thank you.

## The World Soul Healing, Peace and Enlightenment Movement

In June 2008 I held a Soul Healing and Enlightenment retreat in Quebec, Canada. Nearly five hundred people gathered for the retreat. During my teaching, the Divine guided me instantly in the moment:

> *Zhi Gang,*
> *Create the World Soul Healing, Peace and Enlighten-*
> *ment Movement. The key service of this movement is*
> *to sing and chant Divine Soul Songs to offer soul*
> *healing, peace, and enlightenment to the world.*

I immediately shared this divine guidance with all the participants. This divine calling received an enthusiastic response on the spot. We formed a ten-member Founding Committee to lead all of the participants at the retreat as the first group of general members. We decided to gather with the public in a half-hour teleconference every Tuesday to focus on singing four major Divine Soul Songs as service:

- Divine Soul Song *Love, Peace and Harmony*
- Divine Soul Song of Yin Yang
- Divine Soul Song of Five Elements
- Divine Soul Song *God Gives His Heart to Me*

We held our first weekly Divine Sacred Soul Song Singing Gathering teleconference on July 1, 2008, right after the retreat ended. Nearly one thousand people joined us from around the world. The number of participants continues to increase. We have expanded this service to five days a week, Monday through Friday. You have already learned in this book how one person singing a Divine Soul Song can offer healing, rejuvenation, and transformation to all universes. Imagine how much greater is the power of a thousand people singing Divine Soul Songs together. My goal is to have millions of people participating regularly. This is a divine service for you, humanity, Mother Earth, and all universes. I am honored to invite you and your loved ones to join this service.

## The Third Divine Universal Law: The Universal Law of Message Energy Matter

Message Energy Matter is the third Divine Universal Law.

### MESSAGE ENERGY MATTER THEORY

In 1988 my most beloved spiritual father, Dr. and Master Zhi Chen Guo, was teaching a group of students. He suddenly understood that his integrated concept of message, energy, and matter *is* the Tao, and an indisputable law of nature. In other words, Message Energy Matter Theory is applicable to and valid in any aspect of human life, in any kind of space, and in any universe, down to every action and even every intention. It is a universal law.

The Message Energy Matter Theory states:

*Message is soul or spirit.*
*Matter and energy are carriers of message.*

*Message can directly affect the transformation between*
*matter inside cells and energy outside of cells.*

Everything in the universe is made of matter. Matter is infinitely divisible. The smallest unit of matter is the information
wave, or *message*. Messages accumulate to form energy, so energy
can also be considered to be "tiny," or refined, matter. In modern
science, this was expressed by Einstein in his renowned formula
of mass-energy equivalence: $E = mc^2$.

When a volcano erupts, matter converts to energy. In an
earthquake, the vibration of matter also explodes into energy. In
the body, cells consist of matter. Cells are constantly vibrating—
expanding and contracting. When a cell contracts, some cell
matter transforms to energy, which moves out of the cell into the
body space. When a cell expands, some energy in the body space
returns to the cell to become matter.

Let me give an example of energy transforming to matter
inside the body. There is a famous statement in *The Yellow
Emperor's Internal Classic*:

**Ju zhe cheng xing; san zhe cheng feng.**

The literal meaning of these words is accumulation (*ju*), thing
(*zhe*), becomes (*cheng*), shape (*xing*), dissipation (*san*), thing
(*zhe*), becomes (*cheng*), wind (*feng*), but the statement can be
translated as:

*When energy accumulates, it becomes a form.*
*When energy dissipates, the form disappears, just like*
*    the wind flowing away.*

This is an energy and spiritual secret that explains how a tumor or cancer is formed. When energy accumulates in a specific part of the body, a form is produced. This form is a tumor or cancer. Dissipate the energy and this form will disappear. Tumors and cancers will disappear. This is an example of how energy (tiny matter) accumulates to transform to matter and how matter dissipates to transform to energy.

As I already said, energy is also matter. Energy is minute particles of matter. When this tiny matter gets even tinier, it becomes an information wave, or message. Message, energy, and matter in the usual sense are all forms of matter.

The division of matter becomes energy. The division of energy becomes message. The division of message becomes matter. The accumulation of matter becomes energy. The accumulation of energy becomes message. The accumulation of message becomes matter. Message, energy, and matter are interchangeable. Matter and energy are carriers of message. Matter and energy *are* message.

Message can directly adjust and regulate cell and organ functions, heal and prevent illnesses, rejuvenate soul, mind, and body, prolong life, and develop the intelligence of the brain and the potential powers of the soul. Message is soul or spirit. The power of message is the power of soul. Message can purify and uplift the soul and help the soul complete its journey. Message will help all souls join as one to become harmonized. There will be love, peace, and harmony on Mother Earth and in all universes.

THE POWER OF SOUL

In 2006 my book *Soul Mind Body Medicine: A Complete Soul Healing System for Optimum Health and Vitality* was published.

Two of the key wisdoms in this book are that everyone and everything in the universe consists of soul, mind, and body, and that there are three causes of sickness.

The first cause of sickness is soul blockages, which are one's spiritual debts from previous lives and this life. These spiritual debts are bad karma. Over the last several years, I have come to understand deeply that soul blockages are the root blockages of every aspect of life, including health, relationships, and finances.

The second cause of sickness is energy blockages. Five thousand years ago *The Yellow Emperor's Internal Classic* introduced the concept of chi. Guidance for healing in traditional Chinese medicine has been based on this fundamental teaching of the Yellow Emperor: *If chi flows, one is healthy. If chi is blocked, one is sick.* Dr. and Master Guo expanded this concept. As I explained above, when cells contract, matter inside cells transforms into energy outside of cells. When cells expand, energy outside of cells transforms into matter inside cells. Master Guo realized that this cellular transformation between matter and energy is normally in relative balance. If this balance is broken, sickness will occur.

The third cause of sickness is matter blockages. Matter blockages and energy blockages are closely related through the transformation between matter and energy at the cellular level.

Modern scientists talk about message. Soul is message. Soul is spirit. They are the same thing with different names. Energy and matter are the carriers of message. Message is the soul. Message directs the transformation between matter inside cells and energy outside of cells. Soul healing is the application of soul frequency, vibration, and direction to adjust and balance the transformation between the matter inside cells and energy outside of cells. Soul is the boss for human beings. Soul is the boss for life. Soul can promote energy flow and blood flow. Soul can remove energy and matter blockages and balance the transformation between matter inside cells and energy outside of cells.

What can be done about soul blockages? For example, if your body soul has a blockage, which is bad karma, how can you address it? One approach is to ask the higher saints, holy saints, Taoist saints, buddhas, lamas, gurus, and ascended masters in Heaven to help you. There are high-level spiritual fathers and mothers in all layers of Heaven. They are in the soul form, not in a physical form. There are also many great spiritual fathers and mothers in physical form on Mother Earth. Ask your physical spiritual fathers and mothers, and ask your heavenly spiritual fathers and mothers, to remove your soul blockages and give you healing.

For example, millions of people honor Jesus. Jesus was given divine abilities for healing. Bible stories about his healings have inspired millions of people. Jesus is not in a physical form now, but in the soul form Jesus remains an unconditional universal servant. You can ask Jesus to give you a healing blessing anytime, anywhere. It is very simple to do:

> *Dear Jesus,*
> *I love you, honor you, and appreciate you.*
> *Please give me a healing for* _____ (make your
>   request).
> *I am very grateful.*
> *Thank you. Thank you. Thank you.*

Then chant repeatedly, silently or aloud:

> *Jesus heals me*
> *Jesus heals me*

*Jesus heals me*
*Jesus heals me . . .*

Remember, to ask Jesus to give you a healing is not to expect that Jesus will immediately heal you. If you have a chronic or life-threatening condition, it takes some time to restore your health. Jesus's soul can definitely heal some cases in seconds, but this does not mean that Jesus's soul can heal all sickness in seconds. Therefore, to do soul healing, remember the teaching I gave to humanity. The teaching is to say *hello* to souls in the universe and totally relax your soul, mind, and body. Connect with the soul you are invoking. Spend time with that soul to receive healing. Generally speaking, spend three to five minutes per time and practice three to five times per day. There are no time limits. If you can spend a half hour or one hour with Jesus's soul, you will receive much more healing from his soul.

Jesus, divine holy saints, Taoist saints, buddhas—all great spiritual fathers and mothers in all layers of Heaven—can do miracles. You can be healed in seconds by invoking them. There is no doubt about it. But remember that many cases need time to be completely healed.

The previous books in my Soul Power Series were *Soul Wisdom* (2008), *Soul Communication* (2008), and *The Power of Soul* (2009). *The Power of Soul* is the authoritative book of the Soul Power Series. Every book in the Soul Power Series carries divine sacred wisdom, knowledge, and practical techniques to empower readers. Each book includes numerous sacred wisdoms and practices that can transform your life. Some people practice Soul Power techniques for a short time. When they do not see significant improvement in healing or life transformation for relationships and finances right away, they make a quick mind judgment.

They say, "Soul healing does not work. These practices and these techniques do not work."

I have been blessed in my life experience. I have studied with teachers who are the national treasures of tai chi, qi gong, kung fu, the *I Ching,* and feng shui in China. I also became a major Taoist lineage holder, a Buddhist lineage holder, and Master Zhi Chen Guo's Worldwide Representative. I have learned many secrets from Grandmasters who are hidden in the mountains; they do not want me to give their names to the public, preferring to remain quiet servants.

I have offered healing for thousands of people through teleconferences, radio and television programs, and over the Internet. Soul healing has touched millions of people worldwide. I have received thousands of heart-touching and moving stories of great healing results. Yet some people have not received significant benefits. Why not? The answer is very simple: *not enough practice.*

I have benefited from the experiences of my great teachers as well as from my own experience in offering healing for forty years. I can say that many miracles, many heart-touching and moving stories have happened. I also want to share that healing does take time. Many people suffer from sickness for thirty or fifty years. You do need to take a few weeks, a few months, or even one or two years to recover completely. Even if it takes you one to two years to recover, is that a long time if you have suffered for thirty or fifty years?

You must practice diligently for one or two hours per day. You can practice for five minutes here, twenty minutes there, and another ten minutes later. But it does need to all add up to one and preferably two hours per day for chronic and life-threatening conditions. Practice diligently and you could recover from a chronic or even a life-threatening condition in two to three months as Walter did; I shared his story in the beginning section of this book on the Soul Power Series. In fact, we have received many heart-touching stories of healing and recovery from liver cancer, kidney failure, serious arthritis, slipped disc, depression, and many, many other conditions. What these people have in common is that they practiced the soul healing techniques that I share in the Soul Power Series seriously and with dedication.

The books of the Soul Power Series reveal soul secrets, wisdom, knowledge, and practical techniques to you and humanity to empower you to heal yourself, heal others, rejuvenate, prolong life, transform every aspect of your life (including relationships and finances), and enlighten your soul, mind, and body. To enlighten the soul could take you hundreds of lifetimes. To enlighten the mind is even more difficult. Some of the biggest blockages in one's spiritual journey are mind-sets. People ask too many questions. They overanalyze and overthink. They have too many doubts. They struggle with ego, attachment, and more.

When you struggle, remember that divine love and light are within you wherever you may be. Divine love and light are available to you anytime. How many people chant *divine love and light, divine love and light, divine love and light, divine love and light* as they sit working or relaxing, as they are driving, or as they are walking? A few people are doing this. But the vast majority of people have not yet started to do this.

Soul healing and soul transformation are not difficult. **The key is to spend time to practice.** In every book of the Soul Power Series, I have transmitted permanent divine soul treasures. In *The Power of Soul* I offer eleven Divine Soul Transplants. In this book I offer nearly twenty Divine Soul Transplants. Each divine treasure is priceless. These treasures have divine power and abilities. Turn them on and follow along with me to do the practices in the books.

In my workshops I may say, "Now let us chant *divine love and light*." Everyone will chant *divine love and light, divine love and light, divine love and light, divine love and light* with me. I lead participants to do this for three to five minutes, and they feel great. They feel the vibration and the blessing. So in these books, when I ask you to practice for three to five minutes, *please do it*. If you do it, you will receive healing, rejuvenation, and life transformation in the moment. If you think, *I will do it later; I will just read the book for now*, you will miss a lot.

I write my books in this way because I want to bring my live teaching to you as you are reading. I bring you my live workshop anywhere and anytime you read this book. Whether you are reading in the morning, afternoon, or evening, whether you are in your home, on a bus, at the beach, or in the mountains, at that moment you are with me in a workshop. Especially if you follow me in the practices I ask you to do, you will really understand that there is no time or space. You are in my workshop. Divine love and light are with you. The Divine is anywhere, anytime. The Divine is everywhere, every time. No time, no space. If you really understand this, then healing, rejuvenation, transformation of every aspect of life, and enlightenment will come to you, your loved ones, humanity, Mother Earth, and all universes sooner.

## Divine Soul Song of Message Energy Matter

I received the Message Energy Matter teaching in 2002 from Master and Dr. Zhi Chen Guo. His teaching made me understand that everything in the universe is made of matter. Matter vibrates to produce energy. Matter and energy are both carriers of message. Message is soul. Soul directs the transformation between matter and energy.

Later, the Divine told me that Message Energy Matter is the third universal law. I am very grateful for Master Guo's and the Divine's teachings.

HOW I RECEIVED THE DIVINE SOUL SONG OF MESSAGE ENERGY MATTER

During the time I was flowing this book, I asked the Divine, "Dear Divine, you taught me that Message Energy Matter is your third universal law. Could you give me a Soul Song for this universal law?"

The Divine told me, "I will give you a download now." The Divine gave me a Divine Soul Transplant of the Divine Soul Song of Message Energy Matter. This is a huge crystal light soul that the Divine transmitted to my soul. I didn't sing this Soul Song right away. I just received the transmission. The words and the melody of the Soul Song were stored within the transmission. Six days later, while I was still in the midst of writing this book, two of my students and I went to a restaurant. As we were waiting for our meals to arrive, I connected with the Divine Soul Transplant. I said:

> Dear Divine Soul Transplant of the Divine Soul Song
>     of Message Energy Matter,
> I love you, honor you, and bow down to you.
> Please release this Divine Soul Song to me.

When I had asked for this Divine Soul Song, the Divine gave me a Divine Soul Transplant, a permanent divine soul. This soul carries the divine wisdom, knowledge, and power, along with the words and melody of the Divine Soul Song of Message Energy Matter, but I didn't ask for the Divine Soul Song to come out when I received this divine soul. The divine treasure is stored permanently with my soul. I can invoke and connect with the treasure anytime, anywhere.

This is soul communication. It is the same as when you connect with the Divine. Anytime you connect with the Divine, you will receive a response from the Divine. Anytime you connect with holy saints and buddhas, you will receive responses from them also. Soul communication enables you to receive these responses. Soul communication gives you instant teaching, instant guidance, and instant blessing. In this case, when I invoked the Divine Soul Transplant of the Divine Soul Song of Message Energy Matter, I received instant teaching. The words and melody came out at the same time. This Divine Soul Song has only four lines:

> *Transform message, energy, matter*
> *Transform message, energy, matter*
> *Enlighten message, energy, matter*
> *Enlighten message, energy, matter*

See figure 41 for the music of this Divine Soul Song.

Different people carry different frequencies of message, energy, and matter. Everything in the universe carries different frequencies of message, energy, and matter. The Divine Soul Song of Message Energy Matter can transform the frequency of every human being and every soul in the universe to the frequency of Divine Message Energy Matter. Therefore, to sing or chant the words of this Divine Soul Song:

*Transform message, energy, matter*
*Transform message, energy, matter*
*Enlighten message, energy, matter*
*Enlighten message, energy, matter*

is to transform everyone's and everything's frequency to divine frequency.


APPLY THE DIVINE SOUL SONG OF MESSAGE ENERGY MATTER
TO HEAL, REJUVENATE, AND TRANSFORM YOU, HUMANITY,
MOTHER EARTH, AND ALL UNIVERSES

Let's apply this Divine Soul Song to increase trust and remove doubt. These are mind-sets, attitudes, and beliefs that can block your spiritual journey.

*Dear Divine Soul Song of Message Energy Matter,*
*I love you, honor you, and appreciate you.*
*Please bless me to remove doubt and lack of commit-*
*ment on my spiritual journey.*
*Transform these messages to trust and confidence.*
*I am very grateful.*
*Thank you.*

Then sing or chant the words of the Divine Soul Song of Message Energy Matter:

*Transform message, energy, matter*
*Transform message, energy, matter*
*Enlighten message, energy, matter*
*Enlighten message, energy, matter*

Sing or chant for three to five minutes. Then close in the usual way.

Next, let me lead you to offer healing and transformation to all planets:

> *Dear Divine Soul Song of Message Energy Matter,*
> *I love you, honor you, and appreciate you.*
> *Please offer healing and transformation to all planets.*
> *I am very grateful.*
> *Thank you.*

Then sing or chant the words of the Divine Soul Song of Message Energy Matter:

> *Transform message, energy, matter*
> *Transform message, energy, matter*
> *Enlighten message, energy, matter*
> *Enlighten message, energy, matter*

Sing or chant for three to five minutes. Then close:

> *Hao! Hao! Hao!*
> *Thank you. Thank you. Thank you.*

You can apply this Divine Soul Song to offer healing and transformation to yourself and your loved ones for any aspect of life. You can also apply this Divine Soul Song to offer healing and transformation to Mother Earth, stars, galaxies, and all universes.

DIVINE SOUL DOWNLOAD OF THE DIVINE SOUL SONG OF
MESSAGE ENERGY MATTER

In order to transform everyone's and everything's frequency to
divine frequency faster, I am going to offer the next major divine
treasure in this book for every reader. This is the eighteenth Divine Soul Download offered to readers of this book. It is named:

### Divine Soul Transplant of the Divine Soul Song
### of Message Energy Matter

This will be a first-layer golden light soul, not the higher-
layer crystal light soul that I received.

Prepare! Sit up straight. Put the tip of your tongue near the
roof of your mouth. Totally relax. Open your heart and soul to
receive this divine treasure. Tell the Divine: *Dear Divine, I am
very grateful and honored to receive this permanent divine soul. I am
ready to receive it. Thank you.* In the next thirty seconds the Divine will download it to your soul.

### Divine Soul Transplant of the Divine Soul Song
### of Message Energy Matter
### Silent download!

Now close your eyes for thirty seconds to receive this major
divine soul treasure.

> *Hao! Hao! Hao!*
> *Thank you. Thank you. Thank you.*

Thank you, Divine.
Let's practice! I will lead you to apply the Divine Soul Trans-

plant of the Divine Soul Song of Message Energy Matter to bless your water and your food before you eat a meal and before you drink a beverage. Or you may wish to bless the water in a river and in an ocean. Do it with me now:

> *Dear divine soul of the Divine Soul Song of Message*
>   *Energy Matter downloaded to my soul,*
> *I love you, honor you, and appreciate you.*
> *Please turn on to bless this food, this water, this river,*
>   *this ocean.*
> *I am very grateful.*
> *Thank you. Thank you. Thank you.*

Then sing or chant the words of the Divine Soul Song of Message Energy Matter for three to five minutes, silently or aloud:

> *Transform message, energy, matter*
> *Transform message, energy, matter*
> *Enlighten message, energy, matter*
> *Enlighten message, energy, matter*

Close in the usual way.

The next practice is to transform the message, energy, and matter of the whole body. This is a vital practice for rejuvenation and long life. Do it with me now:

> *Dear divine soul of the Divine Soul Song of Message*
>   *Energy Matter downloaded to my soul,*
> *I love you, honor you, and appreciate you.*
> *Please turn on to rejuvenate every one of my systems,*

*organs, cells, cell units, DNA and RNA, spaces be-*
*tween cells, and smallest matter inside my cells, and*
*transform the frequencies of their message, energy,*
*and matter to the frequencies of divine message, en-*
*ergy, and matter.*
*I am very grateful.*
*Thank you. Thank you. Thank you.*

Then sing or chant the words of the Divine Soul Song of
Message Energy Matter for three to five minutes. Close in the
usual way.

### The Fourth Divine Universal Law: The Universal Law of Universal Service

In the beginning section of this book on the Soul Power Series, I
shared how I received the Divine Universal Law of Universal
Service from the Divine in 2003. You may want to reread this
now (pages xix–xxi).

The Divine is a universal servant. The sun and the moon are
universal servants. Everyone and everything is a universal servant, including animals, plants, oceans, mountains, a machine, a
house, a business, planets, and stars. Everyone and everything
serves the universe in its own way, offering the seven aspects of
universal service: universal love, universal forgiveness, universal
peace, universal healing, universal blessing, universal harmony,
and universal enlightenment. The purpose of life is to serve.

## Divine Soul Song of Universal Service

The Divine Soul Song of Universal Service is another newly released divine practical soul treasure for healing, boosting energy, vitality, stamina, and immunity, preventing sickness, rejuvenation, and prolonging life; for balancing Heaven, Earth, and human beings; and for healing humanity, Mother Earth, planets, stars, galaxies, and universes.

HOW I RECEIVED THE DIVINE SOUL SONG
OF UNIVERSAL SERVICE

At my Soul Healing and Enlightenment Retreat in Mt. Shasta, California, in November 2006, as I was teaching about universal service, the Divine interrupted to give me the Divine Soul Song of Universal Service:

> *Lu la li lu la li lu*
> *Lu la li lu la li lu*
> *La li li lu la li lu la*
> *La li li lu la li lu la*
>
> *I am a universal servant*
> *You are a universal servant*
> *We serve humanity unconditionally*
> *We serve all souls unconditionally*

See figure 42 for the music of this Divine Soul Song.

Universal service is the fourth Divine Universal Law.

The purpose of life is to serve. To serve is to transform. To serve is to uplift your soul standing. To serve is to reach advanced soul enlightenment. This Divine Soul Song is very powerful. You can apply it to offer divine healing and transformation to yourself, humanity, Mother Earth, and all universes.

APPLY THE DIVINE SOUL SONG OF UNIVERSAL SERVICE TO HEAL, REJUVENATE, AND TRANSFORM YOU, HUMANITY, MOTHER EARTH, AND ALL UNIVERSES

Let me lead you to apply this Divine Soul Song to offer rejuvenation to Mother Earth:

> *Dear Divine Soul Song of Universal Service,*
> *I love you, honor you, and appreciate you.*
> *Please offer a blessing of rejuvenation to Mother Earth,*
> *    to her air, land, and water, and to all who dwell*
> *    upon her.*
> *I am very grateful.*
> *Thank you.*

Then sing or chant the words of the Divine Soul Song of Universal Service, silently or aloud:

> *I am a universal servant*
> *You are a universal servant*
> *We serve humanity unconditionally*
> *We serve all souls unconditionally*

Sing or chant for three to five minutes. Then close:

> *Hao! Hao! Hao!*
> *Thank you. Thank you. Thank you.*

Next, join me in applying this Divine Soul Song to offer healing and transformation to all stars and galaxies:

> *Dear Divine Soul Song of Universal Service,*
> *I love you, honor you, and appreciate you.*
> *Please offer a healing to all stars and all galaxies in*
> *all universes, and a blessing to transform their con-*
> *sciousnesses to align with divine consciousness.*
> *I am very grateful.*
> *Thank you.*

Then sing or chant the words of the Divine Soul Song of Universal Service:

> *I am a universal servant*
> *You are a universal servant*
> *We serve humanity unconditionally*
> *We serve all souls unconditionally*

Sing or chant for three to five minutes. Then close:

> *Hao! Hao! Hao!*
> *Thank you. Thank you. Thank you.*

DIVINE SOUL DOWNLOAD OF THE DIVINE SOUL SONG OF UNIVERSAL SERVICE

Now I am honored to offer the nineteenth and final major permanent divine treasure to readers of this book. This Divine Soul Download is named:

## Divine Soul Transplant of the
## Divine Soul Song of Universal Service

Prepare! Sit up straight. Put the tip of your tongue near the roof of your mouth. Totally relax. Open your heart and soul to receive this divine treasure. Tell the Divine: *Dear Divine, I am very grateful and honored to receive this permanent divine soul. I am ready to receive it. Thank you.* In the next thirty seconds the Divine will download it to your soul.

## Divine Soul Transplant of the
## Divine Soul Song of Universal Service
## Silent download!

Now close your eyes for thirty seconds to receive this major divine soul treasure.

*Hao! Hao! Hao!*
*Thank you. Thank you. Thank you.*

Thank you, Divine.

Let me show you how to apply this divine treasure to offer a healing to all of your ancestors. Practice with me now:

> *Dear divine soul of the Divine Soul Song of Universal*
> *    Service downloaded to my soul,*
> *I love you, honor you, and appreciate you.*
> *Please turn on to offer a healing for the physical, emo-*
> *    tional, mental, and spiritual bodies of my parents,*
> *    my grandparents, and all of my ancestors in all of*
> *    my lifetimes.*

*I am very grateful.*
*Thank you. Thank you. Thank you.*

Then sing or chant the words of the Divine Soul Song of Universal Service for three to five minutes:

*I am a universal servant*
*You are a universal servant*
*We serve humanity unconditionally*
*We serve all souls unconditionally*

Close in the usual way:

*Hao! Hao! Hao!*
*Thank you. Thank you. Thank you.*

Remember that there is no time, no space. This blessing will serve all of your parents, all of your grandparents, and all of your ancestors, whether they are in a physical form or in soul form. They may have transitioned. They may have reincarnated again. It doesn't matter. This blessing will bless their present lives and their future lives. It will bless your present life and your future lives. It will bless your children and all of your descendants.

The Divine has given us treasures that can be used in such a simple way to offer such great service. We are very honored, humbled, and grateful. We cannot thank the Divine enough.

Next let me lead you to offer healing and transformation to all universes. Practice like this:

*Dear divine soul of the Divine Soul Song of Universal*
*Service downloaded to my soul,*

*I love you, honor you, and appreciate you.*
*Please turn on to offer healing and transformation to*
*    all universes.*
*I am very grateful.*
*Thank you. Thank you. Thank you.*

Then sing or chant the words of the Divine Soul Song of Universal Service for three to five minutes:

*I am a universal servant*
*You are a universal servant*
*We serve humanity unconditionally*
*We serve all souls unconditionally*

Close in the usual way.

Finally, let's apply this divine soul treasure to bless us to be unconditional universal servants. In this time of Mother Earth's transition and purification, humanity, Mother Earth, and the Divine need more pure, enlightened, unconditional universal servants. Join me now:

*Dear divine soul of the Divine Soul Song of Universal*
*    Service downloaded to my soul,*
*I love you, honor you, and appreciate you.*
*Please turn on to bless me to be an unconditional uni-*
*    versal servant.*
*Fully align my soul, heart, and consciousness with the*
*    Divine's soul, heart, and consciousness.*
*Remove all blockages on this path.*
*I am very grateful.*
*Thank you. Thank you. Thank you.*

Then sing or chant the words of the Divine Soul Song of Universal Service for three to five minutes, silently or aloud:

> *I am a universal servant*
> *You are a universal servant*
> *We serve humanity unconditionally*
> *We serve all souls unconditionally*

Close in the usual way:

> *Hao! Hao! Hao!*
> *Thank you. Thank you. Thank you.*

## Summary

The four main universal laws are the Tao for everyone and everything in all universes to follow. Follow this Tao to receive healing and life transformation for your life and the life of the universe.

The Divine has given us Divine Soul Songs of these four universal laws. The Divine has given us the Divine's treasures and tools to transform all humanity, animals, Mother Earth, all planets, all stars, all galaxies, and all universes because Divine Soul Songs:

- carry divine frequency and vibration that can transform the consciousness of humanity, animals, and all souls
- carry divine love that can melt all blockages and transform all life
- carry divine forgiveness that can bring inner peace and inner joy

- carry divine compassion that can boost energy, stamina, vitality, and immunity
- carry divine light that can heal, prevent sickness, rejuvenate, prolong life, transform every aspect of life (including relationships and finances), and enlighten soul, mind, and body

Life depends on movement. For a human being, this movement is cellular movement. Cellular movement creates vibration and frequency. Divine Soul Songs carry divine vibration and frequency. Divine Soul Songs will transform the frequency of humanity to heal and transform every aspect of our lives. Mother Earth, all universes, and all souls have their vibration and frequency. Divine Soul Songs will transform the frequency of everyone and everything to heal, rejuvenate, and transform every aspect of creation.

# 4

# *Experiences of Divine Soul Song*

*A*s I HAVE shared throughout this book, the benefits that Divine Soul Songs bring to humanity, Mother Earth, and all souls of all universes are beyond comprehension. I have received hundreds of stories of healing, blessing, and life transformation from Divine Soul Songs. In this chapter, I will share some of the stories I have received from people worldwide on their experiences with Divine Soul Songs.

These stories represent a small sample of the hundreds I have received. My heart and soul are touched by the feedback given by the public and my students alike. I am honored to be the messenger of Divine Soul Songs. I am grateful and honored to share these stories. I thank all those who submitted their stories. I thank the Divine for the opportunity to serve humanity, Mother Earth, and all universes with Divine Soul Songs.

I will continue to serve all souls through Divine Soul Songs. Divine Soul Song is the divine direction for healing, rejuvenation, transformation, and enlightenment in the Soul Light Era. I am honored to be a servant of the Divine, Divine Soul Songs, humanity, Mother Earth, all universes, and all souls.

Your heart and soul will be touched by these stories of healing, rejuvenation, transformation of relationship and finances, and enlightenment.

## Healing

Divine Soul Songs can heal soul, mind, and body. Divine Soul Songs can heal the physical, emotional, mental, and spiritual bodies. Divine Soul Songs can heal you, others, all humanity, Mother Earth, and all universes.

### DIVINE SOUL SONGS TRANSFORM PANCREATIC CANCER

I have been a student of Master Sha since May 2007. I am a certified Divine Soul Song Singer, Soul Healing Teacher and Healer, and Master Teacher and Healer in training. I have received wonderful divine treasures from Master Sha, for which I cannot thank him or the Divine enough. I am very happy to share my story about Divine Soul Songs.

I was diagnosed with pancreatic cancer one week after the Soul Healing and Enlightenment retreat in Quebec, Canada, in June 2008. I was told I would not live longer than six months—not beyond Christmas, if that long.

I chant the Divine Soul Song of Yin Yang and the Divine Soul Song of Five Elements, as well as my own Soul Song, for many hours every day. When I chant, I am at one with nature, the universes, and all souls.

After practicing these Divine Soul Songs for just over three months, I learned that the results of my tumor marker blood test for my cancer had improved by 80 percent since June 2008. At this time I don't need any medications or other treatment.

I want to emphasize the importance of chanting. Chanting these Divine Soul Songs is critical for healing. Everyone has the same opportunity I had to transform his or her soul, mind, and body. Together we can transform everyone's soul, mind, and body.

I will continue to chant. Every minute of every day, I am looking forward to being totally transformed and healed of pancreatic cancer soon. You cannot chant the Divine Soul Songs too much.

—L. Z.

Germany

## PMS TAMED BY THE DIVINE SOUL SONG
*LOVE, PEACE AND HARMONY*

I have had severe PMS (premenstrual syndrome) for over thirty years. I consulted a PMS specialist, who rated my symptoms nine on a scale of one to ten, with ten being the most severe. The only reason I was not rated a ten was that I do not become physically violent. I have consulted various doctors and tried a number of methods to alleviate this condition, but to limited avail.

On days when I have PMS, I can become so angry that I cannot think and can barely function in any way. Today was one such day. I took vitamin B, St. John's Wort, and Evening Primrose Oil (as my doctors suggested), to no avail.

Then I played Master Sha's CD of the Divine Soul Song *Love, Peace and Harmony* and asked this Soul Song to help me to feel serene and peaceful. *Yeah, right,* I thought. I did not expect it to help, as I was feeling extremely angry after a day when one thing after another had gone wrong.

Within minutes I *was* serene and peaceful. My mind was calm. This was a miracle beyond words. I picked up the phone and apologized to a friend whom I had told off earlier in the day when I was at the height of my PMS. The phone call went extremely well, as I was relaxed, peaceful, and loving.

I cannot emphasize enough what a miracle this is. Thank you so much, Master Sha! Thank you, Divine!

—N. L.

British Columbia, Canada

## DEEP TRANSFORMATION USING DIVINE SOUL SONG CD WITH A CLIENT

I have many wonderful stories from using Soul Song in my psychotherapy practice.

This story is about a client with an extensive history of sexual assault and verbal, emotional, and mental abuse. I gave this client Master Sha's CD *Soul Song for Healing and Rejuvenation of Brain and Spinal Column.*

Here is what her soul expressed to me through soul communication:

> *Many levels of healing have occurred since listening to the Soul Song for Healing and Rejuvenation of Brain and Spinal Column. I listen to it constantly. I now feel such peace and contentment. I have never experienced such deep inner peace as I do now. This is so far beyond what I am used to feeling: fear, terror, distrust, chaos. The Soul Song*

*has brought about such deep peace in my soul, mind, and body. My tragic past was filled with violence, helplessness, and assault, and now I am able to let go of it, bit by bit. My dreams are now peaceful. My whole soul, mind, and body are being healed, layer by layer. The very root of my fear is fading into peaceful contentment. My life is now something not to be feared and dreaded, but lived day to day in gratitude to God. I look forward to the continued unfolding of my healing. My gratitude is difficult to express in words, so I sing my thanks to the Divine. Thank you. Thank you. Thank you.*

—E. L.
North Carolina

## DIVINE SOUL SONG *LOVE, PEACE AND HARMONY* SOOTHES STRESS AND ANXIETY

I find it very effective to sing the Divine Soul Song *Love, Peace and Harmony* whenever I feel a little bit stressed or anxious in my day-to-day life. I soon feel the calming effect of this Divine Soul Song throughout my body.

—T. A.
British Columbia, Canada

## ANGER HEALED BY 95 PERCENT

I ordered Master Sha's *Soul Song for Healing Anger* CD, and as soon as I received it, I played it all night on repeat mode. When I awoke the next morning, I was 95 percent free of my anger over a certain situation. I felt so much better and did not have the constant mind chatter and anguish about this particular situation.

Master Sha, your Soul Songs are truly a blessing. Thank you for this wonderful gift of being almost completely anger-free.

—A. G.

Kentucky


DIVINE SOUL SONG *LOVE, PEACE AND HARMONY*
SAVED MY LIFE

I was introduced to Master Sha and his teachings at a workshop in the late summer of 2006. Two months earlier, I had been held up at gunpoint, and I was totally traumatized. I had been living in a state of constant fear and anxiety. The most ordinary events, such as a cloud moving across the sun, could send me into a panic attack. Life was pretty much unbearable, and sleep for any length of time was almost impossible.

After the workshop with Master Sha, I began attending the free morning group practice teleconferences and weekly Divine Soul Song teleconferences on Tuesday and Saturday. I learned to sing and chant the Divine Soul Song *Love, Peace and Harmony*. I began to experience feelings of peace and safety. In the beginning, tears would roll down my cheeks as I sang *Love, Peace and Harmony*. When I would awaken in the night with a panic attack, I would chant the words *love, peace, and harmony* over and over. Soon my mind would quiet and I would fall back asleep, getting the rest I so badly needed. All I did was repeat these three simple words, and I experienced extraordinary results. It was a miracle.

I began to sing this Divine Soul Song constantly. I sang it aloud. I sang it silently. I sang it driving to work, at work, and driving home from work. I sang it when the panic would begin. I sang it when I experienced peace. The more I sang, the more the love, peace, and harmony of the song became my reality. The fear and darkness disappeared.

I strongly encourage everyone to read what Master Sha has written about this Divine Soul Song. He speaks of how imperative it is to love ourselves first—soul, heart, mind, and body—and how only then can we truly offer unconditional love to others. Love without conditions. Love without expectations. Love without attachment. For me, this beautiful Divine Soul Song, *Love, Peace and Harmony,* holds one of the most profound and yet simplest teachings of life—certainly of my life and of my spiritual journey. I have now been singing this Divine Soul Song for over two years and I am still moved to tears by its words, its melody, and the blessing, healing, and peace it conveys to me and to all humanity. For me, its full richness and depths are still unknown; the teaching, wisdom, and knowledge it carries continue to unfold.

I cannot thank the Divine and his servant, Master Zhi Gang Sha, enough. This Divine Soul Song *Love, Peace and Harmony* is truly one of the sweetest things in my life. I invite all of you to experience this for yourself. I shall be eternally grateful to the Divine and to Master Sha for the gift and blessing of all of the Divine Soul Songs and for the additional life-transforming experience of becoming a certified Divine Soul Song Singer.

—M. T.
Idaho

A REMARKABLE HEALING OF A BACK INJURY

I often experience intense back pain as a result of a previous injury. I see a chiropractor regularly for adjustments, but they do not hold for very long, leaving me to deal with intense pain.

I first heard Master Sha's *Soul Song for Healing and Rejuvenation of Brain and Spinal Column* during a Sunday Divine Blessings teleconference. I requested a healing for my back from this Divine Soul Song and immediately began to feel tingling sensations up and down my back. As these sensations continued, the pain decreased in intensity. I was amazed that the pain was beginning to dissipate after only a few minutes of listening to this Soul Song. Even though I requested a healing for back pain, I felt wave after wave of tingling throughout my entire body, and I realized that I was receiving other healing as well. It was remarkable to feel this transformation in my body. As I continued to listen to the Divine Soul Song, these sensations continued. After listening for only ten minutes, my back felt great. I was so excited about this new Divine Soul Song that I had to have a copy of it as soon as possible.

I soon received my *Soul Song for Healing and Rejuvenation of Brain and Spinal Column* CD, and when I played it for the first time, I was completely mesmerized by its exquisite beauty. I felt the presences of the Divine and many spiritual beings. I felt as though I was being held deeply and tenderly in their love. I could not get enough of this Divine Soul Song, so I began playing it twenty-four hours a day. I love waking up and falling asleep to it. I now have many of Master Sha's Divine Soul Song CDs, and I love them all.

I am so grateful for this gift of Soul Song from the Divine. I am so grateful to Master Sha.

—J. T.

Montana

## TRANSFORMING DARK EMOTIONAL PAIN INTO VIBRANT LIGHT

I had an unfortunate conversation with a loved one moments before I was to facilitate a Soul Wisdom, Healing, and Enlightenment workshop. The exchange was very painful and untimely. With only moments to gather my wits and presence, I knew I needed something to uplift me, to bring me back into balance by transforming the mental/emotional upheaval that was churning in my stomach and in my mind.

I played Master Sha's CD of the Divine Soul Song *Love, Peace and Harmony* and sang with him. Love, peace, and harmony were almost instantaneously ignited in my entire being. It was the miracle I needed at that moment. Not only was I able to transform emotional turmoil into an enlightened presence, I was able to teach the workshop participants from an even deeper level of wisdom.

I am so grateful for the experience, even though it was initially difficult. I released an old pattern and realized a new ability, and others received healing benefits as well. I feel extremely fortunate to have access to a spiritual teacher with whom I can sing and receive healing anytime, anywhere.

Master Sha, an eternity is not enough time to thank you and the Divine. Please accept my very humble gratitude, sent with an

image of thousands of lotus flowers filling the space around you.
I would give those to you if I could.

—J. L.

Oregon


## SOUL SONG BLESSING RESTORES VISION

Singing a Soul Song as a blessing is a most amazing experience.
The healing blessing comes from the Divine in the form of a
song, and I am frequently the one who is most astounded by the
results.

One day I was on the phone with an elderly lady of eighty-
three years. She explained that her vision was blurry and she
thought she may have had a mild stroke. I asked her what she was
doing at the moment. "I am driving down the highway," she said.
I asked if she would like a healing blessing for her eyes, and she
replied, "Yes, I will take anything." She was able to pull off the
highway, and, as a certified Divine Soul Song Singer, I sang a
Soul Song blessing for two minutes—one minute out loud and
one minute silently. At the end of the blessing she said nothing.

I waited. Silence.

Finally, I asked how she felt. She said, "I feel fine."

Another lengthy silence followed. "Are you all right?" I asked.
She responded, "Yes, I'm all right."

Silence. I waited.

Then she shared, "The reason I didn't speak was because tears
were streaming down my cheeks. When I opened my eyes after
the blessing, I could clearly see the trees on the other side of the
highway! Before the blessing they had been blurry. Thank you
very much."

I told her to thank the Divine in her own way, for it was the Divine who gave the blessing, not me. She did. I, however, was the one who was truly amazed and thankful, because all I did was step aside and sing Soul Song for two minutes; the Divine did the rest.

Thank you, Master Sha, and thank you, Divine, for making all of this possible.

—J. B.
Southern United States

## Rejuvenation

Divine Soul Songs can rejuvenate soul, mind, and body. Divine Soul Songs can rejuvenate systems, organs, cells, cell units, DNA, RNA, spaces between the cells, and the smallest matter in the cells. Divine Soul Songs can rejuvenate pets, nature, Mother Earth, all planets, all stars, and all galaxies.

### GENTLE EXPANSION, DEEP WELL-BEING, AND CALM JOY

Whenever I listen to the *Soul Song for Healing and Rejuvenation of Heart,* I notice an almost immediate gentle expansion and sense of deep well-being. My heart feels deeply and physically touched, and a sense of deep gratitude and love arises. When the soul of my heart hears this song, it awakens and rises up to greet and embrace the divine blessings that gently flow from Master Sha's Soul Song.

The new message creates many physical responses. I notice the energy across my heart smoothing and spreading from the lower left chamber up to the right atrium. The sense of balance and gentle expansion continues. I notice my breath becoming deeper. My lungs take on an almost clear-light quality. I am aware of better cardiac function and better oxygenation of my blood.

I am aware of the blood and chi flowing down my arms to my fingertips and down both legs as well. With my Third Eye I can see the tiny blood vessels dilate and improve circulation to every cell in my body. The sense of balance and gentle expansion that clears space around every cell, organ, and organ system continues. I experience a calm joy. Every soul of every cell is suffused with a special, gentle heart Soul Song light, and the sense of balance and deep calm is present everywhere.

I have listened to the *Soul Song for Healing and Rejuvenation of Heart* many times. Now, when I simply hear Master Sha say, "Soul Song for Healing and Rejuvenation of Heart" at the beginning of the song, I have an immediate response of deep well-being, balance, and calm joy as my entire body, mind, emotions, and soul come into an amazing sense of balance and renewal.

I am deeply grateful for this gift. I thank Master Sha from the bottom of my newly healed heart.

—P. S.

California


TRANSFORMATION FROM CHANTING SOUL SONGS FOR WORLD PEACE

Before I knew Master Sha, I never thought that I would chant. It was somewhat foreign to me. Master Sha's teachings changed all that.

The Eleven Days of Sacred Soul Song Singing for World Peace was extraordinary. I experienced an energy boost like I hadn't had for nearly thirty years, and I still feel its effects days later.

Everything, including my thinking and attitude, went into a different gear. I also sleep better and live much more in the moment. My already great relationship with my husband has moved to an even higher level.

All of this may have started earlier, but it became so much more apparent during the eleven days of chanting the Divine Soul Songs of Yin Yang and Five Elements for world peace.

—C. V.

Florida

## SOUL SONG FOR HEALING AND REJUVENATION OF LOWER BACK BRINGS INCREASED FLEXIBILITY

I have been suffering from arthritis in my lower back for nineteen years, making it very difficult to put my socks on each morning.

After downloading Master Sha's Soul Songs, I was inspired to do an experiment. Before I went to sleep one night, I put the *Soul Song for Healing and Rejuvenation of Lower Back* on repeat mode at a low volume. I decided to put the Soul Song to the test—have it play all night while I slept and see if I felt any different in the morning.

The next morning I was quite surprised to discover I could do something I had not been able to do in years. The way I normally have to put my socks on is to lean back while sitting on the bed, swing my foot up, grab it with my hand, rest it on my knee, slide my sock on, and then repeat this procedure for the other foot. After playing the *Soul Song for Healing and Rejuvenation of*

*Lower Back* all night, I was able to just bend forward, lift my foot up, and put my socks on like a normal person. I had at least 50 percent more flexibility in my lower back after just one night! Remarkable! This was all the proof I needed; Master Sha's Soul Songs are *extremely* effective. I can't wait to continue listening to all of them every day (and night). Thank you, Master Sha.

—R. R.

New York


DIVINE SOUL SONGS INCREASE ENERGY, STAMINA,
AND VITALITY

Like many people, I have a very demanding job and work long hours. It seems as though there are never enough hours to complete everything I need to do. However, I love my job and can't imagine doing anything else.

A few months ago, I learned the Divine Soul Songs of Yin Yang and Five Elements. I have chanted them for an hour every day since then. I chant in the shower and while driving the car—whenever and wherever I can. I make sure that one way or another, I fit at least one hour of this practice into my day each and every day. The difference this has made in my energy, stamina, and vitality is amazing. I can keep going much longer and stronger than ever before. In addition, I'm saving money because I now have an alternative to coffee when I need that extra blast of energy!

—R. B.

Hawaii

## Transformation of Relationships

Divine Soul Songs can transform your relationships with a spouse, other family members, friends, enemies, teachers, colleagues at work, animals, organizations, technology, nature, and more. Divine Soul Songs can transform past, present, and future relationships.

### SOUL SONG HEALS RELATIONSHIP WITH A FRIEND

Over the last ten years or so, my friend and I have had a few issues between us that we have not been able to fully resolve. Then we listened to the *Soul Song for Healing Grief and Sadness* together, and we were able to move beyond our old mind-sets and enter into a place of openness, acceptance, and forgiveness. This Soul Song brought light to our relationship, and together we have brought our friendship to a level not previously possible. It is as if we now have a common denominator, something that binds the relationship more than the issue does. We have established a heart-to-heart connection.

All this has come from listening to the *Soul Song for Healing Grief and Sadness* just once! Thank you so much!

—J. M.

Pennsylvania

### DIVINE SOUL SONG ERASES TWO-THOUSAND MILES

I single-handedly raised two beautiful daughters from the ages of one and three. As we had no other family we could rely on, the challenges were great. Relationships among the three of us were sometimes difficult. However, we also developed a special bond that is at times missing in two-parent households or in those with extended family.

My daughters learned several things from our team of three: courage, the value of being independent, and that they could do just about anything. However, as self-reliance was the key to making things work, these girls, young adults now, have often been hesitant to fully share, or to ask for my advice.

Over the past few months, major issues have come up for both daughters. Despite this, their sharing with me has been minimal. Recently, I began chanting the profound Divine Soul Song *Love, Peace and Harmony* periodically throughout the day to open and expand our relationships. This Divine Soul Song is unlimited in its blessings and gifts to humanity, encompassing the total realm of divine transformation of anything in any given moment.

Before long, my phone began ringing, erasing the two thousand miles between my daughters and me. Our relationships were transformed by expanded love, healing, sharing, and learning. One of Master Sha's favorite statements, "Do not hesitate," filled my daughters' minds and hearts through the Divine Soul Song *Love, Peace and Harmony*. I now have improved relationships with my daughters, filled more than ever with love, sharing, learning, laughter, and wisdom.

—J. S.

New Mexico

MOTHER AND DAUGHTER PRACTICE

The very simple yet powerful tool of Soul Song has helped my relationship with my ninety-six-year-old mother so much. Because I am her sole caretaker, things—and I—can get pretty tense at times. I sing the Divine Soul Song *Love, Peace and Harmony* when I begin to feel stressed, and it truly does transform the situation and the environment. It relaxes my mind and changes me. I am more at peace, and my interactions with my mother become more harmonious.

My mother and I often sing Divine Soul Songs together, especially when she is feeling weak. We sing the Divine Soul Songs of Yin Yang and Five Elements, and she always feels better afterward. Divine Soul Songs are something new for my mother to learn, which is good for her mental functioning. And she enjoys them! Practicing Divine Soul Songs is something we can do together that is beneficial on every level of our beings. It gives her strength, it balances her emotions, and it is a meaningful, helpful, special activity we can do together. Having a spiritual practice that heals as a part of our lives is such a blessing.

I am so grateful to have these simple, effective ways to help my mother and nurture our relationship. We have been blessed by Divine Soul Songs.

—B.N.

Florida

## DIVINE SOUL SONG RESTORES LOVE, PEACE, AND HARMONY

One of my friends is very sensitive and emotional. Sometimes she makes me so upset and angry that I don't know what to do. Master Sha teaches that you can chant Divine Soul Songs to heal and transform your relationships, so I decided to try it.

One day I encountered some challenges with this friend. I did not want to argue with her. Instead I sang my favorite Divine Soul Song, *Love, Peace and Harmony.* My tears stopped flowing and my heart was filled with love, peace, and harmony again. Later, my friend and I made up.

I am grateful to the Divine and to Master Sha for the Soul
Songs.
—S. H.
California

## OLD MIND-SETS AND ATTITUDES ARE DISSIPATING

Singing Soul Songs has become a natural part of my life. For me,
a day without Soul Song is like a day without food. I have been
especially happy with how I now handle myself in my marriage
when difficult circumstances arise. I simply begin singing Soul
Song—sometimes silently, sometimes aloud—and my less-than-
positive emotions immediately begin to transform.

Using Soul Song to uplift myself in challenging situations is
helping me to see and experience others in a new light. My actions are transformed by having a new vantage point of seeing
what really is important. Old mind-sets and attitudes that fed
the ego and limited my framework of life are dissipating. Unconditional love, understanding, compassion, and forgiveness are
claiming more of my inner space and spilling over into my relationships. Acting, instead of *reacting,* is becoming my natural
state of consciousness.

Soul Song is nothing short of a magic wand that generates
higher vibrational frequencies, thereby manifesting more peace
on the planet, starting in my own home. My marriage has improved because I am no longer waiting for my partner to change.
I have changed: I am happier and growing.

One of the key benefits of singing my own Soul Song and
using it in my life is that I am becoming less attached to what my
personality "thinks" should be happening in my relationships.
There is a flow of universal knowingness, creating more calm in

my everyday outlook, thoughts, and actions. Without Soul Song I would not experience nature's flow as I experience it now and my primary relationships would involve more suffering.

Freedom comes with knowing and using Soul Song. It is a freedom that grows love on its branches and gives light to create the fruit that will, in turn, give more life in a purer form.

Soul Song gives me ways to fill my heart and bridge relationships with greater fulfillment. Soul Song, thank you for always being there. You are reliable, true, and real, and a magnificent gift of love. Master Sha and Divine, how nurturing of you to share such an extraordinary treasure so that we may experience strength and a new way to live. Thank you, all of you. I honor, respect, and bow to you in humble gratitude.

—J. L.
Oregon


## I COULD NOT HAVE IMAGINED SUCH A PROFOUND HEALING

I participated in the Eleven Days of Divine Sacred Soul Song Singing for World Peace, and the most beautiful healing occurred for my relationship with my daughter.

My daughter suffered tremendously as a result of my divorce thirteen years ago, and since then it was as though I had lost her; the soul-to-soul connection was lost. I could not have imagined that such a profound healing would take place at the level of the soul: reconnection and the healing of past hurts.

Words are limited to express my gratitude for this experience. Thank you.

—C. T.
Quebec, Canada

## Transformation of Finances

Divine Soul Songs can transform finances and businesses. They can help you gain virtue, which is spiritual currency that can be exchanged for physical currency.

### CHANTING DIVINE SOUL SONGS OF YIN YANG AND FIVE ELEMENTS BRINGS MANY NEW STUDENTS

I participated in the Eleven Days of Divine Sacred Soul Song Singing for World Peace. Prior to this, I had not been able to get many students to my classes. During these eleven days, I received many calls from people interested in attending my classes. It has been years since I have received so many phone calls!

This was an incredible blessing, and I am so grateful for these wonderful gifts of Soul Song.

—C. T.
Quebec, Canada


### SOUL SONG BLESSING BRINGS NEW JOB

Some time ago, Master Sha had a daily Soul Song blessing on his website. He would record a brief Soul Song each day, and visitors to the website could listen to it and request a healing blessing.

At the time, I was working at a job I liked, but I needed to earn more money to meet my financial obligations and continue my studies. I listened to and requested a financial blessing from Master Sha's Soul Song. To my surprise, I received a phone call ten days later from someone I had worked with years before, asking me to apply for a position at the hospital where she was now an assistant vice president. I was astounded.

I applied for and got the job. This was a blessing beyond words. The new job paid 70 percent more than my prior job had. Securing this particular job not only helped me financially but enabled me to be of greater service.

The power of Divine Soul Songs is truly beyond my comprehension. I am so very grateful to the Divine and to Master Sha for the opportunity to receive these teachings and blessings.

—A Grateful Student

## Enlightenment

Divine Soul Songs can enlighten your soul, mind, and body. Divine Soul Songs can enlighten humanity and all souls.

### THE EXPERIENCE OF SINGING MY SOUL SONG

My experience with Soul Song developed over many months.

I found that as I sang my Soul Song, my Message Center opened in the most profound way. I started hearing the translation of my Soul Song in English, my native language. I heard words like *praise, joy,* and *love* fill the room. This was in September 2007.

My husband had been ill for some time and made his transition in December 2007. I sang my Soul Song for hours beside him the night he passed. I had the realization that singing Soul Song for those making their transition to the Soul World is one of the greatest acts of service we can offer.

This was months before Master Sha's first Soul Song Singer and Divine Soul Song Singer Certification Training Programs were announced. Since participating in these programs, the power of my Soul Song has increased so much. I know that my Soul Song is expanding my Message Center, even as my Message Center gives me my Soul Song. The interplay between the divine blessings and the precious service is beyond words.

I am so honored and blessed to have this divine treasure in my life.

—R. D.

Texas


## MY HEART WAS TOUCHED BY GOD

I met Master Sha for the first time in February 2008, when I participated in a two-day workshop in Frankfurt, Germany. On the first day, Master Sha led the workshop participants in singing *Love, Peace and Harmony* with him. After singing this Soul Song for forty-five minutes, I felt as if my heart, or rather my Message Center, was touched by God, and I started to cry. Suddenly I realized that God was in the room with us, and that everything Master Sha had said and done was true.

Once home, I played the *Love, Peace and Harmony* CD and sang along. All of a sudden my two-year-old daughter said, "There! Man!" and pointed to a spot in the air. At first I thought that I misheard, but she kept repeating, "There! Man went!" and walked toward the spot. At that moment I realized that my daughter had seen a light being in the room. That being had been drawn by the Divine Soul Song *Love, Peace and Harmony*. This Soul Song had spoken to this soul.

I now sing *Love, Peace and Harmony* and *God Gives His Heart to Me* all the time with my daughter, who loves these Divine Soul Songs and has learned how to sing them. Thank you very much,

God and Master Sha, for these beautiful experiences and for being with me in my life.

—M. S.

Germany

## SOMETHING INSIDE ME WOKE UP

I first heard about Master Sha a few months ago, when my wife discovered the www.drsha.com website. I was amazed that Master Sha knew how to heal and enlighten the soul. At first, this was unbelievable, but then I realized that after a long spiritual search and several teachers, I had finally found a spiritual master who spoke my language!

I attended the Soul Healing and Enlightenment Retreat in Quebec, Canada, and it changed my life. Learning to sing the Divine Soul Songs of Yin Yang and Five Elements and the Divine Soul Songs *Love, Peace and Harmony* and *God Gives His Heart to Me* transported me to another place and time. Something inside me woke up and remembered this incredible music. I had heard and sung this music before; it felt so familiar. As I continue to sing these wonderful Soul Songs, I feel myself transforming into the being I have wanted to become for so long and was always meant to be.

My Soul Language emerged during the Soul Healing and Enlightenment Retreat. Since then, my Soul Language has grown stronger and my Soul Song has emerged. Day by day, my Soul Song is becoming more powerful. When I sing my Soul Song, I can hear the silence between my thoughts, just as the sun breaks between the clouds. In the silent spaces, I receive messages from the Divine and the highest souls. The messages are not audible or visual—just simple knowing presented through my right brain as higher thought, if you will. I am currently learning to translate these messages.

Since learning Soul Song, my connection with truth has made an incredible shift forward. I have become a more loving person. I also now use this marvelous gift of Soul Song to send healing blessings to others.

There are no words to describe all of this, only that I am so very grateful and appreciative to the Divine and to Master Sha.

—D. M.

Washington


## THE VAST BENEFITS OF SINGING SOUL SONG

Since becoming a Certified Divine Soul Song Singer, I have noticed incredible improvement in many areas of my life, including health, relationships, finances, and success at work. But perhaps the most startling discovery has been the dramatic improvement in my clarity and awareness in relation to the world in which I live. It is as if I have had my windows washed and can now see clearly.

Soul Song is a tool that is a *must* for soul enlightenment. It is the fastest route to the truth and to the realization of your true self. Singing a song to experience bliss is a wonderful practice for the world in which we live, and at the same time so very natural and practical in its application and benefit.

—C. K.

California

## ALLOW THE ESSENCE OF EACH DIVINE SOUL SONG TO TOUCH YOUR HEART AND SOUL

Soul peace. Soul love. Soul light. Soul compassion. These are just a few of the qualities that are given through Soul Song, yet it is the soul essence that comes deep from within each Soul Song that I feel as the song of the soul is sung. I have experienced many different aspects of healing and blessings through the use of Soul Song. It is a gift that I am very, very grateful to have been given, as it allows the truest and purest essence of the Divine and my soul to meld and become one. There are no thoughts, no words—only the love, light, and all else that is to come through the notes, the sounds, the voice.

These are clearly felt when listening to the Soul Songs sung by Master Sha: the feeling and presence of the Divine pouring love, light, compassion, joy, and so much more into our hearts and souls for our healing and transformation. They are felt as we allow our souls to sing from the depths of their being, bringing forth healing, blessings, and gifts that are meant for each of us to share and experience. It allows us to experience the truest sense of oneness as we connect heart to heart and soul to soul with one another.

The Divine Soul Songs have allowed transformation to manifest in my own life. I have experienced deep healing and blessings, bringing my soul further along its spiritual journey. I find that listening to the Soul Songs recorded by Master Sha brings me solace and comfort during times of intense pain, allowing the love and light to transform what has come up for me. The sounds allow my soul to soar to the Divine's heart and rest there, receiving so much in return. I allow the comfort of the Divine's heart, the love, and all that is given me to bathe my heart and soul. That is the priceless gift each one of us receives unconditionally. And for those gifts received, I in turn sing the song of my soul, expressing her gratitude, her honor, and her deepest humility for what has been given to me in its purest essence.

I thank the Divine. I thank Master Sha. I thank my own soul for expressing its love and light unconditionally in service to all souls, to humanity, and to countless universes. May all souls experience these precious songs of the soul and allow healing, transformation, and blessings to manifest in their lives. Open the heart. Open the soul. Open to the love, the light, the beauty, and the gifts that will serve you unconditionally through Soul Song. Soul Song is a most priceless treasure.

—C. M.
New Jersey


## SOUL SONGS TRANSFORM A NEIGHBORHOOD IN UNEXPECTED WAYS

Each day I walk my dogs up and down my neighborhood street. As I walk, I sing various Soul Songs: *Love, Peace and Harmony, God Gives His Heart to Me,* and others. Whenever I learn a new song, I sing it in addition to my own Soul Songs. Recently, I have been singing the Divine Soul Songs of Yin Yang and Five Elements.

Until recently, people on our street hardly knew each other. Then, out of nowhere, my neighbor across the street organized a block party. What a surprise! I have lived on my street for twenty-seven years and this is the first block party we have had. It was great: it broke the ice and allowed my next-door neighbor and our family to speak to each other after twenty years of silence over a silly problem.

There are other amazing things happening in my neighborhood. People stop, wave, smile, and talk. I was able to give one lady a healing blessing that helped her arthritis, and she no longer needs her cane. The dogs are even friendlier to each other and want to play together. The whole atmosphere of our street has changed.

Thank you, Soul Songs. Thank you, Master Sha. Thank you, Divine!

—D. F.

Hawaii

## FURTHER OPENING OF MY HEART THROUGH
*LOVE, PEACE AND HARMONY*

It was orientation night of the Soul Healing and Enlightenment Retreat in Lake Junaluska, North Carolina, in March 2007. I remember this very clearly.

Master Sha made a surprise visit. While on stage, he asked everyone to make a request for their one most important wish for the entire upcoming week-long retreat. This was an easy one for me, as I had been to six soul retreats by this time. I requested further enlightenment of my mind. I had learned from Master Sha's teachings that the mind is the biggest blockage on the spiritual journey. To receive a blessing to move closer to mind enlightenment, or perhaps even to reach it, is a priceless gift for your soul journey.

Master Sha asked that everyone sit up straight and open their hearts and souls. For the first time in public, he played a freshly

minted recording of a preliminary version of the Divine Soul
Song *Love, Peace and Harmony* with instrumental accompaniment. The music was heavenly. Master Sha began to sing with
the music and offered one of the most powerful divine blessings
I had received up to that day.

I was standing at the back of the room with several other
students. Although Master Sha asked us to sit, I could not. I
had to dance. My soul wanted to dance, so I did soul dancing.
The students around me were all compelled to soul dance as
well.

The divine love, forgiveness, compassion, light, and virtue
radiating through Master Sha and the *Love, Peace and Harmony*
CD came pouring into my heart. It filled me up, nourished me,
and transformed me. Master Sha teaches that the heart houses
the mind and soul. For my request, this is exactly where the blessing went. It blessed my request and so much more. As I moved,
we were no longer in an auditorium. We were in Heaven's Temple. I saw so many saints, buddhas, Taoist masters, angels, and all
forms of divine or heavenly beings on stage with Master Sha and
all around the room. Heaven had melded with Mother Earth in
that forty-minute blessing and remained melded for the whole
retreat following that special night. There was no separation.
And I was in the most beautiful place I had ever been.

I danced. My heart opened. I danced even more. My heart
opened even more. I surrendered to the moment, to the blessing,
to the Divine, and my heart opened and opened and opened
even more. I felt it physically expand within my upper chest. At
the same time, with my Third Eye I saw the divine blessings
breaking through some black circles that had been around my
heart, preventing it from opening easily and further. As they
shattered, my heart totally filled my entire upper chest.

The feeling was so freeing. The love was so peaceful and intense. The forgiveness was amazing. The compassion was deep and powerful. The light was almost blinding. The further opening of my spiritual channels was sacred. The experience was beyond words.

I left that night changed forever. The changes have stayed with me and even expanded beyond that night. My ability to love, forgive, offer compassion, and experience inner peace and joy in my life has increased. It continues to increase because the bondages around my heart were removed. The Divine Soul Song blessing that night has allowed my mind to become more enlightened over time. Have I reached mind enlightenment? I do not know. But I do know I am closer and closer each day. This would not have been possible without that divine blessing.

If this life-transforming divine blessing were all I received in that retreat, it would have been beyond worth traveling across the country for. If that were the only divine blessing I ever received in this lifetime, it would be totally priceless and precious. I will never forget that night.

My love and thanks go to Master Sha, to the Divine, and to *Love, Peace and Harmony.*

—D. L.

California

## UNSHAKABLE FAITH

On the night of September 1, 2008, I began to feel the start of a troublesome headache. It began mildly, but soon gained strength. The pain became so great that it hurt to the point of nausea. I attempted to do self-healing, but the intensity of the pain precluded me from working effectively. I then decided to go to bed and relax as much as possible before continuing. Little did I know what was about to happen.

As soon as I lay down, the beautiful Goddess of Compassion, Ling Hui Sheng Shi (also known as Guan Yin) appeared beside me. She extended her arms and put her left hand over my crown chakra and her right hand near my torso. I then saw a beautiful light emanating from her Message Center and connecting to mine. Instantly, I fell asleep.

I slept soundly throughout the night. When I awoke the next morning, the headache was completely gone. But even more astounding, I awoke with a completely new outlook. Divine peace, calm, and well-being filled me to the brim. From my new perspective, all was well in the world. I had an outpouring of love and compassion that came from deep within my soul.

The days and weeks prior to this had been disturbing ones. I often thought about people who were behaving badly and who were being recklessly hurtful. I worked hard on the forgiveness practices, and I had gotten to the point of mastery, but I still felt dissatisfied—as though "something" was missing.

Then it dawned on me. When I awoke that morning, I was moved beyond forgiveness. My heart was filled with love. I saw the world through the eyes of love—deep, precious, divine love. In that moment of realization, I felt completely connected to everyone and everything. I fully realized that everything has a soul. Everything is of God, and we are one.

Master Sha often says that knowledge comes in layers. For two and a half years, I had understood that everything has a soul, but a deeper grasp of this wisdom came later. My world was forever changed through an enhanced insight into this simple statement.

I was then shown an image of Christ on the cross. This sacred image holds special meaning for me. It moves me to tears in the deepest way. I am always amazed at how Jesus could be filled with so much love that he could not only forgive, he could love those who were killing him. I do not profess mastery over the sanctity of this wisdom, but I can genuinely say that I experienced a taste of divine unconditional love on the morning of September 2, 2008.

As I wondered what could have prompted such an exquisite healing, an inspired thought entered my mind. I realized that the process could not have happened if my soul frequencies had not been elevated to a level high enough to receive the blessings from the beautiful goddess. I then heard the Divine Soul Songs of Yin Yang and Five Elements play in my head, and I knew it was a message. I put the two pieces together and realized that the result of chanting this song for more than a month—in preparation to teach it to others—had prepared my soul to receive such an incredible gift.

I can say without a doubt that Divine Soul Songs work in a powerful way. They prepared me to receive a most beautiful blessing. My life has been transformed because of this experience, and I know it could happen for others too! I dearly encourage everyone to sing Soul Songs from the heart and allow the heart to be filled with divine love.

—P. S. U.

Hawaii


DIVINE SOUL SONGS IN MY LIFE

I have purchased every one of Master Sha's Divine Soul Song CDs and have them playing constantly in the background—on a little boom box in my dining/living room, on my computer, which is almost always powered on and which you can usually find me in front of, and in my car whenever I am in it. I haven't yet reached the level of technological "with it-ness" where I have an iPod or other MP3 player, but if and when I do, I know my playlists will be filled with Divine Soul Songs! I would also love to be able to figure out how to use Divine Soul Songs as ring-tones on my cell phone.

I also sing Divine Soul Songs at every opportunity. For sure, I do this in Master Sha's Divine Soul Song Singing Gathering for the World Soul Healing, Peace and Enlightenment Movement and his other teleconferences and classes, as well as those work-shops and retreats I am able to attend. But I also sing on my own—sometimes along with the CDs I have playing, sometimes independent of, but in harmony with, them. I sing my own Soul Song as a certified Divine Soul Song Singer. I can sing for many minutes or even just a few seconds at a time. When I am not consciously singing, I often ask my soul and my "inner" souls (of my systems, organs, cells, etc.) to sing or chant Divine Soul Songs. I teach Divine Soul Songs in every workshop I offer and to as many people as possible in casual encounters.

Why do I do all this? Well, first of all, I love them simply as music and sound. They really resonate with me. They bring in-stant peace and healing—and sometimes excitement, reverence, and joy, just as your favorite music or songs do for you. But the real reason is that they are incredibly healing, rejuvenating, and transformative. I don't have any single miraculous story about Divine Soul Songs yet, but I can point to many aspects of my life and being that have been transformed: from having great en-ergy—more energy than ever even though I am in my seventh decade—to visible signs of rejuvenation such as my skin, to excellent health, to quick recovery on those rare occasions when I do become ill, to removal of the last vestiges of anger and other forms of negativity, to the welcome presence of inner confidence, inner peace, inner joy, and the Divine in my life and in and around me. Although I cannot attribute all of these benefits completely to Divine Soul Songs, I strongly believe they have contributed tremendously to my personal transformation, a transformation that is visible and palpable to many I interact with, from my closest loved ones to complete strangers.

These paragraphs are entitled "Divine Soul Songs in My Life," but it would be more accurate to say that Divine Soul Songs, in a very real sense, *are* my life. Divine Soul Songs are me. I am Divine Soul Songs. I would not be the same being without Divine Soul Songs. I am honored and extremely blessed. I cannot thank Master Sha and the Divine enough for giving these treasures to us.

Thank you. Thank you. Thank you.

—N. N.

# Conclusion

MOTHER EARTH IS in transition now. We are experiencing more and more natural and manmade disasters, including earthquakes, tsunamis, hurricanes, droughts, floods, famines, wars, and major financial challenges. Many people are scared, worried, angry, upset, depressed, and anxious. Many people are confused.

Mother Earth's transition is the purification process of Mother Earth and humanity. After Mother Earth goes through this transition period, humanity will turn to love, peace, and harmony. At this historic period, it is most important to be strong and grounded. It is most important to heal yourself, your loved ones, humanity, Mother Earth, and all universes. Divine Soul Songs are sacred divine soul treasures to heal and transform you, your loved ones, humanity, Mother Earth, and all universes.

Divine Soul Songs carry divine consciousness, vibration, and frequency. Divine consciousness, vibration, and frequency can transform the consciousness, vibration, and frequency of you, your loved ones, humanity, Mother Earth, and all universes.

Divine Soul Songs carry divine love, forgiveness, compassion, and light.

Divine love melts all blockages and transforms all life.

Divine forgiveness brings inner peace and inner joy.

Divine compassion boosts energy, stamina, vitality, and immunity.

Divine light heals, prevents illness, rejuvenates, and prolongs life.

Divine Soul Songs can heal and transform every aspect of life, including relationships and finances.

Divine Soul Songs can purify the soul, mind, and body of humanity. Divine Soul Songs can purify the soul, mind, and body of Mother Earth. Divine Soul Songs can purify the soul, mind, and body of all universes.

You can sing or chant the words to Divine Soul Songs to receive healing and life transformation for yourself. You can sing or chant Divine Soul Songs to heal and transform your loved ones. You can sing or chant Divine Soul Songs to heal and transform humanity, Mother Earth, and all universes.

If millions and billions of people were to sing Divine Soul Songs, the healing and life transformation would be beyond words and thoughts. The power of Divine Soul Songs is unlimited, unpredictable, and unimaginable.

Divine Soul Songs can vibrate in every human being, every animal, every plant, every house, every building, every street, every organization, every website, every ocean, every mountain, every forest, every corner of Mother Earth, every planet, every star, every galaxy, and every universe.

Divine Soul Songs are practical divine treasures to heal, rejuvenate, and transform you, humanity, Mother Earth, and all universes.

*Chanting Chanting Chanting*
*Divine chanting is healing*
*Chanting Chanting Chanting*
*Divine chanting is rejuvenating*

*Singing Singing Singing*
*Divine singing is transforming*
*Singing Singing Singing*
*Divine singing is enlightening*

*Humanity is waiting for divine chanting*
*All souls are waiting for divine singing*
*Divine chanting removes all blockages*
*Divine singing brings inner joy*

*Divine is chanting and singing*
*Humanity and all souls are nourishing*
*Humanity and all souls are chanting and singing*
*World love, peace and harmony are coming*

*World love, peace and harmony are coming*

*World love, peace and harmony are coming*

*I love my heart and soul*
*I love all humanity*
*Join hearts and souls together*
*Love, peace and harmony*
*Love, peace and harmony*

# Acknowledgments

$\mathcal{I}$ DEEPLY HONOR AND appreciate the Divine. The Divine is above my head to offer the entire teaching for this book. I flowed the Divine's words and the Divine's teaching to write this book.

I deeply honor and appreciate Dr. and Master Zhi Chen Guo, the founder of Zhi Neng Medicine and Body Space Medicine. He has taught me many soul secrets and much soul wisdom, knowledge, and practice. Without his teaching and training, I could never have written the Soul Power Series. I deeply honor and appreciate his teaching and training. He has prepared me very well to be a servant of humanity and the Divine. He is my most beloved spiritual father forever.

I deeply honor and appreciate all of my masters, including those of tai chi, qi gong, kung fu, the *I Ching,* feng shui, conventional modern medicine, and traditional Chinese medicine.

I deeply honor and appreciate my other major spiritual fathers who do not want me to give their names to the public. They want to be silent servants.

I deeply honor and appreciate my teachers in elementary

school, middle school, high school, and university. Without their teaching, I could not have reached my current condition.

I deeply honor and appreciate my twelve Assistant Teachers. They are Marilyn Smith, Peter Hudoba, Allan Chuck, Shu Chin Hsu, Patricia Smith, Joyce Brown, Francisco Quintero, Peggy Werner, Michael Stevens, Lynne Nusyna, Patty Baker, and David Lusch. They are total GOLD servants for humanity and the Divine. They have made great contributions to the mission. I thank them all.

I deeply honor and appreciate my hundreds of certified Soul Healing Teachers and Healers, certified Master Teachers and Healers of Soul Healing and Enlightenment, and certified Divine Master Teachers and Healers; my more than one hundred Divine Writers; my Divine Editors; and hundreds of Divine Professionals. They have made great contributions to the Divine Mission. I thank them all.

I deeply honor and appreciate Dr. Maya Angelou for writing such a beautiful foreword for this book. I thank her for her heartfelt support.

I deeply honor and appreciate Rev. Michael Beckwith for writing a foreword for the Soul Power Series. I thank him for his heartfelt support.

I deeply honor and appreciate Allan Chuck as the final editor of this book. He is the final editor for the Soul Power Series, of which this book is the fourth to be published in one year, as well as for two of my earlier books, *Soul Mind Body Medicine* and *Power Healing*. His contribution to the mission is great. I deeply appreciate him.

I deeply appreciate and honor Jun Yen Jiang. His orchestrations and arrangements of the seven Divine Soul Songs in this book are beautiful, loving, moving, and heart-touching. He is now a Divine Soul Music Composer. He receives divine music from Heaven and writes out what he hears. I'm very grateful for all the music he is flowing from Heaven for the mission. I deeply appreciate him.

I deeply honor and appreciate Elaine Ward, Diana Gold Holland, May Chew, Rick Riecker, Brian Wilson, and other Divine Editors for their editorial contributions to my books. I thank them for their great contributions to the mission.

I deeply honor and appreciate Nicole Potter for taking the photographs in this book and Lynda Chaplin for providing many of the diagrams in this book.

I deeply honor and appreciate Sarah Ginsberg and Stephen Koszler for their contributions to the creation of the audio version of this book.

I thank all the people who shared their life-transforming Divine Soul Song stories for this book.

I deeply appreciate all of my students and friends worldwide for their warm responses to the Soul Power Series and my teaching and service. I have traveled worldwide to meet thousands and thousands of people. I thank you all for giving me the opportunity to serve you.

I am a totally dedicated servant for humanity, all souls, and the Divine. I am honored to serve each of you.

Finally and very importantly, I deeply honor and appreciate my wife and three children for their love and heartfelt support of my mission. I thank them deeply.

*I love my heart and soul*
*I love all humanity*
*Join hearts and souls together*
*Love, peace and harmony*
*Love, peace and harmony*

# A Special Gift

As a special gift for you, I am including a thirty-one-minute audio CD in this book. The seven tracks of this CD offer extensive samples of five of the Divine Soul Songs that are the main subjects of this book:

Track 1    Divine Soul Song *Love, Peace and Harmony*
Track 2    Divine Soul Song *God Gives His Heart to Me*
Track 3    Divine Soul Song of Compassion
Track 4    Divine Soul Song of Yin Yang Energy Circle
Track 5    Divine Soul Song of Yin Yang Matter Circle
Track 6    Divine Soul Song of Yin Yang
Track 7    Divine Soul Song of Five Elements

Enjoy the melodies. Enjoy the lyrics. Enjoy the beautiful arrangements by Divine Soul Music Composer Jun Yen Jiang with instrumental and choral support. Enjoy the divine frequency and vibration that carry divine love, forgiveness, compassion, and light.

Learn the melodies. Learn the lyrics. This will empower you to benefit fully from all of the practices presented in this book. You will also be able to sing these Divine Soul Songs anytime, anywhere to receive and offer their blessings. Each of these Divine Soul Songs is available in a full-length CD version that can be found on my website.

Divine Soul Songs and Divine Soul Music are your servants. I wish you will receive great benefits from these divine servants.

Thank you. Thank you. Thank you.

# Dr. Sha's Teachings and Services

## Other Books and Audiobooks

*Power Healing: The Four Keys to Energizing Your Body, Mind & Spirit.* HarperSanFrancisco, 2002.

*Soul Mind Body Medicine: A Complete Soul Healing System for Optimum Health and Vitality.* New World Library, 2006.

*Living Divine Relationships.* Heaven's Library, 2006.

*Body Space Medicine* by Dr. Zhi Chen Guo (foreword by Dr. Sha). Heaven's Library, 2007.

*Soul Wisdom: Practical Soul Treasures to Transform Your Life* (revised edition). Heaven's Library/Atria, 2008. Also available as an audiobook.

*Soul Communication: Opening Your Spiritual Channels for Success and Fulfillment* (revised edition). Heaven's Library/Atria, 2008. Also available as an audiobook.

*The Power of Soul: The Way to Heal, Rejuvenate, Transform, and Enlighten All Life.* Heaven's Library/Atria, 2009. Also available as an audiobook.

## Multimedia eBook

*Soul Mind Body Medicine: A Complete Soul Healing System for Optimum Health and Vitality.* Heaven's Library/Alive! eBooks Network, 2008; www.heavenslibrary.com. Includes one hour of new audio content and one hour of new video content with Dr. Sha.

## Healing, Blessing, and Life Transformation

Divine Sacred Soul Song Singing Teleconference for the World Soul Healing, Peace and Enlightenment Movement, Monday through Friday, 5:30–6:00 PM Pacific Time. Register once at www.drsha.com for this ongoing Divine Soul Song singing service.

Divine Remote Group Healing, Rejuvenation, and Transformation Teleconference Session with Master Sha, Sunday, 5:00–6:00 PM Pacific Time.

Divine Soul Downloads, Karma Cleansings, Divine Soul Orders, and other Divine Blessings (www.drsha.com).

## CDs and DVDs

*The Voice of the Universe: Power Healing Music.* Qi Records, 2002. Four powerful universal mantras for the Soul Light Era recorded by Dr. Sha:

- *God's Light*
- *Universal Light*
- *Shining Soul Light*
- *Follow Nature's Way*

*The Music of Soul Dance.* Institute of Soul Healing and Enlightenment, 2007. A ten-CD boxed set of Heaven's music to inspire and help guide your Soul Dance.

*Blessings from Heaven.* Institute of Soul Healing and Enlightenment, 2007. Divine Soul Music by Divine Composer Jun Yen Jiang and Dr. Sha.

*Love, Peace and Harmony.* Institute of Soul Healing and Enlightenment, 2007. The first Soul Song given by the Divine to Dr. Sha and humanity.

*God Gives His Heart to Me.* Institute of Soul Healing and Enlightenment, 2008. The second Soul Song given by the Divine to Dr. Sha and humanity.

*Divine Soul Song of Compassion.* Institute of Soul Healing and Enlightenment, 2009.

*Divine Soul Songs of Yin Yang and Five Elements.* Institute of Soul Healing and Enlightenment, 2009.

*Soul Songs for Healing and Rejuvenation.* www.MasterShaSoul Song.com, 2008–2009. Divine Soul Songs for healing and rejuvenating various organs, systems, and parts of the body; for balancing emotions; and for weight loss.

*Power Healing to Self-Heal Ten Common Conditions.* Institute of Soul Healing and Enlightenment, 2004. On this DVD, Dr. Sha teaches the Four Power Techniques to self-heal:

- Anxiety
- Back pain
- Carpal tunnel syndrome
- Common cold
- Constipation
- Energy boosting
- Headache

- Knee pain
- Menopause
- Weight loss

Dr. Sha also offers personal blessings for each condition.

*Power Healing with Master Zhi Gang Sha: Learn Four Power Techniques to Heal Yourself.* Institute of Soul Healing and Enlightenment, 2006. This four-DVD set offers a comprehensive teaching of the wisdom, knowledge, and practices of Power Healing and Soul Mind Body Medicine. All aspects of Body Power, Sound Power, Mind Power, and Soul Power are covered in depth. Dr. Sha reveals and explains many secret teachings and leads you in practices.

www.DrSha.com
www.HeavensLibrary.com
1.888.3396815
DrSha@DrSha.com

"This inspiring documentary has masterfully captured the vital healing work and global mission of Dr. Guo and Dr. Sha."

*– Dr. Michael Bernard Beckwith – Founder, Agape International Spiritual Center*

This film reveals profound soul secrets and shares the wisdom, knowledge, and practices of Dr. Guo's Body Space Medicine and Dr. Sha's Soul Mind Body Medicine. Millions of people in China have studied with Dr. Guo, who is Dr. Sha's most beloved spiritual father. Dr. Guo is "the master who can cure the incurable." After Dr. Sha heals her ailing father, American filmmaker Sande Zeig accompanies Dr. Sha to China to visit his mentor. At Dr. Guo's clinic, she captures first-ever footage of breakthrough healing practices involving special herbs, unique fire massage, and revolutionary self-healing techniques. These two Soul Masters have a special bond. They are united in their commitment to serve others. As you see them heal and teach, your heart and soul will be touched. Experience the delight, inspiration, wonder, and gratitude that *Soul Masters* brings.

In English and Mandarin with English subtitles. Also in French, German, Japanese, Mandarin and Spanish.

**PPV Video Streaming and DVD at**
# www.soulmastersmovie.com